# Lt Joshua Woodhouse RN

4

14

# Preface

A web site has been made whose main purpose is to be a repository for all the letters, documents, emails, investigations, Inquest Tape Recordings, Inquest Transcripts, and the electronic animations of the US Navy witness accounts that support this book and have been quoted in this book.

The web site has the web address of my son's name, www.joshuawoodhouse.com

# Lt Joshua Woodhouse

My son, Lt Joshua Woodhouse RN, died in suspicious circumstances whilst serving his country on board HMS Ocean, in August, 2010.

His employers, the Royal Navy, who should have done their utmost to unravel all the suspicious circumstances surrounding my son's death, did the very opposite.

However, there is a small glimmer of hope, and this is the reason I write this book.

My son's Inquest was held in November, 2012, two years and three months after his death.

The Jury at my son's Inquest did not know that much vital information had been denied us by the Coroner.

The Jury did not know that the Coroner had refused to include the only three independent eye witnesses as live witnesses in my son's Inquest.

The Jury did not know the Coroner had forbidden our legal team from asking any questions that would in any way investigate foul play.

Despite these great hindrances by the Coroner, the Jury was very clear in their rejection of the account given by the Royal Navy, the MOD, and the Special Investigation Branch (SIB) of the Royal Navy Military Police (MP).

I recount the events as they occurred. These are my experiences of the Military Justice given to my son in the United Kingdom of Great Britain.

## HMS Ocean Friends and Family Day

HMS Ocean was due to go on a deployment to the USA on the 10th June, 2010. To top this, the Queen was paying a Royal Visit to the ship on Thursday, 3rd June, followed by Friends and Family Day on Friday, 4th June.

All was excitement, all was joy on HMS Ocean.

My son was also infected with this joy, with this happiness.

My husband and I travelled to Plymouth, Devon, to partake in the Friends and Family Day of Friday, 4th June, 2010. This was a wonderful opportunity to see where my son Joshua worked. To see his working environment, sleeping quarters, eating quarters, in essence to see HMS Ocean, one of our country's finest military ships.

My son was our host for the day and showed us round HMS Ocean. True to form I took countless photographs, the whole day was fascinating, and it was a joy to see my son in his work environment.

## Family Farewell Bon Voyage Meal

On Sunday 6th June, 2010 my son drove up to our family home and we had our customary celebratory Sunday lunch whenever he went off or returned from a deployment. This particular deployment would last about four months. It was a dream deployment and Joshua was greatly looking forward to it.

The ship would be staying at the US military base in Florida for four weeks when the ship's company would take their two week vacation so that only half the ship would be manned during this time.

Joshua was also greatly looking forward to his two week leave in Florida and his fiancée would be flying down to meet him. He had arranged among other things a swim with the dolphins as a birthday present for his fiancée. We found out later he had also arranged to hire a true blue American car, a Mustang. When in the US of A, do as the Americans do.

We had our Sunday lunch with my son's favourite dish and dessert and for tea I had made a surprise chocolate Bon Voyage cake. We were so happy for Joshua. Joshua was so happy.

And so we waved goodbye to Joshua.

On Thursday, 10<sup>th</sup> June, 2010, HMS Ocean left the UK headed for the USA with Joshua on board.

## The Emails

My son emailed and so we heard about life on board HMS Ocean. They had arrived in the USA, Florida, and the beaches were as beautiful as the brochures paint them. My son arranged a few impromptu BBQs on the beach for his team. He said it was so easy; buy the games, the beach balls, the food, and the rest flows. He was always thinking of others, his team. He wanted to help make the whole experience memorable for them. He wanted them to enjoy this dream deployment in the USA, in Florida.

## The Phone call

On the 6<sup>th</sup> August, 2010, we received the phone call that every parent dreads. Our son Joshua had fallen 40 feet and was in intensive care in Jacksonville, Florida. The whole family would be flown to be by his side immediately.

The Military runs a scheme whereby the family of wounded military personnel are flown immediately to be by their side.

No words can express our pain and anguish. How did this happen? What happened?

## The Journey

The military would be flying the entire family over to Jacksonville, Florida, to see Joshua, all from different locations and different times.

We did not know the state of his injuries, we knew nothing. We were travelling and the text messages were flying. One of our sons thought that they would put Joshua into an induced coma till his body could recover.

I think it was only my daughter who knew we were being flown out to see Joshua die.

In the midst of these trying circumstances, my husband and I could not shake off the certain knowledge that our dear God is only good.

And so we journeyed towards Florida. It seemed to take so long to get to Joshua. On the last leg of the journey, as we headed towards Florida, I remember the sun setting and the darkness covering the land. We were due to land sometime in the evening and the rest of the family, besides my eldest son, were due to also arrive sometime in the evening too.

It was now 9pm and we were close to arriving in Jacksonville, Florida. The time had come.

We touched down at 9:24pm. In the crowds there were two men in white Navy uniform waiting for us. This was too much for me. My husband did the honours. I suddenly saw the rest of the family, my second son, my daughter, and Joshua's fiancé. We presumed that they had arrived some time ago.

We found out later that both aircraft touched down at exactly the same time – 9:24pm.
How could this be?
Even the captain found this extraordinary. I was comforted by this as I felt it was another sign of the good hand of our God upon us. He was showing us His signature in these tiny impossibilities to let us know He was with us. He was there. This was all in His will.

## The Hospital

We were taken in two cars to the hospital. My husband and I were in the first car with the captain. I asked about Joshua's condition. We were told that the hospital would brief us.

We arrived in the hospital and were taken to see the doctor on duty together with a welfare worker who handed round the tissues.

The doctor told us that Joshua had head injuries and that his chances of survival were the nearest you could possibly get to zero.

We were told that Joshua had landed on his head on a metal surface, his skull had been split, and that his brain was badly damaged.

The doctor explained the tests they had done on Joshua to monitor his nerve signals. He explained that Joshua's responses confirmed that the brain had been damaged beyond repair so that Joshua could not survive.

We were told that they were keeping him alive on a ventilator and they repeated that his chances of survival were the nearest you could possibly get to zero.

There were many tears.

We were then allowed to see him. I looked down a corridor of rooms, where was he? I walked quickly looking in each room. Where was he? And then I saw the room with Joshua on the bed.

I took Joshua's hand and he squeezed my hand in response. Thank you, my dear Heavenly Father.

Joshua's head was covered in a bandage, but his face was still beautiful. Beside the bruises, his face was untouched. He had tubes. He had a breathing tube in his mouth. He could not breathe unaided.

His eyes were closed, but he squeezed my hand when I arrived. He was there. He knew we were there.

He squeezed the hands of the others.

We had joy and sorrow. We had joy that we were there with Joshua. We had joy that he responded to us.

It was time to leave. We were taken to a motel near the hospital which the Navy had booked for us. They told us that they would collect us the following morning, Sunday, 8th August, 2010. We would first go to the airport to collect my eldest son and then the whole family would be taken to the hospital to be with Joshua.

Captain Blount brought the head of the engineering department and a driver with him. They all spent the day in the hospital to ensure we were alright and also to be our transport.

As we did not want to be an undue burden on the Captain, we discussed the possibility of hiring a car. This was arranged the following day, Monday.

The days became a blur. I do not know on which day a particular event happened, so I recount some of the following in no particular order.

I remember three doctors in total.

I believe it was on the Sunday that the doctor in charge was a very pleasant woman. She spoke to us about Joshua's condition. She asked whether we would like to see the scans. My husband and I were the only members of the family who wanted to see them.

We sat with her just outside Joshua's hospital room as she showed us the scans of Joshua's head. She showed us where his head had been cracked open. There was a perfect break from ear to ear.

She explained to us that the brain had received such a huge blow that it had swollen. If the skull had not been broken, then the swelling would have pushed downwards on the nerves at the base of the skull and Joshua would have died within twelve hours of his fall.

She said, 'I believe God kept Joshua alive for you to see him.'

We have always been comforted by these words.

Another interesting thing was how the doctors remarked on more than one occasion that Joshua had a very good, strong, young heart. They told us with great admiration that his heart needed no help from them at all, it was so strong.

At another time we were approached by two women with regard to donating Joshua's organs, especially his heart. They wanted his heart.

I knew in the past that Joshua had subscribed to an organ donor charity and wore a wrist band to that effect, but I did not know about the present time. Joshua's fiancée was not happy to donate any of his organs, and therefore we were content to abide by this decision.

Joshua lived a total of four days from his fall. We were at the hospital for his last three days.

We sat there and we took turns in holding his hands, just talking to him. It was a joy to talk to him, to be with him. We were greatly encouraged that he did respond to us. He squeezed our hands on many occasions.

We were under the mistaken impression that we would have Joshua there for at least one to two weeks. But we were wrong.

The third doctor we saw was a very kindly man who told us that they had been battling to keep Joshua's chemical blood balances in control all weekend as his brain was no longer doing this mundane job. The doctor mentioned that if we left Joshua alive any longer, his organs would start failing and yes, they could keep him alive for a few more days, but it would be at the cost of intrusive operations. Did we want that?

This was hard news. We had to make a decision and soon.

That night we all spoke and decided that Joshua was to be taken off the ventilator at 9pm the following day, Tuesday, 10th August. Tuesday would be our last day with Joshua.

And so Tuesday came.

It was now 9pm, Tuesday. I so wanted to be with Joshua during his last moments. We went to a little room and we thought the nurse would tell us when it was all over. Instead she asked us if we would like to be with him during his last moments. They would remove the ventilator from his mouth. I gather it was not a pleasant sight and they wished to do it in private, after which the nurse would call us.

I, my husband, and Joshua's fiancé waited outside Joshua's room. My two other sons were downstairs; it was too much for them.

My husband and I stood arm in arm and sang a hymn from memory. The tears flowed. Joshua's fiancé stood nearby covered in a blanket shivering and crying. The kindly welfare officer covered her in a blanket and held her.

We were called to go into Joshua's room. There was my boy.

I sat at Joshua's right hand, my husband sat at his left. Joshua's fiancé could not bring herself to come in – not yet.

And we saw our boy die.

My comfort was that my dear Lord Jesus allowed Joshua to repent and to be saved. There is none righteous, no, not one.

My comfort is that my dear Lord Jesus Himself carried my boy home, and we look forward to going home too, where

*the Lamb which is in the midst of the throne shall feed them, and shall lead them unto living fountains of waters: and God shall wipe away all tears from their eyes.*
Revelations 7:17

# The Next Day

It was Wednesday, 11th August, 2010. Joshua had gone home on Tuesday, 10th August, 9:31pm.

We were invited to go on board HMS Ocean on Wednesday, 11th August, 2010. My husband and I accepted the invitation and went on board. We had met the ship's padre, Ron Martin, the night Joshua died at the hospital and spoke to him downstairs on our way out of the hospital. He had asked to speak to us whilst Joshua was alive, but our time with Joshua was so short I tried to guard it.

So we went to the ship and the Ship's Padre did the honours and took us around. We wanted to see where Joshua fell from.

Before HMS Ocean set sail for America there was a Friends and Family Open Day on the ship on the 4th June, 2010. Joshua was our host as he showed us around HMS Ocean and looked after us for the entire day. I took many photos of the day as is my usual practice. These photos would prove invaluable in the future.

Now that our boy was dead, and we were no longer by his side, we could go to the ship. We wanted to find out what had happened.

When we first arrived in America, one of our party had gone on the ship whilst Joshua was still alive. They wanted to find out whether Joshua had done anything he should not have done and whether Joshua had omitted to do anything he should have done. They were assured by Captain Blount that Joshua had done nothing amiss. This was a comfort to us.

The question still remained, what happened? This is one of the reasons that we accepted the invitation to go on board HMS Ocean.

The Padre, Ron Martin, took us to the LCVP bay from where Joshua fell. The bay was empty.

We were told that Joshua was on top of the LCVP whilst it was in the bay. From the conversations I gathered that a LCVP was one of the small boats that were held in the side of the ship, in this bay. We were told that Joshua jumped off the LCVP and somehow he fell over the side onto another LCVP in the water below.

Ron Martin drew our attention to the story of the paralytic man in Mark's

Gospel, Chapter 4. This was a comfort to us. We prayed in the LCVP bay.

In our travels to the lunch room we stopped and spoke to Joshua's boss, Steve Ward, who was in charge of the engineering department. At the time I did not know what rank he held. Steve Ward spoke to me and told me that they were discussing what memorial to have in memory of Joshua. He told me that one of the ideas was to have a wooden bench with a plaque on it with Joshua's name. He then said to me 'and we will sit on Joshua'. I found this very strange and made no reaction. As he saw no reaction, he made a point of repeating the statement.

After many months I happened to mention this statement to my eldest son, who said that Steve Ward repeated the very same statement to him at Joshua's funeral and he too got the impression that something was not right.

We had lunch with Joshua's fellow officers in the officers' mess. We also met the Royal Marine captain who happened to be a friend of Joshua.

## Royal Navy Breaking the Law

Whilst Joshua was still alive, the Executive Officer (who was now in charge of the ship whilst Captain Blount resumed his holiday), the Padre, and one other Navy man wanted to discuss something very important with us. A meeting was arranged over lunchtime with all the family present. I wondered what this important topic was, that they needed to discuss it with us whilst my son was still alive, while we had so little time remaining to be with him.

We were told that Joshua had signed into a scheme whereby should he die an instant payment of about twelve thousand pounds is made to his Next of Kin.

We were told by the Executive Officer, the Padre, and the other officer, that they wanted the money to go to Joshua's fiancée, even though she was not Joshua's Next of Kin.

You must understand, Joshua was dying, we were all reeling, and this request had the appearance of being very philanthropic.

However, my husband was totally unhappy about the whole affair, as he knew immediately that it was not the money that was the issue, but the Next of Kin status, which the Royal Navy wished to deprive us of.

My husband knew that by giving the money to my son's fiancée we stood a very good chance of losing our Next of Kin legal status according to English law.

My husband was unhappy about this and stated that we are Next of Kin, and not Joshua's fiancé. The Executive Officer, the Padre, and the other RN member did not care for my husband's opinion.

In fact the Executive Officer stated on his way out, "We have ways and means"

As the months progressed we saw that in planning this meeting the intentions of the Royal Navy were quite calculated.

We were totally unprepared with regard to the subject matter of the meeting. We were subjected to emotional blackmail to agree to give Joshua's payout to his fiancée and thus lose our status as Joshua's Next of Kin. Our legal status as Joshua's Next of Kin was imperative as we fought to find out how Joshua came to die.

The Royal Navy only wanted to deal with Joshua's fiancée and not us. By making this decision and bypassing the legal Next of Kin, the Royal Navy not only broke the law, but they broke Joshua's wish to have his parents as his Next of Kin, as explained in the next chapter.

## Prepare a Will Joshua

For many months, even years, my husband always encouraged our sons to make a will. Not because they were married, but because their jobs were dangerous.

On the last Sunday before Joshua left on the HMS Ocean deployment to America, we had one of our traditional farewell Sunday lunches where we wished Joshua every happiness and safety on this upcoming deployment.

After the Sunday lunch whilst we were having coffee, my husband once again endeavoured to get Joshua to make a will. The rest of the family smiled as we saw Dad trying once again to get Joshua to make a will.

My husband told Joshua again how very important it was that he should make his will, especially before another deployment.

Joshua specifically and firmly said to his father, 'It's okay Dad, I have everything under control.'

What does that mean?

Exactly what it says.

Joshua did have everything under control. He was expecting to be away in this deployment for four to five months and he had put all his affairs in order.

Joshua knew that we, his parents, were the legal Next of Kin, and that is exactly how he wanted it to remain whilst he was away on this deployment.

When the Royal Navy broke English Law and gave Joshua's pay out to Joshua's fiancée, they did it against Joshua's wishes and without Joshua's authority and they did it without our authority.

This was just another example of the Military justice that we experienced as a family, and it would not only continue but it would get even worse.

## Before We Left America

We wanted to know how Joshua fell, how Joshua died. We wanted to know what did in fact happen.

Despite one of our party being told that Joshua had done the job in question exactly as it was always done, we still did not know what exactly happened. We were given snippets of information. We were told that Joshua jumped from the roof of the LCVP and slipped and fell and it was just bad luck that another LCVP happened to be underneath at the time.

I wanted to find out how he fell. How did this happen? We were told that the SIB Military Police, (the military equivalent of the CID) flew over immediately to investigate my son's death.

We were told that the ship had also conducted their own investigation into Joshua's death and that we would be sent a copy of this report. We waited for over four months for this report that had been finished and signed even before Joshua was dead. Yet we were not allowed to see it till just a few days before Christmas.

We were led to believe that professionals were investigating Joshua's death, and therefore we assumed that they would do a professional job, which entails doing an honest job. It entails having moral integrity.

Two men went to do a job and only one came back. On these grounds alone my son's death could immediately be classified as suspicious.

## The Trip Back to the UK

We stayed in America whilst a post mortem was carried out on Joshua's body and we left Monday, 16th August, six days after Joshua died. We flew back to the UK to bury our son. We were to fly on the same aircraft as Joshua but for some reason there was a mix up and Joshua's body was on a different flight leaving one hour later.

We arrived in the UK, Tuesday 17th August, in the morning. The weather was overcast, grey, cold, and wet. It was perfectly in keeping with how we felt.

The Royal Navy had arranged a party to accept Joshua's body honourably.

Joshua left Plymouth on the 10th June, on board HMS Ocean headed for America. A dream deployment. He was so happy; he had looked forward to this trip. And this is how he returned – in a coffin.

## The Three US Navy Witnesses

The welfare officer liaising the day to day running of all the things that needed to be arranged for the funeral, the flights, the accommodation, mentioned that three US Navy personnel had witnessed Joshua's fall.

Understandably, the entire family were very interested to hear this information and immediately quizzed the social worker about this.

The following day she told us that no US Navy personnel witnessed the fall. We did not believe her.

## The Fine Military Funeral

Joshua was to have another post mortem, this time in the UK, after which he would be buried. We were put up in self-catering family accommodation in Southsea, whilst we waited to bury my son.

HMS Ocean flew the Padre, Ron Martin, to the UK to take the funeral service. We were very grateful to have someone who knew Joshua.

On Friday, 27th August, 2010, the Royal Navy gave Joshua a funeral with full military honours. We were told that they had their flags fly at half-mast on all their ships. We were grateful, and yet ...... there were under tones.

What is really going on here? We, as a family, were still stunned and numbed by the death of my son, but even in these circumstances we noticed the undertones.

Steve Ward, the head of the engineering department where Joshua served, had been flown to the funeral to represent Captain Blount. He read Captain Blount's message at the service. It was obvious this was a great trial to him.

At the 'wake' after the funeral Steve Ward spoke to my husband and said to him in an exasperated tone, 'Are you satisfied now?'

Back in Florida at the hospital while Joshua was still alive, it was plainly obvious to the entire family that Steve Ward resented spending the whole day at the hospital, putting in a presence out of respect for Joshua.

Now at the funeral, it was equally obvious that Steve Ward resented being there. And as I found out much later, he gave his 'sit on Joshua' jibe not just to me, but also to my eldest son, this time at the funeral.

What were the relations between Joshua and Cdr Steve Ward, head of the Engineering department?

The Royal Navy gave Joshua a fine military funeral and people were kind to us, for which we were most grateful. But there was a price to pay.

We were soon to find out what this price was.

## HMS Ocean returns October, 2010 – It's all Joshua's Fault

HMS Ocean returned to the UK end of October. Joshua's fiancée had a few issues that she personally wanted to deal with and hence met the ship as it came into home waters in Plymouth. Joshua's fiancée spoke with Captain Blount.

Joshua's fiancée informed us that Captain Blount had told her that the Ship's Investigation had been completed and that the news was not good. He was endeavouring to prepare her for the shock. He was telling her that the report put all the blame for Joshua's death on Joshua himself.

What a turn around this was.

It was Captain Blount who informed one of our party that Joshua had done the job in question in exactly the way it had always been done and had not done anything he should not have done. And yet here he was preparing the family for the report which says the very reverse of what he told us whilst in Florida.

All this time I was waiting for news of the SIB investigation into my son's death that would diligently uncover the truth about how my son came to fall. This was their job, after all, to carry out a full criminal investigation into my son's death.

And all this time, we were given nothing. We had no account of how Joshua came to fall and die. All we knew was that the Ship had done an investigation, and now we were told that HMS Ocean was blaming him for his own death.

And more than that; we were informed that the Royal Navy sent a post to all its ships, with an emotive message saying that they had just come from the funeral of a young officer who died needlessly because he didn't obey the Health and Safety on board HM Ships.

Officially it was all Joshua's fault.

## Next of Kin – November, 2010

The Royal Navy blamed my son for his own death. We had no intimation that they would do this. The Royal Navy did not even bother to tell us; instead they informed my son's fiancée. Shocked and reeling from the news, I was angered.

It was very clear that the Royal Navy wanted to make Joshua's fiancée the Next of Kin.

By giving Joshua's fiancée the initial pay-out, and Joshua's pension which the Royal Navy did illegally, they wanted to push us out of the way.

There was too much at stake here.

They had a suspicious death on their hands and they needed the parents out of the way.

On the 4th November, 2010, I immediately emailed Captain Blount, Commodore P.M. Bennett, and Vice Admiral R.J. Ibbotson to say that, by English law, my husband and I were Joshua's Next of Kin, and we had not rescinded that right.

> *"My husband and I hereby wish to inform you that by English law, we are Lt Joshua Woodhouse's Next of Kin, nor have we rescinded this right to any other party."*

I also wrote that my son's fiancé's receipt of money in no way stripped us of our Next of Kin status.

> *"I would like to add that as my son's fiancée, XYZ, was in financial need, following my son's death, my husband and I were more than happy that the Royal Navy gave the £12000 cash payment to her immediately. We are also more than happy that she is, we believe, due to receive a pension from the Navy.*
>
> *However, the fact that we are happy for XYZ to have received this money, does in no way mean that we have rescinded our right as Joshua's Next of Kin, as stipulated by English Law, irrespective what the Navy has decided in their own internal administrative policies and workings."*

My husband and I were content for Joshua's fiancé to have Joshua's pay-out, and his pension but we never rescinded our rights as my son's legal Next of Kin.

On the 24th November, 2010, we received a letter from Commodore Mike Mansergh, Director Naval Personnel basically saying, of course the Navy recognises us as the Next of Kin.

## The Immediate Ship's Investigation – December, 18th, 2010

Following the news that the Immediate Ship's Investigation (ISI) blamed my son entirely for his own death, contrary to everything we had been told when we were in Florida, I needed to see it. Therefore in my email to the Royal Navy of the 4th November, 2010, informing them that my husband and I were the legal Next of Kin, I asked to be notified of all information to do with my son's death, which included the ISI.

> "We understand some report has been completed on HMS Ocean, and we, the Next of Kin, have not been informed."

and

> "Will you please ensure that my husband and I, as the legal Next of Kin of Lt. Joshua Woodhouse, are kept informed of any developments, past, present, and future in relation to all my son's affairs."

I emailed Captain Blount on the 16th November, asking for this investigation (the email can be seen on the website)

> "I have been informed that the investigation into Joshua's accident conducted by HMS Ocean has been completed.
>
> Please may (my husband) and I, as legal Next of Kin, have a copy of your investigation."

The following day, we received an email reply saying (see the website) −

> "The Investigation you refer to in your email below was conducted immediately after Josh's accident and was completed within days."

We found out that the HMS Ocean ISI was indeed completed within days. It was actually completed and signed before my son was even dead, and yet the Royal Navy would not give us a copy of this report till over four months later.

November passed, it was now December, and we were still waiting.

O yes, we did know one more thing. We now knew since November, 2010, that the Royal Navy blamed my son totally for his own death.

We waited and waited. At long last we received the Ship's Investigation by email on the 18th December, 2010, from Commodore Mansergh's office. Four months after Joshua died and four months after they had completed it.

Thoughtful Christmas present, Royal Navy.

Why such a long delay? Why were we kept in the dark for so long?

Why was it that you 'knew' it was all my son's fault, and yet you made sure we knew nothing? Nothing at all.

# Putting the Puzzle Pieces Together

And now we come to the ISI that was finally in our hands on 18th December, 2010.

I should be grateful that we had something, anything, giving an account of how my son died. I understand that other military families have to wait sometimes years and only receive the information just before the Inquest.

As you travel with us through time in our quest to find out how my son came to die, you will see that obtaining any information on my son's death was like obtaining state secrets. There was a big impenetrable mountain on the road of justice and it was called the Coroner – Coroner David Horsley.

From December, 2010, when we received the ISI until February, 2012, one year two months later, the Coroner only released one document to us – my son's Post Mortem.

As I understand it, the only reason that we received the ISI was because it was Royal Navy policy, else I doubt very much we would have received any information at all.

# The Immediate Ship's Investigation (ISI) – making sense of it

There was so much in the investigation that made no sense. I did not even know what a LCVP is or what it looked like, nor a wheelhouse, nor a wheelhouse roof. We had to try to find out. We scoured the internet and all the pictures we had taken during the Royal Navy Friends and Family Day just before Joshua left for the American deployment.

When an insurance company receives an account of an accident, it requests drawings, maps, explanations, else the account is meaningless.

Two days after receiving the ISI, on the 20th December, 2010, I emailed Commodore Mansergh, asking for supporting information, as I could make no sense of the investigation without it. I needed to know what the LCVP looked like, to have plans and pictures of it, and how it fitted into HMS Ocean.

> *"Mrs.XYZ has mentioned in her email that*
>
> *Can I reassure you that the Commodore, while content for me*

*to respond to you directly, has asked me to convey to you his reassurance that you should continue to feel free to contact him directly with any issues in future that you think would be more appropriately addressed by him personally.*

*There is one more point that I would be most grateful if you would please help me with regard to my son's fatal fall on HMS Ocean.*

*I am unable to make much sense of the account in the Ship's Investigation without using a great deal of guesswork and making far too many assumptions, most of which will be totally incorrect.*

*I therefore need some supporting documentation. I have listed below some of the things that would help me to understand how my son came by his death"* –

(see his full email on website)

This is no different to what an insurance company requires when they receive some strange and wonderful account of an accident.

Commodore Mansergh replied on the 22nd December, telling me that he had asked a team to obtain the information for me. (see his full email on website)

However, by the 23rd December, I received another email from Commodore Mansergh saying *"that most, if not all, of the additional documentation and details that you seek is contained in the Royal Navy Special Investigation Branch (SIB) report"* therefore the person to ask is the Coroner. (see his full email on website)

In the fullness of time we only ever received the summary of the SIB Report, not the full report itself. This summary had no plans and dimensions of the LCVP, and no pictures. We were being fobbed off and told to go to the Coroner and ask him for the SIB report, which would have all the plans and pictures I was asking for. Hmmm.

I asked Commodore Mansergh again for the plans and pictures of the LCVP from which my son fell. (see the website) After all, whilst in Florida, one of our party was taken on the LCVP, and we were shown round the LCVP Bay. At that time we were too stunned to take photographs and start amassing information. Nobody told us that the location of my son's fall was top secret or that it would become top secret as soon as it got into the Coroner's hands.

Commodore Mansergh replied on the 23rd December (see website), saying that he would ask his team on their return from Christmas leave how best to provide me with the pictures I needed. I didn't think I would get them, though I do think they tried to help us in obtaining these photographs. On the 25th February, 2011, I received confirmation that I would not get any supporting photographs or plans of a LCVP, or of the LCVP Bay. (see email on website)

We were back to square one. How were we to understand the account of the events leading up to my son's death, with no knowledge of the place from where he fell?

The amazing thing was that my son's fall occurred on the outside of the ship and not in some internal corridor or passageway in that huge internal military labyrinth HMS Ocean. This was a great blessing as it allowed us to obtain a multitude of pictures from the internet as we tried urgently to make sense of the ISI in order to find out how and why my son fell from one of the LCVPs.

The ISI is almost exclusively the account of the one man who was with my son right up to the time when he fell. This man is Petty Officer (PO) Matthew Fulton.

If one were to read this account without any idea or what a LCVP looks like, or without any idea of what a LCVP Bay looks like, or without any idea of what the wheelhouse roof looks like, and without any idea of the cramped area on the wheelhouse roof, then the account might possibly sound plausible.

Everything sounds perfectly plausible in the dark. It is the light that reveals the subterfuge.

## On Our Own – Plans and Pictures

Where could we get plans and pictures of the LCVP and the LCVP Bay in order to try to make some sense of the Ship's Investigation? And what exactly is a LCVP?

All Christmas we scoured the internet and were very grateful for any bits of information we were able to obtain.

My husband also contacted a ships' model maker, Jecobin, asking whether we could buy the plans of HMS Ocean. The company would not charge us, but posted us the plans immediately and free of charge. We were grateful for their help and kindness.

We spent Christmas poring over these plans of the ship, of the LCVP Bay, of the LCVP, trying to understand how the LCVP worked, how it was lowered into the water, where it was positioned on HMS Ocean, working out how you climb up onto the LCVP once you are in the LCVP Bay. What was a Davit? Where was it? How was the Davit related to the LCVP? Where were the flexible Davit hoses? How many Davits were there for each LCVP? All this in our desperate efforts to try to make sense of the ISI and my son's last moments before his fatal fall.

What happened to my son?

The more we studied the plans, the pictures, and the more we pored over the account in the Ship's Investigation and did our multiple re-enactments, the more obvious it was that the account given by PO Fulton was not plausible.

Had the Special Investigation Branch (SIB) Military Police taken even half the trouble we did when they were flown from the UK to Florida? Time was to reveal to us that they had not. Time was also to reveal to us that they had not even thought it worthwhile to have a re-enactment of the events.

## What was PO Fulton's Account of the Events?

Let us now consider PO Fulton's account of my son's last moments.

I will now go through our thinking as we read and re-enacted what can only be called PO Fulton's account of my son's last moments. I have shown all our diagrams which we made for ourselves as we endeavoured to bring PO Fulton's account to life. One of the pictures was given to us the week before the Inquest, and all the others are our own diagrams and pictures.

I shall now proceed with the events according to PO Fulton.

On Friday 6th August, 2010, before 9am my son arrived in one of the LCVP Workshops called 4T, in order to find out from PO Fulton whether or not the flexible Davit hoses had been changed. My son had been informed that they had been and PO Fulton told my son that they had not been changed.

PO Fulton suggested that they go up immediately to the LCVP and check the manufacturer's label.

My son was due to start his two week holiday on Tuesday, 10th August, and was looking forward to seeing his fiancée, who would be flying over from the

UK.

My son wanted all his work left in good order before he started his leave.

HMS Ocean carries four LCVPs which are housed in four LCVP Bays, two on each side of the ship.

On the day that my son fell, there were two LCVPs in the water below, and two LCVPs in the Bays. Each LCVP had a name, NM, N2, N3, and N4.

The picture below shows the position of the LCVPs at the time.

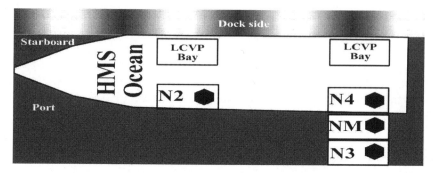

The following picture was taken at the time of my son's fall which the Coroner only gave to the legal team ten days before my son's Inquest.

According to PO Fulton, he and my son went to the LCVP bay, where N4 was housed. They then climbed the ladder to board LCVP N4 itself in order to check the flexible davit hoses.

There was a sheer, forty to fifty foot drop on one side of the LCVP, and the two LCVPs, (NM and N3), were in the water directly beneath them; Engineering Technician (ET) Myers and PO Dot Cottam were working on the LCVPs in the water. According to ET Myers, LCVP N3 had the engine running. The two Davits hold the LCVP in the LCVP Bay. According to PO Fulton they first went to check the Davit near the front (bow) of the LCVP (see Davit 1 in the picture above). From this position they could not see the flexible Davit hose labels.

According to PO Fulton, they then went to check Davit 2 that was near the wheelhouse of LCVP N4.

According to PO Fulton, he then decided to climb up onto the roof of the wheelhouse.

According to PO Fulton, my son followed and also climbed up onto the wheelhouse roof to join him.

According to PO Fulton, we have two men on the cramped wheelhouse roof, where a man is unable to stand, but can merely crouch.

According to PO Fulton they obtained the information they required. The flexible hoses had in fact been changed.

According to PO Fulton, he decided to climb back down to the deck of the LCVP by taking a different route, the longer back route across the wheelhouse roof which had a multitude of equipment on it.

According to PO Fulton, who now says that he saw nothing, as his back was turned, he heard a thud, then 'Whoa, Whoa, Whoa', then a scream.

> "Almost immediately after the initial thud, he heard Lt Woodhouse's voice say something that sounded like 'Whoa, Whoa, Whoa' (as if he had lost his balance) followed by a scream."

My son's scream was no ordinary scream. I have calculated that it would last about 1.5 seconds. No one has to exert their imagination to know that this 1.5 second scream would be a loud scream, a scream full of terror and anguish. This was not a shout. It was a loud, terrified scream.

After hearing my son's scream, PO Fulton happily continued down to the deck of the LCVP via the back of the wheelhouse roof. My son's terrified scream appears to have made little impact on him.

So PO Fulton now arrives onto the deck of the LCVP by the back of the wheelhouse. The scream still has made no impact on him. We now read that once on the deck of the LCVP, he

> "initially presumed that Lt Woodhouse had merely jumped and lost his balance in the LCVP, so he went around to the front of the wheelhouse expecting to see him on the deck"

But what is ET Myers reaction to my son's terrified 1.5 second scream?

We read that ET Myers was working on LCVP N3 in the water below. ET Myers tells us that LCVP N3 had the engine running. Above this noise ET Myers heard my son's loud, terrified scream. My son had not even landed and the scream was so loud, so anguished, that ET Myers immediately looked up and saw my son as he was falling.

What a difference this is from PO Fulton's reaction on hearing my son's scream. PO Fulton continues his journey to the back of the wheelhouse roof, but ET Myers, startled by the loud, urgent scream, looks up in horror to see my son falling and then instantly starts shouting an alarm.

What happens next? Are there any other sounds? There is the sound of my son's head hitting the metal LCVP. The force of my son's head landing on a metal surface split his skull from ear to ear.

PO Dot Cottam, who was inside the engine bay of LCVP N3 in the water below, heard this loud thud. This is despite the fact that he was in a small, confined space. ET Myers immediately started shouting to raise an alarm.

ET Myers ran to where PO Dot Cottam was, to alert him of my son's fall.

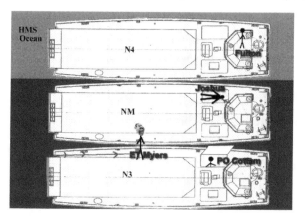

13. *ET4* **(Myers)** *immediately raised a loud vocal alarm and **continued shouting**. However due to the noise of N3's engine he assessed that PO3 (2)* **(Dot Cottam)** *could not hear him and therefore crossed to the engine bay access hatch to ensure that the PO could hear his LVA* **(loud vocal alarm).** *On exiting from the engine bay PO3 (2)* **(Dot Cottam)** *was informed that "an officer had just fallen". PO 3 (2)* **(Dot Cottam)** *then joined ET 4* **(Myers)** *in **continuing to raise the alarm**.*

We read that ET Myers realised that PO Dot Cottam had not heard the scream or the loud shouting to raise an alarm, so
Myers "***continued shouting***" as he headed towards PO Dot Cottam.

Now that PO Dot Cottam has been alerted, he immediately joins ET Myers, and starts shouting too.

Therefore with regard to the scream and shouts, what exactly has taken place?

Firstly, we have my son's loud, terrified scream, after which he lies silent forever. I have roughly estimated this scream would have had a duration of 1.5 seconds.

Next we have the very loud thud/bang as my son hits the metal surface of the LCVP with his head.

After that we have ET Myers' loud, urgent shouting, and raising of an alarm.

Then we have the two men, Myers and PO Dot Cottam, urgently shouting in unison and raising an alarm. We now have double the noise and double the alarm and double the urgency. There is a man in a pool of blood right in front of them. Time is of the essence if they are to save his life.

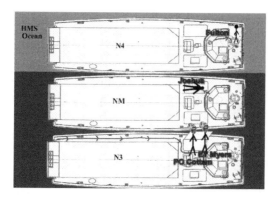

All this time that the air is filled with heart wrenching urgent shouts, alarm shouts, what is PO Fulton doing?

Ah, he is wondering what could possibly have happened to my son. He is still gently walking around LCVP N4.

He is so intrigued as to where my son is that he goes first to the front of the wheelhouse to see whether he is there.

> 15. *Having climbed down from the roof of the wheelhouse, PO2 (1)* **(PO Fulton)** *initially presumed that Lt Woodhouse had merely jumped and lost his balance in the LCVP,* **so he went around to the front of the wheelhouse expecting to see him on the deck.**

He does not find my son at the front of the wheelhouse, where he presumed he was, and where he was expecting to find him. It doesn't occur to him to look over the side. The urgent shouts and alarm calls mean nothing to PO Fulton. If my son's terrified scream made no impact on him, then urgent shouts would make even less impact.

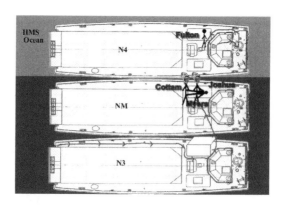

This gets stranger and stranger. All this time, the two men below are shouting urgently, and raising an alarm.

But PO Fulton is still wondering where my son is. Now that he does not see my son by the front of the wheelhouse, he then assumes that he has fallen into the LCVP Bay. O yes, this is where he must be. In fact, he says that now that he sees that my son is not on the LCVP at all, he quickly climbs down to the LCVP Bay as he now wishes to assist.

> *When he observed that Lt Woodhouse was not there, he assumed that he had fallen down into the LCVP Bay below and so quickly climbed down to assist.*

This is another strange impossibility. He suspects my son fell and landed in the LCVP Bay. In order for my son to have landed in the LCVP Bay below, he would have to have grown wings, flown off the LCVP, and then somehow have propelled himself backwards so that he lands in the Bay. Impossible.

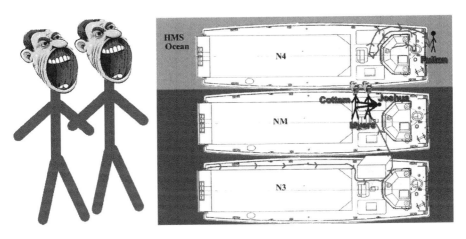

All the time that PO Fulton is wondering where my son is, ET Myers and PO Dot Cottam continue shouting out an alarm.

We now read that the shouting and the alarms were so loud that other members of the ship's company arrived in the LCVP Bay from inside the recesses of HMS Ocean to see what was going on. They were told to get the alarm piped.

> *16. At this stage other members of the Ship's Company had heard the LVA but were enquiring whether it was real or not. ET4 (1) **(Myers)** re-iterated the alarm by the use of the phrase "safeguard" and told*

*those personnel that had arrived in the LCVP Bay to "get it piped".*

These people heard the loud shouting and heard the alarm from inside HMS Ocean, but PO Fulton, who is right on the scene, is still wondering what could possibly have happened to my son.

According to PO Fulton, he has now arrived in the LCVP Bay and sees that my son in not in the Bay. It is only now that he decides to look over the side of the ship. O where is Joshua? Where could he possibly have got to?

All the while that PO Fulton is perplexed, wondering where my son is, and making a pretence of searching for my son, we have firstly my son's loud terrified scream, then we have the loud bang as my son's head hits the metal LCVP, then we have ET Myers' urgent shouts, and lastly we have ET Myers and PO Dot Cottam's joint united shouts and alarm calls.

I do not believe PO Fulton's account of the events.

Two men went to do a job, and only one came back, and his account is the closest you can get to a fairy tale.

## On Our Own

The Royal Navy would not help. This was getting too close to the bone for them. In fact they had acted positively. It was all my son's fault. They had given us a fine military funeral; why ever were we not satisfied?

The more we pored over the many pictures and plans and the one Ship's Investigation, the more we were convinced that there were questions which needed answering.

What was to be done?

It did not appear that anyone else thought PO Fulton's account in the ISI was even slightly suspicious. We felt very alone. I felt as if we were the only ones in the world who could see that his account was contrived.

I emailed many charities, organisations that I found on the internet asking for help, for advice. What could be done? I was desperate. Who could help? Who was there who would even be prepared to listen?

Who was there who would even believe us?

# Contacting the Coroner

We found the circumstances of my son's death described in the ISI highly suspicious. What could we do?

We needed to see the criminal investigation done by the SIB, Military Police. How could we get this investigation?

I had been told to contact Coroner David Horsley and request this vital document.

On the 30th December, 2010, I emailed the Coroner informing him we were the next of kin and asked when we might be able to see the SIB criminal investigation into my son's death.

On the 1st January, 2011, I received the normal, non-committal official email letting me know I will just have to wait until he, the Coroner, saw fit to divulge information. I quote from his email below -

> "At the moment, I have not received either of the 2 reports to which you refer. The SIB report will I expect be more relevant to my investigation. Once I have gathered all the evidence I consider necessary and appropriate for the Inquest, I will take a view on what Inquest documents can be released to interested persons.
>
> I hope this assists you"

(see email correspondence with Coroner David Horsley on website)

We would just have to wait.

Prolong the waiting and prolong the time and then all uncomfortable problems will just disappear. Time has a funny habit of covering all irrelevant little problems like a suspicious death. All that is needed is a huge pile of papers and a long distance of time, time, and more time.

But there is a suspicious death, time is of the essence, not only to investigate it but also to stop a recurrence. Time is of the essence.

# Contacting the Police – 1st January, 2011

What was to be done to get an investigation into my son's suspicious death? It was obvious from the Coroner 's email that we would have to wait a long time before we saw the criminal investigation done by the SIB, Military Police, into my son's death, and we never did see it. We only saw a summary of it.

I emailed the Police and asked if they would investigate the suspicious circumstances surrounding my son's death.

Paul Barton, Detective Chief Inspector, Hampshire Constabulary, replied, telling me that my son's death would continue to be dealt with by the SIB, Military Police, unless there was clear evidence of a crime and the Coroner directed otherwise.

> *"My understanding is that you are not satisfied with the investigation by SIB and you would like Hampshire Constabulary to investigate.*
>
> *I must advise you that under normal circumstances, any death involving military personnel during operational deployment would be dealt with by SIB **unless there was clear evidence of a crime** and **the Coroner directed otherwise.** The SIB is independent from the MOD and will be acting on behalf of the Coroner."*

Paul Barton, Detective Chief Inspector, Hampshire Constabulary also discussed my son's death with the Coroner who informed the Chief Inspector that he was satisfied that my son's death should remain with the SIB.

> *I have today discussed this case with Mr Horsley and at this moment in time **he is satisfied** that the investigation into Joshua's death is suitable to remain with SIB. He has not as yet received the findings on the investigation and therefore cannot comment at this stage as to whether or not the investigation was thorough.*
>
> (see emails to Hampshire Constabulary on website)

What clear evidence of a crime is needed before the case is handed over to the Police? Are the suspicious circumstances in the Immediate Ship's Investigation not reason enough for an investigation?

Two men went to do a job and only one came back, and his account is so implausible that a child would know that it has been knocked together.

It appears that this is not enough information to warrant an investigation by the Police.

Next, I am informed that the Coroner has the power to hand a death over to the Police for them to investigate. This fits in with what I read online regarding the duties of a Coroner. As soon as there is any suspicion of foul play, the Coroner is to immediately stop his investigation and hand it over to the Police.

We were to find over the coming months that despite the fact that as the information got more and more suspicious, the Coroner abused his position as HM Coroner, and refused to hand my son's suspicious death to the Police to investigate. And yet he did even more than this.

The Coroner impeded justice by covering, and hiding, and denying us information and then even denying us the opportunity to ask any questions pertaining to my son's suspicious death at his Inquest.

## Who Can Help?

There was no one to help. The Police did not want to know. The Coroner is the very impediment to justice.

Who can help? Who even cares that my son died in suspicious circumstances?

How do we get more than that one tiny bit of information into how my son died? The one report on my son's death elicited more questions than answers. It revealed a big gaping hole of dark secrecy that is Military Justice.

How do you get anyone to investigate a suspicious death in the Military?

I wrote many emails to all sorts of organisations which I found online, but to no avail. How could they help? Who can take on the Military?

## Contacting the Royal British Legion

Whilst waiting to bury my son in August, 2010, we were given information on a new service that the Royal British Legion had recently started for military families. We were told that the Royal British Legion was now giving free Inquest Advice to families.

What did I know of Inquests? I didn't know too much about their purpose as I had not needed to.

My son's fiancée availed herself of the service immediately.

As I was now flaying around like a drowning man looking for anybody to help us investigate my son's suspicious death, my thoughts turned to the Royal British Legion and their Independent Inquest Advice for military families. Perhaps they could help us where none other would or could.

I did not want to piggy back on the RBL lawyer that was helping my son's fiancée. I did not want to burden or distress my son's fiancée with our thoughts.

I therefore emailed the Royal British Legion using a pseudonym. However, they knew by the circumstances that it was my son Joshua. I was told that it was not unusual for different members of the same family to have different lawyers advise and represent them.

We therefore gratefully accepted the help of the Royal British Legion who assigned a different lawyer to help us.

Right from the very beginning I informed the Royal British Legion that our main concern was to have my son's suspicious death investigated, as seen by my email of the 9th January, 2011 -

> *"To return to our main concern, my husband and I believe that the circumstances surrounding my son's fall warrant a Police Investigation. I am in touch with Hampshire Constabulary as I am asking them to hold a Police Investigation into my son's fall. We also believe there is an urgency to have this investigated.*
>
> *We would be pleased to hear whether or not the British Legion would be able to help my husband and I in any way, bearing in mind our first and foremost concern is to determine whether my son's fall was in fact due to an accident."*

> (see email correspondence on website)

Our objective was to find out how Joshua died, as the only report in his death, the ISI, pointed to highly suspicious circumstances.

The Ship's Investigation was demanding a deeper investigation into my son's death.

Had this taken place?

# The Royal British Legion – Life Savers

Without the Royal British Legion, my son's case would have been steamrolled in the usual fashion by the MOD and the Coroner.

We say thank you to the people in the Royal British Legion who saw the great oppression of military families by the Coronial system and the MOD, and who stepped in to help us, to give us a voice; for taking on the MOD and the Coroner, for fighting a battle that we could not fight, that we had no idea how to fight. A battle we could not possibly fight whilst still reeling from our great personal loss.

I shall now recount some of the events as the Royal British Legion pick up the baton.

# Has PO Fulton Been Put Into Custody?

The Royal Navy and the MOD were hiding behind the Coroner. This is very convenient.

They would not give us any information besides the one solitary Ship's Investigation. I gather we were treated better than most military families, who only receive a report days before the Inquest.

If the wheels of Military Justice turn slowly enough, perhaps the only people who think this death is suspicious would have worn themselves out and possibly died, and then there will be nobody to question the strange circumstances surrounding my son's death.

I needed to have some indication as to how seriously the SIB, Military Police were treating my son's death. Did they think it was suspicious? I needed to know long before the Inquest, which could be many years away. How could I find out?

On the one hand we knew that all of Joshua's records were being meticulously gone through – his health records, educational records, even up to his health and safety course training. But what about the records of the only man with my son when he fell to his death?

Aaah, a thought! There was a way I could find out whether or not the Coroner, the MOD, the RN, and the SIB Military Police considered my son's death as suspicious. Had PO Fulton been put in custody? I needed to know.

In my very first phone call with the RBL Lawyer, I expressed my concern that my son's death was suspicious. It was important to know, and not lose the opportunity of time. I had said as much in my introductory email.

The RBL Lawyer suggested that she ask the Defence Inquest Unit of the MOD whether any charges or disciplinary action was taken against any person.

The answer came back, no.

In fact we got more information than that.

The RBL lawyer informed us that her MOD DIU legal counterpart told her that Joshua was so well liked on the ship, it could not possibly have been foul play.

## Military Justice – so now we knew

So finally we knew. If the only man with my son, PO Fulton, was not in custody, then the authorities were ignoring the suspicious circumstances surrounding my son's death.

The MOD, the SIB Military Police, the Royal Navy, and of course, the Coroner, were not officially treating my son's death as suspicious.

Two men went to do a job and only one came back and his account is completely implausible; yet those placed in authority to investigate a suspicious death were not doing so.

And it was worse than that. HMS Ocean threw their dead officer to the dogs. A dead man cannot defend himself so you can do with him as you please, but first make sure that you give him a fine funeral. Oh and don't forget to put the flags at half-mast.

This is the Military Justice I was experiencing. This is the Military Justice that my son received. They were not treating my son's death as suspicious.

If PO Fulton, the man with my son, was not in custody, then I can logically surmise that the SIB investigation into my son's death has concluded, like the Immediate Ship's Investigation (ISI), that my son was responsible for his own death.

# The Royal British Legion – Why are they Involved?

The RBL lawyer explained the history of the Coronial system to us.

We had previously looked online and understood that the Coroner's main function was to decide on the cause of death, and, more importantly, first and foremost, to make sure it was not due to murder - the legal term being 'foul play'.

But this was only on paper.

The RBL lawyer explained to us that the Coronial system is archaic, about 500 years old, and unlike other judicial systems has not moved with the times. Appealing against this system is very difficult, costly, and well-nigh impossible.

The result is that you have a Coroner who is virtually untouchable and behaves as such. The behaviour of our particular Coroner, Mr David Horsley, is not an isolated case.

The RBL lawyer went on to explain that due to the outcry from Military families at their terrible treatment in the hands of Coroners, the RBL set up the Independent Inquest Advice Service to help military families receive even a small scrap of justice.

Providentially, the Independent Inquest Advice Service was started the month before my son died. We thank our God for His kindness to us for this help from the Royal British Legion.

# The MOD Put their Big Guns onto Joshua's Case

Initially the RBL lawyer had been corresponding with Royal Navy Inquest Advice to find out whether they would be holding a Service Inquiry, to find out whether the SIB report had been sent to the coroner, and to find out whether any charges or disciplinary action had been taken against PO Fulton, the man with my son.

Then in February, 2011, the RBL lawyer told me in a phone call that the MOD had put their 'big guns' onto my son's case and she was not sure why they had done this. She further wrote,

> I have forwarded the forms of authority to Lt Col Freddie Kemp at the
> Defence Inquest Unit (DIU) who has taken over the conduct of this

> *matter from Naval Command. DIU is the tri-service MoD unit that supports the coroner in military inquests.* **I do not know why the Naval Inquest Unit has not retained this case. They usually pass them on where there is a Service Inquiry or complications.** *I will not guess at the motives here? I will be seeing Lt Col Kemp on 7th February and will attempt to gain some insight to this decision and to the issues in the case.*

Why had the MOD put their big guns onto my son's case? Why was this case so important to the MOD?

My personal opinion is that it was not the Health and Safety aspect of my son's case that the MOD feared.

It was that my son's death was steeped in suspicious circumstances and they had to do their utmost to hide these circumstances and pretend they just did not exist.

There must not be a scandal. There must not be even a whiff of a scandal.

Headlines - 'Join the Royal Navy and get murdered'.


## The Royal British Legion Asks for Disclosure

The RBL now has the mammoth task of obtaining information from the Coroner and checking up on this by liaising with the Royal Navy Inquest Support, and then the MOD Defence Inquest Unit.

On the 22nd January, 2011, the RBL lawyer asked first and foremost for disclosure of the SIB Investigation. She was informed that this would only be dealt with once all the information had been gathered.

> *"Mr Gregory has confirmed that the coroner will deal with the issue of disclosure of documents once he has finished gathering all the evidence in this case."*

No commitments there. Very reasonable legal speak. As it turned out, it would be over a whole year later before we were finally given the SIB Investigation, which was only a summary.

By the 26th May, 2011, the RBL lawyer asked again for disclosure of the SIB Investigation.

By the time of the first pre-Inquest on the 18th August, 2011, we still had not received it.

At the first pre-Inquest, when the Coroner was asked again when we might have the SIB investigation, he gave a speech which made it clear that he didn't have to do anything.

## The Royal British Legion Asks for a Pre-Inquest

The RBL lawyer informed us that some Coroners do not even bother to hold a pre-Inquest in which important matters are discussed, such as the scope of the forthcoming Inquest, the witnesses, and such like.

Therefore on the 28th February, 2011, and again on the 9th March, the RBL lawyer enquired whether the Coroner would hold a pre-Inquest. She was told in March that he was still considering this. Then on the 26th May, and 30th June, the RBL lawyer informed the Coroner that we would be in the Portsmouth area during August, 2011, and asked if he would like to hold a pre-Inquest.

Success. The RBL lawyer managed to 'respectfully' persuade the Coroner that it was a good idea to hold a pre-Inquest when we would be in Portsmouth in August, 2011.

## We have a Post Mortem – Joshua's Heart

The Royal British Legion had been pressing for disclosure of documents, amongst these being the Post Mortem.

In March, 2011, the Coroner released my son's Post Mortem.

The RBL lawyer suggested that we have a medical doctor give their professional overview of my son's autopsy. We were informed that there is a panel of doctors made up of retired practitioners who voluntarily give their time to the Legion, and Joshua's autopsy was sent to one of this party.

In mid-April, 2011, the RBL lawyer arranged a telephone conversation to discuss the findings.

She suggested I should sit down, always a bad sign.

She then told me that the doctor who had studied my son's autopsy, a retired military cardiologist, noticed that Joshua had a thickening of the heart. On that evidence alone, he/she came to the conclusion that my son suffered from cardiomyopathy which in his opinion accounted for my son's fall, saying that my son had obviously had a heart-attack, had fainted, and then fallen over the side.

I immediately countered this and told the RBL lawyer that at the hospital every single doctor on each day of Joshua's stay in Intensive Care remarked with the greatest admiration on Joshua's 'good strong young heart'. In fact one doctor even went on to say that despite such a terrible blow received from falling forty six feet and landing on his head, his heart did not miss a beat, nor had it ever need any resuscitation. It was a 'good strong young heart' to quote the doctor's words.

I then went on to say to the RBL lawyer that the hospital even asked us if we would donate Joshua's heart as they wanted it so badly.

She then replied, 'Things are not as clear cut as the MOD would have us believe.'

She told me that this information had to go to the Coroner who could then decide whether or not to investigate the matter further.

Following this news I then went about investigating the matter myself, despite the great disadvantages I faced. I began reading and preparing as much material as I could to refute this false claim should the MOD choose to follow this route at the Inquest.

I also contacted a medical doctor who specialised in cardiomyopathy as opposed to just a cardiologist and sent him my son's autopsy. He replied that it was highly unlikely that my son had suffered a heart attack.

We also ordered a copy of my son's medical records during his last four days at Shands Jacksonville Hospital, which contained highly detailed charts and graphs of his blood levels, blood chemical structure, heart- beat, and blood pressure.

The more I read and the more I studied Joshua's records, in addition to the opinion of the cardiomyopathy specialist, the more outrageous was this claim that my son had had a heart attack and thus fell to his death.

No person having a heart attack has the strength to scream, let alone scream loudly for 1.5 seconds.

## Obtain Legal Representation

The RBL lawyer informed us that the Royal British Legion could only give Inquest advice and could not represent us at the Inquest. She told us that they would routinely refer cases to a group of solicitors in their efforts to help obtain legal representation for a military family at an Inquest.

Here is another example of the kind and practical advice and help given by the Royal British Legion to its military families. Thank you Royal British Legion.

Unfortunately the RBL was unable to find help for us as we were not dependents of my son and the legal firms needed to earn a living.

> Unfortunately, the group of solicitors firms that we usually refer cases to is unable to take on this matter as you are non-dependents and therefore any claim would not have a monetary value and would outweigh the costs of bringing any such litigation. I shall now make further enquiries on your behalf and would suggest that you also start making enquiries through The Law Society, as previously mentioned.

She also stressed the fact that we should seek legal representation as my son's Inquest would be a Jury Inquest and the MOD had put their 'big guns on the case'.

I had told her that when we first received the suspicious ISI, I had tried to obtain legal representation and help for the forthcoming Inquest by contacting a legal firm and outlining my position.

The legal firm explained that they needed to cover their costs, quite rightly, and that there were two routes they could follow to do this.

One was to seek compensation by proving we were financially dependent on my son, which was not the case.

The second route was for them to seek to prove some Health and Safety negligence by the Royal Navy and by this means get a pay-out to cover their fees.

I told the firm that I wanted to find out how my son died, as he died under suspicious circumstances, and I wanted no stone left unturned in trying to investigate this. The legal firm explained that they might be able to ask one or two questions on this subject, but the main thrust of their representation would be to obtain a pay out from the MOD on Health and Safety grounds.

As our objectives were not the same as that of the legal firm, we did not go any further. Therefore when the RBL lawyer suggested that I look for a firm to represent us, I did not make any effort to do so and we decided, as a family, that we would endeavour to represent ourselves at my son's Inquest with the RBL hopefully advising us.

The RBL lawyer was not particularly happy with our decision but completely understood our position and the fact that we could not obtain legal representation in order to find out how my son came to his violent death.

But this did not stop her. She was beavering away in the background and was doing her utmost to help us by seeking free legal representation for us. We could never have accomplished this on our own and we shall ever be grateful.

## Request for Disciplinary Records of HMS Ocean

A family member suggested that we ask for the Disciplinary Records of HMS Ocean, as they could possibly shed some light on my son's death.

We then asked the RBL Lawyer to please ask the Coroner for the Disciplinary Records of HMS Ocean. I explained why it was so important to us.

She kindly added this request and sent a letter to the Coroner on the 26th May, 2011, where she wrote -

> *"Further, they have asked that I make a request for disclosure of the following documents -*
>
> *1. Medical records*
> **2. Disciplinary records in which Joshua may be named**
> *3. The SIB report"*

(see letter to Coroner 26/5/11 on website)

One month later, and there was not even a response from the Coroner. The disciplinary records were very important to us. I asked the RBL lawyer if she would please write again to the Coroner explaining our position and why it was so important to us as we thought my son's death was loaded with suspicious circumstances.

On the 30th June, 2011, she wrote again requesting the disciplinary records of HMS Ocean

> Dear Mr Horsley,
>
> Re: Inquest touching upon the death of Lt Joshua Woodhouse RN
>
> Further to my letter of 26th May 2011, Mrs Woodhouse has requested that I clarify the point regarding her request for the disciplinary records. For the sake of completeness, I am using the wording that Mrs Woodhouse has specified, as follows:-
>
> > **"I would like to have copies of any disciplinary records or disciplinary cautions…..which might have involved my son in any way at all. That would include any records where my son was either the party bringing the disciplinary action/caution or reporting it, or being a witness, or having any participation whatsoever in the action"**

(see Letter to Coroner 30/6/11 on website)

By the 12th July, she informed us of the Coroner's response –

> "The coroner has indicated that **he will not be calling for the disciplinary records as he does not feel that they are relevant** to his investigation. I seem to recall that Lt Col Kemp had indicated that there was nothing in the records and that all accounts indicated that Joshua was well liked. "

The Coroner does not consider that the Disciplinary Records of HMS Ocean are relevant to the investigation of this suspicious death.

I thought the Coroner's job was first and foremost to ensure that there are no suspicious circumstances in the death, and if there are, then he is to immediately hand the investigation over to the Police for the experts to investigate.

Are we not dealing with a suspicious death? Two men went to do a job and only one came back and his account is just not plausible.

And so I asked the RBL lawyer to once again please ask the Coroner for the Disciplinary Records of HMS Ocean.

Why didn't the Coroner consider the Disciplinary Records of HMS Ocean relevant? Is it because he has already decided the outcome of the Inquest? Just another unfortunate accident and purely the fault of the unfortunate individual?

I therefore asked the RBL lawyer to please ask yet again, and this time to yet again use our own wording. How could we possibly spell it out to the Coroner? Two men went to do a job and only one came back alive, and his account is riddled with holes. Surely this is crying out to be investigated? What must one do to get a suspicious death properly investigated in the UK?

The RBL lawyer kindly wrote once again on our behalf to the Coroner on the 2nd August, 2011, and I quote from this letter below -

> *"Mrs Woodhouse notes your comments about the relevance of the disciplinary records. She has asked that I clarify her position and expressly asked that I inform you of her concerns and that I send a copy this letter to her.*
>
> *"We need to see the disciplinary records for the following reason:*
>
> - *If my son had disciplined someone, then that could give the person disciplined a motive for murdering my son. The person who actually did the murder might not necessarily have been the person disciplined, but a friend, relative or in another relationship to the disciplined person.*
> - ***Failure to allow us to see the disciplinary records would mean the possibility that my son has been murdered has already been discounted by the coroner."***

Why did we do this? We believed that my son's death was highly suspicious and that there was a high possibility that there was Foul Play in his death. How could we get this across to the Coroner without spelling it out?

The answer from the Coroner was again 'no'.

Except this time there was a difference. I was informed that the Coroner was 'out of sorts' at being asked.

Why was the Coroner out of sorts? Was it perhaps that the reason given for failure to release the disciplinary records had hit the bull's eye?

## Meeting the RBL Lawyer – 11th August, 2011

The RBL lawyer had suggested that the Coroner hold a pre-Inquest in August, 2011 as we would be in the Portsmouth area.

During this time it was also arranged for us to meet her.

It was at this first meeting where three members of our family were present that the RBL lawyer could see that there were deep questions about the official account, as given in the ISI, and that we had based this opinion on clear and logical arguments.

We showed her some of the work we had done in obtaining photographs and plans in order to make sense of PO Fulton's account of my son's last moments before his fall.

It was a very profitable meeting and it was a pleasure to meet the woman who helped us so greatly.

## Coroner David Horsley Informed Early of Foul Play Suspicions

At this meeting the RBL lawyer informed us that she had seen the Coroner recently and that he was not well pleased at our comments regarding the concealment of the Disciplinary Records where we stated –

> *"Failure to allow us to see the disciplinary records would mean the possibility that my son has been murdered has already been discounted by the coroner."*

She told us that the Coroner had countered this accusation by saying that if we believed my son's death was due to foul play we should have informed him right at the very beginning.

Aaah, but the Coroner had been informed.

When I contacted Detective Chief Inspector Paul Barton, Hampshire Constabulary in January, 2011, with our concerns that my son had died in suspicious circumstances, he had immediately discussed this with Coroner. I quote Inspector Barton's email of 8/1/2011 –

> *"I must advise you that under normal circumstances, any death involving military personnel during operational deployment would be dealt with by SIB unless there was clear evidence of a crime and the Coroner directed otherwise. The SIB are independent from the MOD and will be acting on behalf of the Coroner.*
>
> ***I have today discussed this case with Mr Horsley*** *and at this moment in time he is satisfied that the investigation into Joshua's death is suitable to remain with SIB. He has not as yet received the findings on the investigation and therefore cannot comment at this stage as to whether or not the investigation was thorough."*

The Coroner had been notified right at the very beginning and yet he was pleading ignorance and throwing the blame back on us.

He had been informed by Chief Inspector Barton of our concerns before even receiving the SIB Investigation.

Therefore a normal person would instantly be on the alert to see why the parents believed such a thing. Were there any grounds for such a belief? What reasons could they possibly have to believe such a thing? This warranted a very careful evaluation of the investigations that were soon to fall on the Coroner's desk.

Instead, the Coroner pleaded that he didn't even know we believed Joshua had died in suspicious circumstance.

The RBL lawyer was very pleased to have copies of my email correspondence with Detective Chief Inspector Paul Barton so that she could send them to the Coroner.

## Unexpected Help – a London Barrister

It was at this meeting that the RBL lawyer informed us that she had found a London barrister who volunteered to represent us at no charge whatsoever and at very short notice. The first pre-Inquest was just one week away, and he had an enormous amount of work to do just to familiarise himself with the case and prepare for the pre-Inquest.

This news was totally unexpected and it took many days for the enormity of such an event to fully hit us.

However, we did have reservations in the sense that we did not know the calibre of this man that had so generously offered to help us, nor did we know the motives.

We were therefore looking forward to meeting this London barrister, and at the same time we were also intrigued by the man. How did such a wonderful event occur?

## The Royal British Legion – Thank you

To the Royal British Legion and to all the public who loyally support them and their work, we say thank you.

Inadequate words, but that is all we have.

We were informed that now that a London Barrister had volunteered to take on Joshua's case and fight for him, they had officially handed over the baton to him. They would always be on hand to help and would be there right up to the Inquest, but legally they would no longer be at the forefront of the battle. Instead they would continue to beaver away in the background, supporting and helping and advising the London barrister whenever required.

What had the Royal British Legion done for us?

I shall list some of the things they have done for us, for our son Joshua, and they are not listed in order of importance, for they are all of great value to us. It is because of the work of the Royal British Legion that we had a miniscule of a fighting chance, that we were even allowed to gasp out a word of protest against the might of the Coroner, and the might of the MOD.

- It was the Royal British Legion that arranged for a pre-Inquest for us.
- It was the Royal British Legion that found for us a London Barrister who, for no financial gain, but rather at great financial cost to himself, chose to represent Joshua. How did such a thing happen?
- It was the Royal British Legion who obtained the Post Mortem for us.

- It was the Royal British Legion who kept asking for the disclosure of the SIB report.
- It was the Royal British Legion who kept asking for the Disciplinary Records of HMS Ocean.
- It was the Royal British Legion who gave of their personal time and gave me many hours of personal phone calls with updates and advice on my son's case and its progress.

And that does not include all the work done on our behalf that I know nothing about.

## The First Pre-Inquest - 18.08.2011 - Meeting the London Barrister

We were overwhelmed that a London Barrister would volunteer to represent us and at such short notice and we were intrigued to meet him.

We met the London Barrister in the downstairs tea-room of the Portsmouth Guildhall where we were able to have a short discussion before we were summoned to my son's first pre-Inquest.

The London Barrister was courteous and a true gentleman from the very start.

He had had less than one week to prepare for my son's Inquest. In this time he not only read my son's case but prepared a pre-Inquest Review Agenda being a five page document made of thirty two bullet points to discuss at the pre-Inquest.    (see website)

The London Barrister asked us why we suspected foul play in my son's death. We gave him some of our reasons and he did not correct us to say that we were imagining things.

The London Barrister also made it quite clear that he would not be following a route that he did not believe in, or a route that he could not justify, irrespective of our wishes.  He wanted to ensure from the very beginning that we knew what his terms were.  We were perfectly content with this and appreciated his honesty.

## The First Pre-Inquest - 18.08.2011 – One year after Joshua's death

It was now time to be summoned to my son's first pre-Inquest.

My son's fiancée, with her RBL lawyer, was also present at this first pre-Inquest.

The MOD barrister and lawyer sat opposite us exchanging light humorous conversation.

A tissue box had been placed in front of me. It reminded me of the following words in the Bible

> **But woe unto you …. for ye tithe mint and rue and all manner of herbs, and pass over judgment …**

> Luke 11:42

Meticulous with the details, the tissue boxes, but overlooking the weightier matters of righteousness and justice and judgment.

The Coroner entered last.

Amongst the first things the Coroner did was to humiliate the RBL lawyer and interrogate him as to why he was there.

After the grilling of the RBL lawyer, the Coroner turned his attention to the London barrister. He firstly upbraided him for only emailing the suggested pre-Inquest Review Agenda the day before, mentioning what a long document this was that consisted of five whole pages. How was he expected to review such a long document received only the day before?

After the Coroner had grilled the barrister, he then proceeded to use that very document as his agenda for the pre-Inquest.

It also showed me how much preparation the Coroner had made for my son's pre-Inquest. He had not even prepared his own agenda of items to be discussed. Was seven months not long enough for this very important, very busy man to do his work?

And so we proceeded to work through the London barrister's pre-Inquest Review Agenda.

## The First Pre-Inquest - Foul play to be Explored

After listing the properly interested persons for the Inquest in item 1, being the family members, Item 2 of our barrister's Agenda stated the most important aspect of the Inquest, in fact, the whole purpose of any and every Inquest, 'Was there any Foul play?'

> *"The family seek as wide a remit as possible, but can identify the following themes:*
>
> *Adequacy of steps to ensure Health and Safety*
>
> *Any possible Foul play"*

Here is a trained legal man that in the short time that he had to familiarise himself with my son's case by reading the Briefing Note from the Royal British Legion with supporting documentation, the one document from the Royal Navy (the Ship's Investigation) immediately identified the need to give as *"wide a remit as possible"* and to investigate the most important issue of my son's death – was there any *"Foul play"*?

This should be the first and foremost item to consider in any death and this top legal mind put it in the forefront of his request for my son's forthcoming Inquest.

## The First Pre-Inquest - The Coroner claims Foul Play is his first consideration

Now let us consider the Coroner's reaction when yet another person, a trained legal mind, informs him once again of the need to diligently enquire whether or not there was any foul play/unlawful killing in my son's death.

It is also to be borne in mind that just over two weeks earlier, on the 2nd August, the RBL wrote to the Coroner again requesting the Disciplinary Records of HMS Ocean, and this time quoting the following –

> *"Failure to allow us to see the disciplinary records would mean **the possibility that my son has been murdered** has already been discounted by the coroner."*

The Coroner then gave a speech saying that Foul Play was of course his first consideration and the very first thing on his mind when reviewing my son's case. He went on to tell us all how he had exercised his duty well in carefully considering whether there were suspicious circumstances in my son's death.

He then proceeded to inform us that he had concluded from all the evidence in front of him, which he had carefully considered, that there were no suspicious circumstances and therefore no foul play in my son's death.

Considering all the evidence?

What exactly does considering all the evidence mean?

At the very minimum, it means reading the evidence. In his job as HMS Coroner, it should also mean studying it, reviewing it, understanding it, analysing it, knowing the evidence inside out, back to front, and from all angles.

This is the man with all the evidence in front of him and yet he says that he could see no suspicious circumstances in my son's death.

We found many suspicious items in the one document that we have been allowed whilst this man is sitting on all the reports, evidence, and documents, before telling us that he can see no suspicious circumstances in my son's death.

Do all the other reports somehow negate the suspicious items in the ISI?

And there is more. The parents of the dead lieutenant now have fine trained legal help, firstly the Royal British Legion, and now a London Barrister, who are both saying the same things - investigate foul play.

## The First Pre-Inquest - Article 2 – Investigate the Suspicious Death

The third and fourth items in our barrister's Review Agenda concerned Article 2 of the European Convention. Was this engaged?

I am not a legal person and as such, in my limited understanding of the legal implications, I believe this to be a further request for a full Inquiry into the suspicious circumstances surrounding my son's death.

We had been informed that the coroner must decide four questions
    Who?

When?
Where?
How?

with regard to the death in question.

It was pointed out to us that a coroner could easily say that to answer the question of 'How' a person died, they may well say, 'in the hospital bed' completely ignoring the events that led that person to find themselves now lying in a hospital bed.

Consequently the legal team had to request that the 'How' be widened to include 'in what circumstances'. This could only be done by requesting that Article 2 of the European Convention on Human Rights be engaged.

To this the Coroner wanted written submissions from both legal teams to persuade him whether he should or should not investigate my son's suspicious death and 'engage Article 2'

This is my understanding of the request for Article 2.

## The First Pre-Inquest - Jury and Witnesses

Next in our barrister's Review Agenda concerned whether or not to have a Jury at my son's Inquest. To this the Coroner asked for submissions from the legal teams.

They then proceeded to discuss the next points in the Agenda, namely which witnesses to call and which witnesses will only have their statements read out, and these are referred to as Rule 37 Witnesses.

## The First Pre-Inquest - Withholding Evidence

So now we come to Item 15 of the Review Agenda which concerns Disclosure. It is one year since my son's death, and all we had was the one document, the ISI, for which we waited for four months, and the Post Mortem that was released to us in March, 2011.

At this first pre-Inquest the London Barrister requested among other documents the release of the criminal investigation Report conducted by the Special Investigation Branch (SIB) of the Royal Navy Military Police at the time of my son's death one year previously.

The Coroner then informed us all that he might never release the SIB report on my son's death, but that he might just bring the SIB man (whoever that was) to be a witness at the Inquest.

To this the London Barrister replied that it would be very difficult to question a witness when you had no idea what they had written.

I was in shock that such behaviour was occurring before my eyes and in a legal court of the UK.

In sharp contrast, the London Barrister was a true gentleman, never once being ruffled by these absurd statements made to him.

## The First Pre-Inquest - Disciplinary Records Refused

And still on the topic of Disclosure in Item 15 of the Review Agenda, we now come to the request for the Disciplinary Records.

This is another broken record that the Coroner does not want repeated. It was only two weeks previously that the Royal British Legion yet again requested a copy of the disciplinary records of HMS Ocean. Now to be asked again, and this time by a top London barrister, was making the Coroner distinctly and visibly unhappy.

What was going to be the reaction to this repeated request? Let us draw near and see.

The Coroner asked how could he possibly go through all those Disciplinary records. How could we be so absurd to ask such a thing?

I wondered, does HMS Ocean have that many disciplinary records that it would require an inordinate length of time to read through them? What sort of criminal ship is HMS Ocean that the Coroner is so concerned with the great quantity of disciplinary records he would have to study?

I also note that the Coroner, the SIB Military Police, and the MOD went through my son's health records, his educational records, his health and safety training, his study notes, his exam results, and all possible reports with a fine tooth comb, and yet they refused to publicise the disciplinary records of HMS Ocean.

What was being hidden in the Disciplinary records of HMS Ocean?

## The First Pre-Inquest - the SIB work for Me

Among the topics discussed, the SIB were mentioned. The Coroner gave us the backdrop to the Special Investigation Branch of the Royal Navy Military Police, the SIB.

He very proudly stated that the SIB were his men and that the SIB worked for him, and not for the military. They were independent of the Military.

Hmmm. This sounds excellent. An independent investigative police force that worked only for the Coroner, and not the military, and were totally impartial.

When we did receive the summary of the SIB report, I thought back to this time when the Coroner proudly told us that the SIB were his men, and that they worked for him.

Yes, they are your men, and yes, they do work for you.

## The First Pre-Inquest - the Result

What was the result of my son's first pre-Inquest?

Both legal teams had to make written submissions to the Coroner on two important matters –

- Whether to have a Jury at my son's Inquest and
- Whether Article 2 should be engaged and my son granted a full Middleton Enquiry into his death.

Each side had to convince the Coroner, in writing, as to the reasons why he should or should not have a Jury and hold a full Middleton Enquiry, i.e. engage Article 2.

What is a full Middleton Inquiry?

As I understand it, the Coroner has the power to hold just a normal enquiry, saying, for instance, that my son died in his hospital bed, simple, nothing suspicious about that, enquiry closed.

As I understand it, not being a legal person, a full Middleton Enquiry is where the possibility of unlawful killing, aka foul play, is investigated.

A full Middleton Enquiry was never granted to my son. Time would show that my son was denied a fair, criminal investigation into the suspicious circumstances surrounding his death by the SIB, and he was likewise denied a fair inquest into those same suspicious circumstances by the Coroner.

The legal team representing us were forbidden from asking any questions regarding the suspicious circumstances surrounding my son's death at the Inquest.

## The Coroner

From January, 2011, the Royal British Legion (RBL) had taken up the baton and they were representing my son in preparation for his Inquest.

The RBL asked the Coroner when we might have the SIB report, the pivotal report into the circumstances of my son's death. One year after my son's death the report was still denied us. Worse than that, at the pre-Inquest, the Coroner informed one and all that he might never choose to release it.

The RBL asked the Coroner for the disciplinary records of HMS Ocean. Again, refused, and this time refused right till the very end. We have not been allowed to see the Disciplinary records of HMS Ocean.

The RBL asked for my son's Post Mortem, which they obtained.

The RBL asked the Coroner for a pre-Inquest, which was granted.

I often wonder how the Coroner would have treated us had it not been for the Royal British Legion standing for us, standing for my son Joshua.

## The London Barrister Takes the Baton

Here we have a man that appeared from nowhere and took up our son's cause to fight for him at the time when we thought we were once again on our own. We were prepared to fight on our own despite being so ridiculously unfit to do so.

Why would anyone represent my son at his Inquest? This is expensive, costly, demanding, heart wrenching, thankless work.

Thank you for taking the baton from the Royal British Legion and fighting for my son. Thank you for doing it with all your might. Thank you for always treating us as if we were paying clients, influential paying clients. Never once did we feel that we were bothersome to you or that we were a bigger commitment than you had bargained for.

Throughout this entire episode, my family were spectators as we watched the generosity of so many people who selflessly gave of themselves in order to fight for my son against the mighty forces of the MOD and the Coroner and the Military.

I will now recount the events as they occurred.

## London Barrister's Submission – Request for Jury

The London Barrister's first submission to the Coroner regarded arguments as to why the Coroner should hold an Inquest with a Jury.

The London Barrister commences this submission with a request for the two main issues listed below to be examined -

- The Health and Safety issue, to find out what the Health and Safety procedures are on board HMS Ocean as they failed to prevent this tragedy and
- The Foul Play issue

Item 2 refers -

2. *Lieutenant Woodhouse died from head injuries suffered in a fall whilst serving on board HMS Ocean whilst the ship was docked at the Naval Station, Mayport, Florida, USA. The circumstances of his death are the subject of this inquiry and it is submitted that there are many issues that need to be addressed. The family of Lieutenant Woodhouse have submitted that questions not only need to be asked of the **health and safety** procedures on board HMS Ocean that failed to prevent this tragedy but also of the investigation itself in **deciding whether there was any foul play involved**.*

# London Barrister's Submission – Foul Play not Ruled Out

The London Barrister's Submission requesting an Inquest with a Jury gave repeated reasons for investigating Foul Play, pointing out that our family feel that Foul Play has not been ruled out. If it had been ruled out then the London Barrister would have been the first to inform us that he could not pursue this path as it had no grounds. On the contrary, the London Barrister pursued his arguments as to why Foul Play should be investigated.

In Item 18 of his submission, the London Barrister gives multiple reasons why my son's death is suspicious and warrants a full investigation and certainly an Inquest with a Jury.

The London Barrister commences with the first suspicious circumstance; two men went to do a job and only one returned.

> *"Two men climbed onto the wheelhouse of the Landing Craft and only one returned."*

He then points out that no one else saw the moment when my son fell and we have to rely on this man's sole testimony, the man that was with my son. He is showing the large weight that is placed on the sole testimony of the only man with my son, PO Fulton.

> *"According to the evidence of the Petty Officer who accompanied Lieutenant Woodhouse no one else saw the moment when he fell and **it is his sole testimony** that suggests that he exclaimed upon losing his footing."*

The London Barrister points out that this evidence, the evidence of the only man with my son, needs to be tested in a full, independent investigation.

He also mentioned that we, the family, had contacted Hampshire Constabulary in January, 2011 requesting an investigation into my son's death, only to be informed that the SIB Military Police were investigating and therefore Hampshire Constabulary could take no action.

The London Barrister pointed out to the Coroner that this SIB investigation is a military investigation and as such lacks openness and the public scrutiny that a full inquiry should have.

He also pointed out that we still had not been given the results of the SIB

Military Police investigation into my son's death.  It is to be remembered that the London Barrister wrote this one year after my son died when we had only the ISI from the Royal Navy and the Coroner had only released to us one more document, the Post Mortem.

The London Barrister was asking for disclosure.  He was asking for an open and full investigation into my son's suspicious death.

from Item 18 below –

> "According to the evidence of the Petty Officer who accompanied Lieutenant Woodhouse no one else saw the moment when he fell and it is his sole testimony that suggests that he exclaimed upon losing his footing. **This evidence needs to be tested in a full independent investigation.** In January 2011 the family requested that the Hampshire Constabulary investigate Lieutenant Woodhouse's death but were informed by DCI Paul Barton that as the SIB were already investigating they could take no action. **This is a military investigation which lacks the openness and public scrutiny that a full inquiry should have and indeed no formal conclusions from this investigation have yet been made available to the family.**"

In Item 19 of his submission, the London Barrister once again mentions Foul Play, and states that as the family suspect foul play, then the Coroner should consider the views of the family and the requirement of public scrutiny, and therefore provide for fully open and public scrutiny of the suspicious circumstances surrounding my son's death.

> "The Administrative Court was clear in Paul that where the Al-Fayed family **suspected foul play** and expressly desired a Jury for a **proper investigation** then those views should have been taken into account. HM Coroner need not, at this preliminary stage, decide whether any foul play has taken place but rather, should consider the views of the family and the **requirement** of **public scrutiny** in what are undoubtedly extremely sensitive and distressing circumstances. It is submitted that it would be appropriate to exercise the discretion accorded to HM Coroner under section 8(4) of the Coroners Act 1988 to satisfy the wishes of the family and thus to provide for **fully open, public scrutiny** of the **circumstances** surrounding Lieutenant Woodhouse's death."

In his conclusion, he once again points out that there should be an open, public scrutiny of all the evidence regarding my son's suspicious death.

I quote the Barrister's conclusion below –

### Conclusion

> "It is respectfully submitted that the obligation to summon a Jury under Section 8 (3)(d) of the Coroners Act 1988 is engaged in this case. There is a reasonable suspicion, even on the evidence as it stands, that reoccurrence of the tragic circumstances of Lieutenant Woodhouse's death is possible. In addition, or in the alternative, it is an express wish of his family that an inquiry be held in front of a Jury and that **there is open, public scrutiny of all the evidence in this matter**. It is in the best interests of all the parties to the inquiry, including the Royal Navy, that a Jury be summoned for this inquiry."

(see the website for the full submission)

We never did get a fully independent investigation into my son's suspicious death despite these repeated requests. The Coroner did not investigate the suspicious circumstances surrounding my son's death. The Coroner did not hand over my son's suspicious death to the Hampshire Constabulary for them to investigate as he should have done.

## London Barrister's Submission – Request for Full Middleton Inquiry

The London Barrister's second submission to the Coroner regarded arguments as to why the Coroner should hold a full Middleton Inquiry.

A full Middleton Inquiry would allow us to fully inquire into the suspicious circumstances surrounding my son's death. A full Middleton Inquiry would have allowed our legal team to correctly and fully interrogate PO Fulton regarding his strange account of my son's death.

A full Middleton Inquiry would have allowed Foul Play to be investigated.

Two men went to do a job and only one returned and his account is shot with holes, inconsistencies, strange accounts, and behaviour.

Let us look at the London Barrister's second submission to the Coroner requesting a Full Middleton Inquiry into my son's death.   I am not familiar with legal terms and cannot do the submission full justice; hence it is included in its entirety in the web site.

## Suspicious Circumstances Demand Investigation of Foul Play

The suspicious circumstances surrounding my son's death demand that Foul Play should be investigated i.e. that my son is granted a Full Middleton Inquiry or Inquest.

Let us quote from the London Barrister's second submission to the Coroner

In Item 12 he states –

> "It is respectfully submitted that, at the least, the **circumstances** of Lieutenant Woodhouse's death **require a full "Middleton" investigation** in order to prevent a similar tragedy befalling another serviceman."

In Item 13 he mentions the circumstances that warrant a full and open investigation –

> "It is has been made **clear** to HM Coroner that there are a number of issues arising out of the **circumstances** of this incident which the family believe require a **full** and **open** investigation (see the Pre Inquest Review agenda used as a basis for discussion at the hearing on 18 August 2011). They are concerned that a full investigation is required to review the possibility of **foul play** but also that there are a number of factors that indicate a systemic failure on the part of the State in implementing safety precautions and regulations. It is submitted that these two factors provide enough of an indication of a failure by the State or an agent of the State in protecting Lieutenant Woodhouse's article 2 right to life to require a **full "Middleton" inquiry"**

In Item 18 the London Barrister mentions that as my son did not receive a full and independent criminal investigation from Hampshire Constabulary, a full Middleton Inquiry is required to investigate the possibility of foul play and to ensure that my son's death is investigated independently and in great detail.

> "The report does not address a further concern of the family that a **full criminal investigation should have been carried out** with regards to the survivor of the incident or other members of the crew who may have held a grudge against Lieutenant Woodhouse. It is suggested that no one saw the actual moment when he fell from the LVCP and there has been no evidence provided from the SIB investigation that has been carried out. There was no mention in the ships' investigation report as to whether the maintenance was planned or if anyone other than Lieutenant Woodhouse and the Petty Officer knew that they were going aloft. The family asked the Hampshire Constabulary to conduct an investigation but this was refused due to the on-going military investigation. **A full "Middleton" inquiry is required to address the possibility of foul play and provide the independence and detail required under the United Kingdom's Article 2 obligation."**

In Item 20 he mentions once again that the circumstances warrant a full Middleton Inquiry to investigate Foul play –

> "Lieutenant Woodhouse died whilst serving on board HMS Ocean and is entitled to the full protections and rights accorded to him under the European Convention. **The circumstances of his death are still unclear and require an investigation** into whether the United Kingdom was/is in breach of its Article 2 obligations. **Foul play is yet to be ruled out** in a full independent investigation and the mere fact that the Ship's Investigation Report recommended changes to HMS Ocean's safety procedures suggests that the regime at the time was not fit for purpose in protecting the lives of servicemen working on board. This tragic incident should not be repeated and lessons need to be learned where necessary to prevent it happening again. **Only a full "Middleton" inquiry** will meet the requirements of this case."

When we first read the London Barrister's submission, one of the things that struck me was that he repeatedly mentioned that two men went to do a job, and only one came back alive.

For some time we felt like we were the only ones that seemed to find the circumstances of my son's death strange and very suspicious. It was refreshing to find that here was a London Barrister who put a great deal of stress on the fact that two men went to do a job and only one came back alive.  He, too, found it suspicious, so much so that it warranted an investigation.

## MOD's submission to Coroner David Horsley – 21st September, 2011

And now we come to the MOD's submission to the Coroner explaining why the Coroner must not allow a full Middleton Inquiry into my son's death.  A submission that explains why my son's death must not be allowed to have all the facts investigated.

(see full submission on website)

How is it possible to give a sound reason why my son should not be allowed to have an investigation into his suspicious death?

We knew that HMS Ocean in its ISI stated that my son's death was merely a tragic accident.

> *26. There is insufficient evidence to establish the exact reason that caused Lt Woodhouse to fall from N4 LCVP on 6 Aug 10, but based on the evidence provided, it appears to have been a **tragic accident** due to him losing his balance, after having jumped or fallen onto the deck from the wheelhouse roof.*

The Coroner was now our only chance of having my son's suspicious death investigated.  We had to have a Full Middleton Inquiry into his death in order to be able once and for all to find out whether there was Foul Play involved in my son's death.

I did not know that one had to fight to get a suspicious death investigated.  I thought that when the circumstances were suspicious then the death would automatically receive a full criminal investigation.

But here we were, the parents, the spectators, watching legal battles in high places as our barrister had to fight the MOD in order to obtain an investigation into my son's suspicious and violent death.

Why do we have to fight for this fundamental human right in the great United Kingdom?  Have we lost this human right once we decide to join the military and endanger our lives to fight for our country?

Is this how the country treats its military? Is this the Military Justice they give their military?

## MOD's submission to Coroner David Horsley – No Suspicious Circumstances – Really?

Let us see how the MOD can stand up and defend the indefensible.

The MOD's submission is full of legal cotton wool that tells you nothing, so let us go straight to the heart of their argument.

It is summed up in the second last point, item 15, forming his conclusion where the MOD barrister states –

> "Secondly, it is not accepted that it will be appropriate for the Inquest to conduct a *"full "Middleton" inquiry ... to address the possibility of foul play"* as suggested on behalf of the family. ***No evidence whatsoever has emerged from any of the investigations undertaken to date to suggest that foul play is a possibility in this case.***"

One thing that can be said is that the MOD barrister has been totally definite and absolute in his statements to defend the indefensible.

*"No evidence whatsoever"*

Therefore, if one were to find even a tiny bit of evidence that would suggest that foul play was a possibility, then the statement that there is 'no evidence' whatsoever would be found to be false.

What about:
- Two men went to do a job and only one returned – repeated many times by our London barrister.
- The investigation is relying on the account of one man and one man only - suspicious.
- This one man's account happens to be the account of the only man with my son – suspicious.
- The one man with my son, PO Fulton, says that he saw nothing – very suspicious.
- This one man, PO Fulton, wondered where my son was – very suspicious.
- Don't forget the scream. Whilst my son screams, whilst the two men

below shout and raise loud alarms, PO Fulton was still wondering where my son was – very suspicious.

Now let us look at another one of his statements. The MOD barrister says –

> "from any of the investigations"

This to me means that he has seen more than one investigation, whereas we, the family, were only allowed to see the one investigation, the ISI. From this one investigation, we could glean a large selection of very suspicious facts, and yet this MOD barrister, who has more than one investigation before him, cannot glean even one suspicious fact from any of the many investigations before him. Hmmm. Interesting.

We have to also realise that the MOD barrister's submission was made after he had read our barrister's two submissions. Our barrister's submissions are dated 5th September, 2011 and the MOD barrister's submission is dated 21st September, 2011 in which he also quotes from our barrister's submission.

Therefore Collins, the MOD barrister, has had ample time to read all the suspicious circumstances as being the reasons why our barrister stated that my son's death was owed a full investigation through the Coroner's court. Our barrister has spelt it out for both the Coroner and the MOD barrister. Our barrister states in Item 18 of his first submission that two men went to do a job and only one returned.

Item 18
> "Two men climbed onto the wheelhouse of the Landing Craft and only one returned."

Our barrister also mentions in Item 18 that we are relying on the sole testimony of one man – another suspicious circumstance

Item 18
> "According to the evidence of the Petty Officer who accompanied Lieutenant Woodhouse no one else saw the moment when he fell and it is his sole testimony that suggests that he exclaimed upon losing his footing."

Collins, the MOD Barrister has these two suspicious facts placed in his lap, and yet he states in his submission that –

> "No evidence whatsoever has emerged from any of the investigations

*undertaken to date to suggest that foul play is a possibility in this case."*

# The Coroner has to Decide

We have seen that Collins, the MOD barrister, put forward his unsubstantiated statements for not allowing my son to have a full Middleton Enquiry in order to investigate Foul Play.

On the other side, we have seen how my son's barrister put forward his clear reasons why my son's death was owed a Full Middleton Inquiry that would investigate all the evidence surrounding his suspicious death.

Both these submissions landed on the Coroner's desk in September, 2011.

The decision now rested with the Coroner. We would not hear what his decision was until six months later.

Why does one man have the power to deny my son his right to have his suspicious death investigated without at the same time having to give sound reasons for his decisions? A reason other than he 'does not deem it necessary'

There was only one opportunity left to us for all the facts in my son's death to be investigated. This opportunity resided with the Coroner.

So, we waited.

# A Visit to a LCVP

In September, 2011, a few weeks after my son's first pre-Inquest, my husband and I had the opportunity to visit and board a real LCVP, one that was the same model as that from which my son fell from. How did this happen?

When Commodore Mansergh sent us the ISI which stated that my son fell from the LCVP on HMS Ocean, in December, 2010, I could not make much sense of the document. I needed supporting plans and pictures of the LCVP which I requested from Commodore Mansergh.

One cannot say that the LCVP is a top military secret, as it is openly in view of the public where four LCVPs are housed in the sides of HMS Ocean for the entire world to see.

Another reason I asked for photographs was that when we were in Florida my son's fiancée was shown around the LCVP. Nobody told us that it was top secret and that we were not allowed to see where my son fell from.

In December 2010 Commodore Mansergh 's office sent a request to HMS Ocean asking for photographs of the LCVP my son fell from.

However, by the end of February, 2011 I was informed that I could not have these pictures and plans as they fell under the jurisdiction of the Coroner

> "As much as the Naval Service wishes to help you in understanding exactly what happened, we have been advised that provision of the information you seek remains firmly in the jurisdiction of the coroner; and that until he authorises release, the Naval Service has no authority to disclose any such information to you. Regrettably, I have now also been advised that this principle includes the provision by us of any more recent photographs.
>
> If you wish to pursue your outstanding request at this stage, may I recommend that you approach Mr Horsley directly? I will then await instructions from him as to what I can and can't disclose to you at present."

No amount of pictures from the internet can substitute for a visit onto a real LCVP, a LCVP like the one my son fell from. As my son's fiancée had been taken on the LCVP whilst we were in Florida, and as we would be in Portsmouth in September, 2011, I contacted Commodore Mansergh's office again. This time I asked whether we could be shown round a LCVP so as to try to make some sense of the only account of my son's death that we had, the Immediate Ship's Investigation.

Commodore Mansergh's contact point for us was a woman whom he described as 'the expert in Navy Command HQ Inquest Support Section'. This woman went out of her way in her efforts to help us and the result was that a visit was arranged for us to view a LCVP in the Royal Marine Base, Poole, on the 6th September, 2011. What a wonderful opportunity. We were very grateful.

The Royal Navy informed us that we were forbidden to take any photographs. We were only allowed to view the LCVP.

Commodore Mansergh's contact point met us at the Royal Marine Base and it was good to meet the woman who had tried so hard in December 2010 to obtain photographs of the LCVP for us.

The Royal Marines showing us the LCVP were not informed that we were forbidden by some person in the Royal Navy to take any photos, and so they invited us to take as many photographs as we wished.

We were so grateful for this opportunity to see a LCVP, to walk on it, to try to understand what each structure does, and best of all to photograph it in order to try to make sense of the ISI which recounted my son's last moments before his fall.

The pictures we were able to take were invaluable as we endeavoured to piece together PO Fulton's movements and my son's last moments before his fall.

The Royal Marines who showed us round the LCVP could not have been more courteous or kind, for which we are very grateful. We were treated to a beautiful lunch and a cup of tea. They did not try to hurry us out in any way at all. On the contrary they did all in their power to help us.

## Putting together the Puzzle Pieces

For nine months our minds were spinning with all the inconsistencies and discrepancies in the ISI, which is none other than PO Fulton's sole account of the events. We pored over the plans from the model makers of HMS Ocean and we scoured the internet for any pictures of HMS Ocean and the LCVPs. We bounced off ideas and always wrote them down. But there were big gaps. We needed to board a LCVP; we needed to do this on HMS Ocean. We needed to see the scene of my son's fall.

Now that we had kindly been allowed to see a real LCVP at the Marine base in Poole, we were armed with substantial photographs that allowed us to make more headway in our efforts to understand how my son came to fall and die. A visit to HMS Ocean would have been ideal, but we were extremely grateful that we were even allowed to board and see and photograph a LCVP at the Marine base in Poole.

Armed with these latest pictures we set to work to put together all our thoughts, all the plans, all the internet pictures, and all the information that we had gathered since Christmas, 2010, and compile them into readable documents for the legal team which from nowhere appeared to represent us.

We had so many questions, and only one document giving an account of my son's death, the ISI. Only one document.

We were kept in the dark and having to piece together the puzzle pieces ourselves. What about all the other military families who have also been treated in the same manner?
We were privileged in that owing to so many extraordinary circumstances, the MOD, the Coroner, and the Royal Navy, could not keep us as much in the dark as they would wish to do, and as they are accustomed to doing to the majority of bereaved military families.

Now armed with photographs of a real LCVP, we set about further investigating and searching out and exploring the account in the Immediate Ship's Investigation.

We spent the next three months and the next Christmas holiday putting together our thoughts, our analysis, our investigations, into readable bundles for the London barrister to get an idea of some of the issues and background and our concerns and our questions relating to my son's strange, inexplicable death.

The questions. We had so many questions.

## The Puzzle Pieces – What did the Wheelhouse Roof Look Like?

According to the ISI, which is the only document we had of how my son died, my son was on the wheelhouse roof, and then somehow slipped and fell forty six feet onto the LCVP in the water below. PO Fulton is the only man with my son. Therefore Lt Cdr Pickles, Lt Cdr Lucocq, and WO Clapham who carried out the ISI, are showing their complete confidence in PO Fulton's version of the events.

What does the wheelhouse roof look like?

Now that we had photographs of the LCVP we were able to painstakingly construct plans of the wheelhouse roof in order to re-enact my son's last movements according to PO Fulton's account in the ISI.

At this time, I noticed, whilst continuing to trawl the internet, that there were fresh pictures recently published of the very LCVP my son had fallen from, LCVP N4, as it was being raised from the sea onto HMS Ocean. Another God send.

The fixtures on the wheelhouse roof can vary; therefore it was very important to get a picture of the fixtures on the wheelhouse roof of LCVP N4, the very LCVP from which my son was supposed to have fallen.

We wanted to know the exact position of the radar, and the speakers, and the strange bits of equipment on the wheelhouse roof. Other models had this equipment in different places. We needed to know exactly where this equipment was placed. It was very important as we endeavoured to find out whether PO Fulton's account was true.

Some parts of it might appear plausible only if the general public, and Joshua's family, had no idea of the scene of my son's fall.

These are the pictures that I obtained from the internet, and the plans that I made.

**A picture of LCVP N4, the very LCVP that Joshua fell from, being raised onto HMS Ocean in August, 2011. You will notice that the mast is down ready for it to be stowed in the holding bay of HMS Ocean.**

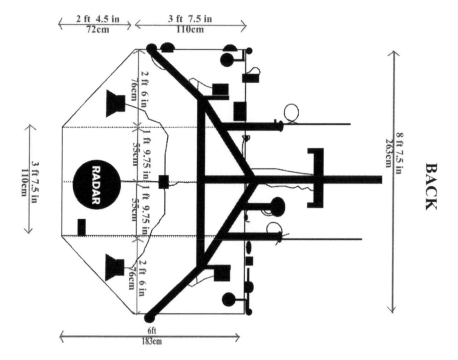

A plan of the wheelhouse roof of LCVP N4 which we had made from internet pictures and from the pictures obtained from our visit to Royal Marine Base, with our measurements. We will always be grateful to the Royal Marines who so willingly and kindly helped us.

## Questions, Questions, Questions –what happened on the Wheelhouse Roof?

The ISI was such an implausible account of the events according to PO Fulton. The events that Lt Cdr Pickles, Lt Cdr Lucocq, WO Clapham and HMS Ocean endorsed. The events that Captain Blount, HMS Ocean's Captain, endorsed. The events that the Royal Navy endorsed.

According to PO Fulton, he and my son went to the LCVP Bay and then climbed onto LCVP N4 in order to check flexible Davit hoses on the LCVP.

> 6. POET(ME)2 (PO Fulton) reports that on the morning of Fri 6 Aug he was in 4T LCVP Workshop supervising the painting of the deck. At approximately 0900 Lt Woodhouse (SSEO) arrived to discuss the status of flexible hoses on the LCVP davits. Lt Woodhouse believed

*that all the hoses had recently been changed, whereas PO2 (1) (PO Fulton) was under the impression that none had been changed. In order to clarify the issue, PO2 (1) (PO Fulton) suggested they go and check the manufacturers label on the hoses.*

*7. In order to check the flexible hoses they needed access to the davits. Due to both Starboard LCVPs (N3 & NM) being disembarked for maintenance, they would have required scaffolding to gain access to the davits, so it was decided that it would be easier to climb up onto one of the LCVPs on the port side (N2 & N4) to have a quick look. They elected to go to the Port Aft LCVP Bay as it was closest.*

Let us hear what PO Fulton tells us happened next -

*10. They initially attempted to check the forward davit, but due to the manufacturers label being inaccessible from the deck of the LCVP, PO2 (PO Fulton) decided to climb up onto the roof of the wheelhouse to gain a closer view of the aft davit. As there is no ladder for this purpose, he used a handrail around the wheelhouse as a step. Lt Woodhouse climbed up the same way and within a minute or two they had obtained the required information*

This is strange behaviour. Looking at the pictures of the LCVP in Bay there does not appear to be much room for a man to get on the wheelhouse roof, let alone stand on the roof.

**Showing LCVP N4 in the holding bay of HMS Ocean**

In the diagram below we have shown the possible crouching places in blue.

84

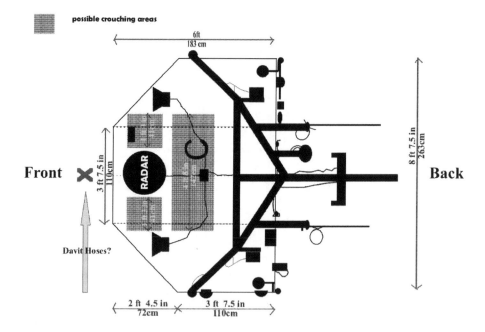

What was very evident from these plans and pictures that we had put together was that the wheelhouse roof had on it a mass of sensitive and expensive equipment, and that there was just enough room for one man to climb onto it, and then to crouch.

This raised even more doubts as to the truthfulness of PO Fulton's account of the events. We had to ask, was Joshua ever on the Wheelhouse roof?

## Questions, Questions, Questions – was Joshua ever on the Wheelhouse Roof?

After making the plans of the wheelhouse roof from all the pictures on the internet and from the pictures from our visit onto a LCVP, the questions were getting louder and more urgent.

Why would my son have followed PO Fulton and climbed up onto the wheelhouse roof to perform an eyeball exercise? The job of checking a manufacturer's label does not need two pairs of eyes.

Where could my son have positioned himself on the wheelhouse roof whilst he was there? On the radar? Why would my son have climbed onto the wheelhouse roof?

This is the account according to PO Fulton, the prime suspect.

But we have more. It is not just PO Fulton, but Lt Cdr Pickles, Lt Cdr Lucocq, WO Clapham, Captain Blount, and HMS Ocean who would have us believe that my son climbed onto the wheelhouse roof, and somehow positioned himself in that cramped, dangerous environment, only to do what? Use his eyes and do the job that PO Fulton was doing?

Questions, questions, questions. We had all these questions, all these 'facts' from the Initial Ship's Investigation that were ridiculous and we were supposed to believe them.

With our limited resources, we tried to do a re-enactment with our diagrams and pictures. And these diagrams and pictures show PO Fulton's account to be suspect.

And then, one and a half years after my son's death, when the Coroner released more documents, what did we find?

There was an independent witness who saw my son clearly, from start to finish. This independent witness stated that my son was not on the wheelhouse roof. This witness saw my son standing comfortably at the back of the wheelhouse and on the deck of the LCVP. This witness saw my son standing in the only place on the LCVP where there was a guard rail.

My son's death was not a simple case of accidental death as PO Fulton, Lt Cdr Pickles, Lt Cdr Lucocq, WO Clapham, Captain Blount, and the Royal Navy wanted us to believe.

## The Safety Number

Why did my son go with PO Fulton to the LCVP? Why didn't my son just let him go by himself? This job was an eyeball exercise, and it did not require two men.

My son went in obedience to Royal Navy regulations. When a man went to do a job, like checking the flexible Davit hoses, the regulations required that a second man accompany him as his Safety Number.

That is the only reason my son went. My son did his utmost to obey the

Health and Safety regulations on the ship.

And what does the Royal Navy do?

The Royal Navy sent a 'post' to all their ships saying that if my son had obeyed Health and Safety regulations he would not have died.

Not only did my son die in highly suspicious circumstances which Lt Cdr Pickles, Lt Cdr Lucocq, WO Clapham, Captain Blount, and the Royal Navy do their utmost to cover, but then they add insult to injury and cast my son's name out as refuse for them to trample on publically.

## Puzzle Pieces – PO Fulton Sees Nothing

The Initial Ship's Investigation was redacted with no names supplied. In it PO2, the only man with my son, is PO Fulton. I have added his name in order to make the Initial Ship's Investigation account a bit easier to understand. In this investigation PO Fulton conveniently says he did not see anything. See item 11 of the Immediate Ship's Investigation below -

> *10. They initially attempted to check the forward davit, but due to the manufacturers label being inaccessible from the deck of the LCVP, PO2 **(PO Fulton)**decided to climb up onto the roof of the wheelhouse to gain a closer view of the aft davit. As there is no ladder for this purpose, he **(PO Fulton)**used a handrail around the wheelhouse as a step. Lt Woodhouse climbed up the same way and within a minute or two they had obtained the required information.*

> *11. Having completed the task, PO2 **(PO Fulton) proceeded to the back of the wheelhouse to climb back down**. As he **(PO Fulton)** was doing so, he **(PO Fulton)**heard a loud thud which he presumed was the sound of Lt Woodhouse jumping down from the front of the wheelhouse onto the deck of the LCVP **(although he did not see anything).** Almost immediately after the initial thud, he **(PO Fulton)** heard Lt Woodhouse's voice say something that sounded like 'Whoa, Whoa, Whoa' (as if he had lost his balance) followed by a scream.*

PO Fulton says he saw nothing; therefore everything is right with the world. I see a formula here. All you have to say is that you saw nothing.

# Puzzle Pieces – Why did PO Fulton return via the back way?

And there is more strange behaviour from PO Fulton.

According to him, my son was on the wheelhouse roof. We have shown that this is hard to believe, and that an independent witness saw my son standing comfortably on the LCVP deck, and not on the wheelhouse roof at all.

Let us continue with his statements.

He says that after he checked the labels on the flexible davit hoses, he decided to get down onto the LCVP by going via the back of the wheelhouse roof.

Why didn't he get back down by the front route, seeing he says that he was at the front of the wheelhouse roof?
The front route is safer, easier, shorter, quicker to descend, and more importantly, has fewer obstacles.

The picture below shows the short, direct, quick, and safer route to take to ascend and descend the wheelhouse roof.

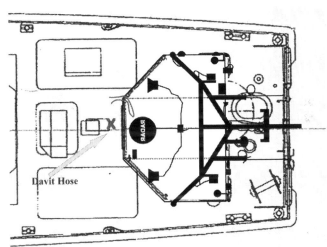

Death - 46ft drop

Here is another picture showing the route that would be more natural to take when ascending and descending the wheelhouse roof. The route is shown in red. I have also made a representation of the Davit in order to show the LCVP when it was in the holding bay of HMS Ocean.

Route to ascend & descend

Davit

PO Fulton tells us that he decided to take the back route. This route is a minefield of obstacles. Taking the back route means that there is more likelihood of damaging the equipment and/or oneself.

It would be natural to avoid taking the back route altogether.

Then there is the other question. How would he descend onto the LCVP deck via the back way?

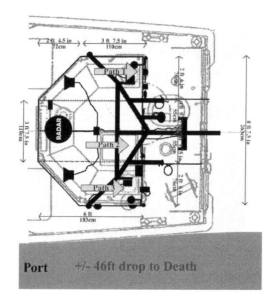

I have sketched out the possible paths that he could take now that he has decided not to take the front way.

What is interesting is to find out what the descent would have looked like. We obtained these photographs from our visit onto a LCVP.

If he chose to take Path 1, then this is what he would have to contend with in his descent.

The distance between the edge of the wheelhouse roof and the first antenna is approximately 2ft 6 inches (81 centimetres)

Here is another picture of the descent via Path 1

Let us now look at Path 2. This shows an area of exit that is approximately 1ft 10in (66 cm) wide. There are obstructions when descending to the deck of the LCVP. It would be very difficult to take this route without tripping up, without damaging one's clothing, oneself, or the equipment.

This picture shows the mast right by path 2.

This picture shows how small the width of path 2 is.

Let us even consider Path 3. This path is right by the 46 foot (14 metre) drop onto the LCVPs in the water below.

The picture below shows the obstructions when descending via Path 3.

The area is about 2ft 6in (76cm) wide, and has these obstructions and wires. In addition this is the path nearest to certain death.

We have to conclude that it was totally unnatural for him to take the back route where the route over the wheelhouse roof was full of obstructions and sensitive equipment.

One has to wonder whether PO Fulton said that he took the back route in order to be able to testify that he never saw anything?

## Questions, Questions, Questions – The Flexible Hoses

So many questions. So many things that did not add up.

The ISI said that my son Joshua came into the LCVP Workshop to discuss the status of flexible hoses on the LCVP davits. Below is an excerpt.

> 6. POET(ME)2 *(PO Fulton)* reports that on the morning of Fri 6 Aug he *(PO Fulton)*was in 4T LCVP Workshop supervising the painting of the deck. At approximately 0900 Lt Woodhouse (SSEO) arrived to discuss the status of flexible hoses on the LCVP davits. Lt Woodhouse believed that all the hoses had recently been changed, whereas PO2 (1) *(PO Fulton)* was under the impression that none had been changed. In order to clarify the issue, PO2 (1) *(PO Fulton)* suggested

*they go and check the manufacturers label on the hoses.*

*7. In order to check the flexible hoses they needed access to the davits. Due to both Starboard LCVPs (N3 & NM) being disembarked for maintenance, they would have required scaffolding to gain access to the davits, so it was decided that it would be easier to climb up onto one of the LCVPs on the port side (N2 & N4) to have a quick look. They elected to go to the Port Aft LCVP Bay as it was closest.*

This is very strange.

Why were records not consulted?

If no records existed, why did both men not consult the person/persons who had changed the flexible hoses or the person in authority?

What made my son certain that the hoses had been changed?

Why was PO Fulton under the impression that none of the hoses had been changed?

What was the result of the hose check? Had the hoses been changed? If so, who had changed them? Had this work been recorded in the record system? If not, why not?

Is this job normally done whilst the LCVP is in the holding bay or are the Davits lowered or is scaffolding put up?

How often are the flexible hoses checked? How many people are required to do this job, and who are they?

My son was a SSEO, Ship's Services Engineering Officer. Was this part of his normal remit or was he covering for someone else whilst they were on leave?

Was this job part of PO Fulton's normal remit or was he covering for someone else whilst they were on leave?

So many questions. We only had one document, the Initial Ship's Investigation, and it was so sparse that all it engendered were more questions.

## The Seat of Power

For one and a half years we had only the ISI and my son's Post Mortem and our minds were spinning with questions, questions, questions.

How did my son come to his death? What really did happen?

Yet all this time, one and a half years of time, the Coroner had the answers to most of these questions.

He was sitting on the three US Navy Witness Statements. The Coroner was also sitting on the Supplementary Ship's Investigation. He was sitting on the SIB Investigation and many more documents that we shall never know about. The Coroner did not release further documents to us till one and a half years after my son's death.

And those are not his only actions. The Coroner told us time and time and time again that he saw no reason to believe there were suspicious circumstances in my son's death, and he had all the documents, and all the documents shouted even more loudly that my son's death was suspicious.

This is Military Justice in the UK.

## Legal Team Increases

The London Barrister was concerned that he would be disqualified from representing us at Joshua's Inquest on some legal point as it was unusual to be represented only by a barrister.

He therefore approached the Royal British Legion with his concerns and they once again set to work to help us.

They were able to find a top London law firm headed by a man of kindness and compassion, which, like the London Barrister, volunteered to give of their time and their efforts selflessly and without charge to represent our son.

It was just before Christmas 2011 that we heard this good news.

On the 17th January, 2012, all the official legal papers had been signed and work commenced immediately.

This also coincided nicely with the completion of the bundles which we had finished collating and putting together over the Christmas holidays and which the legal team received in January, 2012.

# Request for Full Disclosure – SIB Criminal Investigation

Just three days after officially taking over my son's case, the London law firm immediately wrote to the Coroner informing him that they would be representing us, and asking among other things for Full Disclosure. (see letter dated 20.01.2012 on website)

This was another broken record, being repeated ad infinitum. The Coroner had been asked for disclosure from January, 2011, by us, then continually by the Royal British Legion, then the London Barrister, and now one year later, January, 2012, by the London law firm.

The SIB Military Police Criminal Investigation was pivotal to the entire Inquest.

When did the Coroner get a copy of the SIB report? On the 29th November, 2010, we were informed by the Royal Navy that the full SIB investigation had been concluded and the final report issued and would be in the hands of the coroner in the near future. See excerpt of email below

> **Special Investigation Branch Report**
> *You mention that this should be concluded soon. Can my husband and I please see a copy of this full report as well? If we can, what sort of time period might we be looking at?*
>
> *As I write, **the Special Investigation Branch report conducted on behalf of HM Coroner for Portsmouth , Mr David Horsley, has just been concluded and the final report issued.** This has now been passed to the Defence Inquests Unit who will arrange to despatch a copy to the Coroner at the earliest opportunity, taking the Christmas break into account. Although we expect also to receive a copy of the report, we cannot forward you a copy without formal authorisation from Mr Horsley because, as is the case with civilian police reports, these are not routinely disclosed to families in advance of an inquest. Can I respectfully suggest that in due course, you contact the Coroner directly concerning your request for a copy of the Police report? His full postal address is shown below for ease of reference:*

Therefore the Coroner had been sitting on this report for one year and would not release it to us despite repeated requests for its disclosure.

# Request for Full Disclosure – Immediate Ship's Investigation- Unredacted

We had been given the ISI on the 18th December, 2010, just over a year ago. This investigation had been redacted making it difficult to read and understand. In addition it was extremely difficult to make sense of it without accompanying plans and pictures of HMS Ocean and the LCVPs.

In their letter of the 20th January, 2012, the London Law firm requested an unredacted copy of this investigation together with all attachments and statements relied upon. I quote below -

> 1. *The full unredacted version of the Ship's Investigation Report together with all attachments and statements relied upon.*

We were not given the interview notes upon which the ISI was based.

# Request for Board of Inquiry of the MOD

In item 4 of this same letter, the London Law firm asked to see the report by the Board of Inquiry, and if not available, an explanation as to why not considering the circumstances. I quote below –

> *4. If available, a copy of the report by the Board of Inquiry of the ministry of Defence and, if not available, an explanation as to why no such Board of Inquiry has been convened in these circumstances.*

What is interesting is that we had been fobbed off by Commodore Mansergh RN who told us that it was unlikely that there would be a Board of Inquiry. I quote from his letter to us on 24th November, 2010. (see website)

> *The concurrent investigation being undertaken by the Royal Navy's Special Investigation Branch (SIB) for HM Coroner has yet to conclude but is expected to do so shortly. In the light of this report and the completed Ship's Investigation report, the Royal Navy will then consider **whether it is right or necessary** to convene a follow on Service Inquiry (SI), which used to be known as a Board of Inquiry.*

> *Under the Armed Forces Act 2006, which came into effect on 1 October 2008, it is mandatory for the Royal Navy to consider holding a Service Inquiry into the deaths of all its serving members. The key objective of such an inquiry is **to determine the facts of a particular***

*matter* and, where applicable, to make recommendations aimed at preventing a recurrence. However, *if it is considered unlikely that such an inquiry would establish any new relevant facts, or identify any further recommendations* or lessons to be learned over and above those which may have already been identified through the other investigations, arrangements exist for a senior Naval Officer (at Rear Admiral level or above) to dispense with the need to hold such an inquiry.

The legal team deemed the Service Inquiry very important and kept on fighting to have one. In contrast the Royal Navy and the MOD thought my son's death was totally unimportant and not worth troubling with a Service Inquiry seeing as the Ship's Investigation and the SIB Military Police had adequately answered all that needed to be known, in their opinion only.

When the SIB Criminal Investigation Summary was released to us, and this was only a summary, it did not answer our questions and therefore there was even more need to have a Service Inquiry to determine the facts of my son's death.

This Service Inquiry was another item that the legal team was vigorously fighting for.

## Request for Visit to HMS Ocean

Just one week after officially taking over my son's case the London law firm informed us that they would be contacting the MOD asking for a visit to HMS Ocean.

The legal team had seen the inadequacy of the vague Ship's Investigation, which gave no supporting plans, structures, or pictures. They therefore went straight to the bull's eye, and immediately requested a visit to the scene of my son's fall, HMS Ocean.

This is something of course that the Coroner should have done in his capacity as Coroner, and should have done a year ago, but our legal team and the Coroner had different objectives.

On the 1st February, 2012, we were informed by the London law firm that the MOD did reply to their request, stating that the visit was more likely to happen if my husband and I were to be present. As this was too difficult to arrange, it appeared that this door was shut. The MOD added to the obstacles against us.

The London law firm then informed us that they would continue to try to arrange a visit to HMS Ocean, and this time they would try to do so through the Coroner. They would not do this immediately as they were still waiting for a reply to their original letter and all the requests contained in it including disclosure. They had to tread very carefully around the Coroner.

## Coroner Responds – 1st February, 2012

On the 1st February, 2012, the Coroner replied to the London Barrister's submissions of September, 2011, and to the latest letter from the expanded legal team of the 20th January, 2012. See his letter on the website.

This was a long awaited letter. What had he been doing since the time he received the SIB Investigation in January, 2011?

We eagerly read the letter. There were many items the Coroner had been repeatedly asked for from our legal team.

- Could we have disclosure of the pivotal SIB Investigation, together with all supporting documents?
- Were there independent US Navy witnesses? If so we needed to see their accounts.
- We needed to see the full unredacted Immediate Ship's Investigation.
- We need to see all the supporting documents for the Immediate Ship's Investigation.
- What was the Coroner's decision with regard to the two Submissions put before him regarding Foul Play?
- What was the Coroner's decision with regard to the two Submissions concerning having an Inquest with a Jury?
- Had the Coroner set an Inquest date yet?

By God's grace alone, my son had been given a legal team who fought for him, a legal team that just a month previously had increased to include not just the Royal British Legion, a top London barrister, but now also a top London law firm.

I do believe that if it were not for the legal team increasing in size the Coroner would have continued to refuse to do his duty and refuse to give us any disclosure besides the one Post Mortem report.

The main issue that all the team had been fighting for was disclosure. Fighting for over a year for disclosure. Now that there was a full and a formidable legal team taking on my son's fight, the Coroner decided it might be good policy to give a little.

The Coroner informed us –

> "I hope to be in a position very shortly to release to you copies of the statements of the persons names on the list. With these I intend to also provide copies of the documents that I consider to be the appropriate documents for the Inquest's considerations."

Further in his letter of the 1st February, 2012, the Coroner would not give us an Inquest date or any indication when it might be held. The most he gave was that the Inquest would take one week and that he had set a date for another pre-Inquest to be held on the 15th March, 2012.

Let us consider the items that the Coroner gave us. I shall discuss the most important item last.

## Issues to be Examined at the Inquest

After stating that he will be conducting the Inquest with a Jury, the Coroner lists what he has made the heart of the Inquest, what he has allowed the Inquest to investigate. This is none other than Health and Safety Issues.

In his letter of the 1st February, the Coroner wants the Inquest to investigate –

- What Health and Safety training my son received before he joined HMS Ocean.
- The Health and Safety training my son received for the task since joining HMS Ocean.
- The Health and Safety procedures for the entire Royal Navy.
- Whether my son was complying with the Health and Safety training he received.

As a spectator, watching Health and Safety being used to deflect attention away from my son's suspicious death, it is not surprising that it has been given such a bad press and is generally held in contempt.

The whole point of Health and Safety, the reason for its existence, is based on sound, and caring, and valid grounds. However, to see it used in this way causes it to be brought into disrepute and results in the very opposite of what it was designed for.

Here we had the Coroner setting the heart of my son's Inquest on Health and Safety matters, when the weightier matter of a suspicious death was ignored.

## The Witness List

The Coroner gave us a list of his provisional witnesses. These are divided into two categories. The live witnesses, and the written witness statements, called Rule 37 statements, those that would be read out at my son's Inquest.

JOSHUA WOODHOUSE – Provisional Witness List (23/01/2012)

Witnesses:

1. Lt. Commander Day (SIB)

2. PO Fulton (carrying out task with JW)

3. PO Cottam (Working below JW, first on scene)

4. ET Myers (Working below JW, first on scene)

5. Lt. Cmdr Brewer (Safety, Health and Environment Officer, HMS Ocean)

6. COP Lawson (Carried out risk assessments for working on LCVPs on HMS Ocean)

7. Capt. Forsey (Chief of Staff (Engineering) Surface Ships, RN)

8. Andrew Wheeler (SO1, Fleet Command, RN)

9. Dr Borek (Forensic Pathologist)

10. CPO Connolly (Medical Assistant, HMS Ocean)

11. LT CDR Harris (SO2 IFT Brittania Royal Naval College, Dartmouth)

Statements (Rule 37):

1. Statements of 3 USN personnel who witnessed JW's fall.

2. LT. Reynolds (Officer Course Managers, HMS Sultan)

3. PO Skyes-Gelder (Chief Bosun's Mate, HMS Ocean)

4. MNE Tait (LCVP crew member, HMS Ocean)

5. Lt. Hayes (out with JW, night before)

6. Lt. Pitman (out with JW, night before)

7. Lt Pearson (out with JW, night before)

8. Surgeon Capt. Carne (JW's medical history)

9. AURELIAN NICOLAESCU – (Associate Medical Examiner, USA – Florida Autopsy)

We received this list of provisional witnesses before we received the SIB report and all the other disclosure documents that the legal team had fought hard and long for. We still had only one supporting document, the ISI.

We could not tell whether this Provisional Witness List was adequate or not without the disclosure documents.

Let us look at the top of this Provisional Witness List to find the most important witness. This was Lt. Commander Day (SIB). The SIB report is pivotal to the entire Inquest. It is a report on the supposedly full and fair criminal investigation into my son's suspicious death, by a supposedly impartial and trained force.

It would only be reasonable to assume that it was Lt Commander Day who wrote this pivotal SIB Investigation.

The Coroner issued a total of three witness lists. In the first one above, he named the chief SIB witness as Lt Cdr Day. In his second witness list of the 22nd February, 2012, the Coroner named the chief SIB witness as SIB Wilson, who wrote the investigation. In his third witness list of the 12th September, 2012, the Coroner changed his mind and named Lt Cdr Day as the chief SIB witness.

Then lastly at the Inquest, after much playing around with this chief SIB witness, we finally had Lt Cdr Wilson in the stand to actually answer for his report.

And then we considered the Rule 37 Witness statements; these are the witnesses whose statements will only be read out.

We noticed in this list the names of three Lieutenants who were with my son the night before he died.

It was transparent to us what the Coroner wanted to achieve. He wanted to prove that my son was drunk, and what better way than to have witness statements read out rather than having live witnesses to give the background and a full account of the events of the previous night. Yet this too was to change on the 12th September, 2012, just seven weeks before my son's Inquest.

Just before the Inquest the Coroner also changed the SIB witness from Lt Cdr Wilson to Lt Cdr Day.

Why did the Coroner make these two sets of changes? Did an event end of June, 2012, make him change his mind? Was it perhaps the animated re-enactments he received that were the reason for this change?

And last, but certainly not least, we noticed that the three US Navy witnesses we had heard about were assigned to the position of Rule 37 witnesses.

It appeared by this that their statements were totally unimportant, seeing as they were only to be read out. Again bear in mind that we were awaiting the release of these US Navy witness statements; therefore we could make no comment as to whether this was a good or a bad decision of the Coroner to place them in this lowly position.

So we waited for disclosure. Would it be another year, or would it indeed be shortly?

## Coroner David Horsley Makes his Decision on Foul Play

Now I come to the most important item in this letter of 1st February, 2012.

The Coroner informs the legal team of his decision regarding our Barrister's submissions way back in September, 2011.

It was in September, 2011, that the Coroner had received one submission from our London barrister and one from the MOD barrister regarding whether to allow a Full Middleton Inquiry to investigate my son's suspicious death.

The length of time to come to this decision gives one the impression that it is a very difficult decision to make and one that needs careful thought.

Let us look at what the Coroner did write to support his decision to deny my son a full Middleton Inquiry into the suspicious circumstances surrounding my son's death –

> *"**I have no evidence before me to give me reasonable grounds** to suspect that either Lt Woodhouse was unlawfully killed or took his own life."*

The Coroner has all the documents before him, whereas we have one redacted Immediate Ship's Investigation which is still shouting that the events are suspicious. But now we have the promise that he will release to us documents that he considers to be appropriate for the Inquest.

> *"I hope to be in a position very shortly to release to you copies of the statements of the persons names on the list. With these I intend to also provide copies of the documents that I consider to be the appropriate documents for the Inquest's considerations."*

Therefore, the Coroner's decision that he has no evidence before him to give him reasonable grounds to suspect that my son was unlawfully killed must be supported by the documents that he was just about to release to us.

## Documents Arrive – 22/2/2012 – Partial Disclosure

On the 22nd February, 2012, we received news from the legal team that the documents had arrived. I would not call it full disclosure by any stretch of the imagination, so I call it what it is, partial disclosure. Partial disclosure in order to enable the Coroner to distort the facts regarding what actually did happen to my son.

What struck me forcibly was the huge number of documents on Health and Safety. If thrown at anyone, they would be enough to badly wound a person.

It was very difficult not to be angry at the great emphasis laid on the Health and Safety aspect of my son's death, making it very clear that all they wanted to prove was that my son was guilty of breaking some Health and Safety directive and was responsible for his own death. The Coroner and his man SIB Wilson went to great lengths to dig up anything to do with Health and Safety regarding my son, from his initial training, from his records in Britannia Royal Navy College, to every tiny little course he attended.

It was all this unnecessary paper work that added time delays to my son's Inquest, and of course the perfect cover for the Coroner to pretend to be doing his job.

In sharp contrast to the huge amount of needless information on Health and Safety, one was made very aware how little the Coroner and his man SIB Wilson and the establishment valued the only important documents, the documents that had any bearing on the suspicious circumstances surrounding my son's death.

Is this or isn't this a suspicious death?

Also noticeable in this unbalanced investigation into my son's death is the almost total lack of investigation into anything to do with PO Fulton.

My son's movements the night before were investigated. Were PO Fulton's? My son's emails were investigated. Were PO Fulton's? My son's health records were investigated. Were his?

I list below the documents released to us that deal with the suspicious events surrounding my son's death, and these are the documents that I studied.

**Documentation Released to us**

### The Witness Statements.

- The three US Navy witness statements.
- The statements from three Lieutenants.
- The statements from people in LCVP below.
- PO Fulton's statements.

### HMS Ocean.

- Supplementary Ship's Investigation – prepared 12th September, 2010.

### SIB Military Police.

- Summary of Evidence.
- RNP SIB Investigation Process.

We were now able to read and study these documents (see the website). I have recounted below our thoughts, analysis, and personal investigation of the facts and statements contained in these precious documents. We commenced with the accounts by the three US Navy witnesses.

## The Three US Navy Witness Statements.

We had been deliberately starved of these documents for over a year.

One and a half years previously in August, 2010, whilst we were preparing to bury my son, the Navy welfare officer informed us that there had been US Navy witnesses to my son's death. We grasped at this piece of news. This was so encouraging to us. There were witnesses to my son's death. Surely this would be a huge aid in the investigation of his death.

The very next day the Navy welfare officer back tracked and denied any knowledge of anything. Yet, from the time that we heard of the US Navy witnesses, we eagerly desired any information obtained from these witnesses in our efforts to find out how my son came to his death.

When we finally received partial disclosure from the Coroner, we devoured every word, especially the accounts of the three US Navy witnesses. These were the accounts of three 'disinterested', impartial parties. These were the accounts of three people who had witnessed my son's movements on HMS Ocean in those few minutes leading up to his fall, and, ultimately, his death.

## What Did the Three US Navy Witnesses Say?

A US Military ship, USS Mitscher, was passing HMS Ocean just at the time that my son fell ultimately to his death. USS Mitscher was 80 - 100 feet away (according to Witness 3, Los Angeles). The visibility, from the point of view of distance, would have been very good. It was a clear Florida summer day. The US Navy witnesses remarked on the sound made by my son as he hit the metal deck of the LCVP below. They did not hear my son's scream, as this would have been a high pitch, high frequency scream, and would have been lost as it travelled the 80 – 100ft over the water. They heard only the loud bang which would have been at a lower pitch, lower frequency, and therefore would not have been lost as it travelled over the water.

I will start with the Charleston witness, whom I will call Witness 2, Charleston. This US Navy witness was on the bridge of USS Mitscher, and he noticed a man in white walking on the flight deck. He then turned away to do his work, and on looking back saw a man in white overalls fall from HMS Ocean. Witness 2, Charleston, presumed this was one and the same man, but we found out just before the Inquest when further documents were produced that it was not. The man in white walking on the flight deck was wearing shorts. My son, whom Witness 2, Charleston, saw falling, was wearing white overalls.

The other US Navy witness, whom I will call Witness 1, Philippines, was on the midships quarterdeck of USS Mitscher, and his account was more difficult to understand. Witness 1, Philippines, said that he saw feet. Witness 1, Philippines, then tried to describe how he saw my son falling. Like Witness 2, Charleston, Witness 1, Philippines, presumed that the feet he saw when he first looked at HMS Ocean belonged to my son, whom he saw a little while afterwards when he was falling.

We only found out later that the feet he saw did not belong to my son. They belonged to a man who was on a moveable platform doing maintenance work on the side of HMS Ocean, and very near to my son's position. This information had been hidden from us, and only revealed a few days before my son's Inquest.

This information was not pursued or investigated by SIB Wilson, Royal Navy Military Police. It was difficult to understand exactly what Witness 1, Philippines, was telling us, but we studied his account again and again and again.

The third US Navy witness, whom I will call Witness 3, Los Angeles, saw the entire episode from start to finish. His account was also the most systematically recorded account, and we later found out that he was a teacher/instructor in the US Navy, which would explain his clear and methodical manner. Reading his account was like watching a slow motion movie of my son's fall. The account of Witness 3, Los Angeles, was invaluable.

Witness 3, Los Angeles, is the only one who saw the entire episode from start to finish, and I shall therefore be starting with his account.

The entire contents of the three accounts are included for reference on the web site.

# Witness 3, Los Angeles – Clear and Accurate Witness Account

Let us now look at the statements made by Witness 3, Los Angeles.

Continuation of voluntary sworn statement of

███████████

on August 25, 2010

well deck where the man fell from. He peeked his head out of the well deck and looked down and I think he saw the fallen man. He then ran inside the skin of the ship.

While I saw the entire incident happen, I don't think many other people saw it. I know that nobody saw the fall as clearly as I did. I think some people saw something fall overboard, but they did not get a good look. I think some people thought it was a duffle bag or a dummy/OSCAR that fell because they did not get a good look at the fall or didn't want to believe that they realy just saw someone fall like that.

The bridge called down to the fantail and asked if anybody saw what it was that fell. I told ███████ that I saw a man fall and some people were arguing that it was not a man that fell, but I told ██████ that it was a man who slipped and fell. I saw the entire incident clearly. To the best of my knowledge that is what happened. I provided a rough scetch of the positions of the ship and personel and incedent to special agent Gomez.

This statement, consisting of this page and 1 other page(s) was typed for me by █████████ ██████ as we discussed its contents. I have read and understand the above statement. I have been given the opportunity to make any changes or corrections I desire to make and have placed my initials over the changes or corrections. This statement is the truth to the best of my knowledge and belief.

Signature ███████████████████

Sworn to and subscribed before me this _25_ day of _August_ in the year _2010_ at

NCISFO NORFOLK VA

Witness ██████████████████

Representative, Naval Criminal Investigative Service
AUTH: DERIVED FROM ARTICLE 136,
UCMJ (10 U.S.C. 936) AND 5 U.S.C. 303

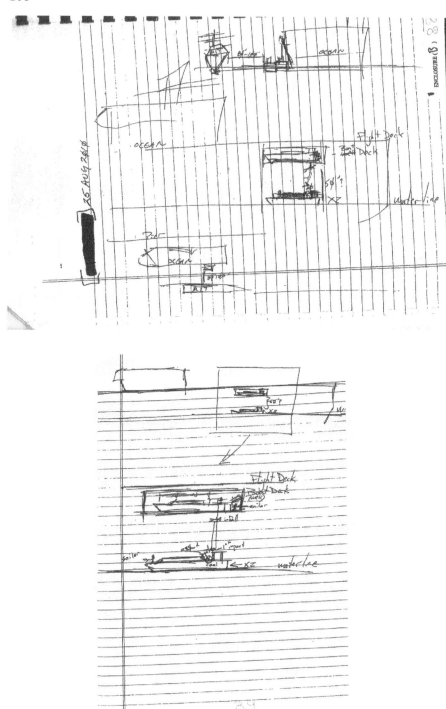

I will endeavour to show why we believe that the account by Witness 3, Los Angeles, is both clear and accurate. His statements, including the smallest details, are confirmed by other witnesses.

Witness 3, Los Angeles, sets the scene to the events that he witnessed. Witness 3, Los Angeles, has gone to great lengths to clearly explain exactly what took place. He watched the events of my son's fall from start to finish. He has provided not only an invaluable, step by step, written account of what happened, but has also made diagrams in order to help us further understand exactly what he saw. These diagrams are a supplement to the very clear account he gives us.

Witness 3, Los Angeles, first sketches the position of the ships for us.

In his first sketch, Witness 3, Los Angeles, accurately shows us the relative positions of HMS Ocean, USS Mitscher, and the 2 LCVPs in the water below. Witness 3, Los Angeles, also gives his estimation of the distance between USS Mitscher and the LCVPs at 80 – 100 feet (24 – 30 metres).

**USS Mitscher**   the 2 LCVPs   **HMS Ocean**

**Witness 3 Los Angeles Diagrams**

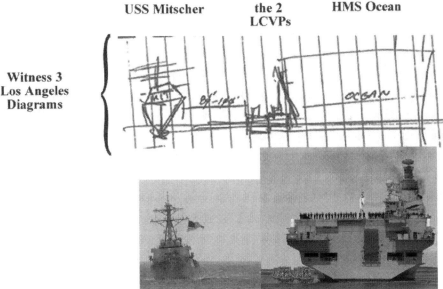

In the representation above, I have added photos of USS Mitscher, HMS Ocean, and the LCVPs in order to show the accuracy of the pencil diagrams that Witness 3, Los Angeles, has drawn for us. The positions of the ships have been verified by other witnesses, namely, ET Myers, Witness 1, Philippines, and Witness 2, Charleston.

Witness 3, Los Angeles, then shows us a side elevation of HMS Ocean with the position of the LCVP in the Bay, and my son, Joshua, standing at the back of the wheelhouse and on the deck of the LCVP. Witness 3, Los Angeles, also draws the position of the two LCVPs in the water below.

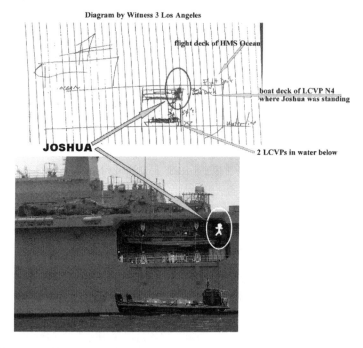

You will notice that Witness 3, Los Angeles, also shows us the height from the LCVP in the bay to the ones in the water below to be about 50 feet (15 ¼ metres).

Witness 3, Los Angeles, has been accurate and clear with the information that he has given us. He even tells us of the position and movements of a sailor in the LCVP below, who we know to be ET Myers.

All these statements show the accuracy of the account by Witness 3, Los Angeles, and they also show the great lengths he has gone to in ensuring that he records all the details for us.

Now that we have verified the accuracy of the statement made by Witness 3 Los Angeles, let us examine them further.

## Witness 3, Los Angeles – Saw the Incident from Start to Finish

Witness 3, Los Angeles, appears to be the only witness who saw the entire incident from start to finish and to have seen it so clearly. Witness 3, Los Angeles, says that he knew that

> *"nobody saw the fall as clearly as I did."*

When my son had just fallen, the bridge of USS Mitscher instantly radioed down to the fantail asking if anyone had seen the fall. They needed to know. There would have been much discussion about the event between the ship's company for Witness 3, Los Angeles, to be able to make the claim that he was the only witness who saw the fall clearly and saw the entire incident happen. Other witnesses would have only seen bits or parts of the events, but Witness 3, Los Angeles, says that he saw the *"entire incident happen"*. He reaffirms this statement and says, *"I saw the entire incident clearly"*

Witness 3, Los Angeles, says –

> *"While **I saw the entire incident happen**, I don't think many other people saw it. **I know that nobody saw the fall as clearly as I did.** I think some people saw something fall overboard, but **they did not get a good look**. I think some people thought it was a duffle bag or a dummy/OSCAR that fell because **they did not get a good look** at the fall or didn't want to believe that they really just saw someone fall like that."*

> *"The bridge called down to the fantail and asked if anybody saw what it was that fell. I told xyz that I saw a man fall and some people were arguing that it was not a man that fell, but I told abc that it was a man who slipped and fell. **I saw the entire incident clearly.**"*

## Witness 3, Los Angeles – Saw Joshua Standing on the LCVP Deck

Let us go back to Witness 3, Los Angeles' statements. Witness 3, Los Angeles, says that he saw Joshua standing on the LCVP deck at the back of the wheelhouse.

Witness 3, Los Angeles, tells us that my son was standing at the back of the LCVP which was in the bay of HMS Ocean.

> *"While I was manning the rails, I noticed a man in a white jumpsuit onboard HMS OCEAN. He stuck out to me because he was wearing all white. I noticed **he was standing on one of OCEAN's landing crafts in a well deck. He was on the aft end.** I saw him grab a stanchion/ part"* (the hand rail) *"of the landing craft, and he appeared to try to proceed to the port side of the craft using the stanchion as leverage/ handle. "*
> *"He appeared to be comfortable doing what he was doing he was not tentative in his actions or motions. He was only using one hand, and I believe it was his right hand."*

Witness 3, Los Angeles, also tells us that Joshua is holding the rail with his right hand.

It is the starting position we are dealing with here. My son was standing at the back of the LCVP on the deck. My son was standing at the back of the wheelhouse.

Witness 3, Los Angeles, has made a diagram and he has put in that diagram all the positions of my son's movements, from his starting position standing comfortably at the back of the LCVP to his fall. I have circled my son's starting position at the back of the LCVP and behind the wheelhouse, and added labels to clarify the diagram.

**Diagram by Witness 3 Los Angeles**

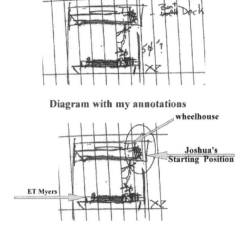

**Diagram with my annotations**

In the picture below I have further recreated this starting position using stick figures and photos of the LCVPs.

The drawings that Witness 3, Los Angeles, has made for us are a very good backup of his highly detailed, written account of the events he witnessed.

## We Have a Problem – Joshua or PO Fulton at the Back of the LCVP?

We have a problem.

Witness 3 Los Angeles shows us my son standing comfortably at the back of the wheelhouse roof. Isn't this where PO Fulton tells us he was standing?

Both statements cannot be true.

## Witness 3, Los Angeles – Joshua is Walking Comfortably

We have noted with what great detail and accuracy Witness 3, Los Angeles, recounts to us the events of that day. In the same manner he accurately and descriptively tells us what my son, Joshua, was doing.

> *"While I was manning the rails, I noticed a man in a white jumpsuit onboard HMS OCEAN. He stuck out to me because he was wearing*

*all white. I noticed he was standing on one of OCEAN's landing crafts in a well deck. He was on the aft end. I saw him grab a stanchion/part"* (the hand rail) *"of the landing craft, and he appeared to try to proceed to the port side of the craft using the stanchion as leverage/handle. "*

**"He appeared to be comfortable doing what he was doing he was not tentative in his actions or motions.** *He was only using one hand, and I believe it was his right hand."*

He says Joshua was standing at the back of the LCVP, on the deck of the LCVP.

He also tells us that my son held the hand rail with one hand and that Joshua was comfortable doing what he was doing, and that Joshua was not tentative in his actions or motions.

It is most likely that he and PO Fulton went to view USS Mitscher as she is sailing past, and before they miss the opportunity. Could it be my son is also enjoying the beautiful Florida morning, with the sparkling sea and glorious Florida sunshine?

## Why is Joshua at the Back of the LCVP?

Was it to view USS Mitscher that my son stood at the back of the LCVP? Why didn't he view USS Mitscher from the front of the wheelhouse or wherever else he happened to be?

The back of the LCVP is the only place on the LCVP that has a guard rail. In addition there is a hand rail encircling the wheelhouse. The back of the LCVP is the safest place to stand.

Not only does my son choose the safest place on the LCVP to stand, but he also holds the hand rail. And we were further told that he took his A4 diary with him when he went to the LCVP with PO Fulton.

This diary was found on the ledge of HMS Ocean after my son's fall. Why had my son placed the A4 diary on the ledge of HMS Ocean? Was it perhaps so that he could have both hands free in order to view USS Mitscher sailing past?

## Witness 3, Los Angeles – Joshua Swings and Rotates

Witness 3, Los Angeles, has told us that my son was walking comfortably towards the port side as USS Mitscher was sailing past.

> *"He appeared to be comfortable doing what he was doing he was not tentative in his actions or motions".*

But now we have a complete and sudden change of direction and speed. My son was walking and walking comfortably.

My son now goes from a very comfortable position to one where, out the blue, he is seen to swing and rotate.

Witness 3, Los Angeles, is the only witness to see my son thrown off balance. He states –

> *"When he swung/rotated his body around to get to the port side, his foot slipped and his hand grip gave way and he fell off of the landing craft"*

We now have a very sudden movement. My son is suddenly swung round - rotated round. A few seconds before we have him moving calmly towards the port side of the LCVP holding onto the rail.

What has caused such a sudden and forcible change to his very calm, careful movements?

## DID HE SLIP ON A GREASY FLOOR?

Did my son slip? SIB Wilson mentions that the deck of the LCVP was slippery.

When a person slips, their feet are literally taken out from under them. Their feet slide forwards, and they land on their bottom. After that, if they are not so fortunate, they continue sliding forwards.

If my son slipped and landed on his bottom, the direction of movement would have been straight ahead. There are two barriers in front of my son, the guard rail and a further foot barrier. Both these barriers would have stopped his continual slide off the deck and down the forty to fifty foot drop.

Both pictures were taken from our visit on a LCVP.

You will notice that the floor of the LCVP has been designed to be a non-slip floor.

This is specifically so that the Royal Marines are able to run on and off the LCVP, probably under fire, and in adverse conditions with wet, muddy, oily, grimy boots. The LCVP has been designed specifically for the worst conditions and therefore the designers have gone to great lengths to ensure that the troops would never slip.

Slipping would not have caused a sudden, rotating movement. In addition the floor has been designed so that slipping does not occur.

It would therefore be reasonable to say that my son did not slip.

## Did Joshua Trip Over an Obstacle?

If my son did not slip, did my son stumble and trip over an obstacle?

We first have to ask whether there are any obstacles in the area where my son was walking.
We must also remember that according to the account of Witness 3, Los Angeles, my son was extremely careful as he moved slowly towards the port side of the LCVP.

> *"He appeared to be comfortable doing what he was doing he was not tentative in his actions or motions.*

Therefore it is highly unlikely that my son would have been clumsy and tripped over an obstacle. What could have caused this sudden movement? What could have caused this sudden change of direction? What could have caused this increase in speed, as my son was seen walking, and walking comfortably?

Then there is the direction to consider. When a person stumbles and trips over an obstacle, the body lurches forward. The head goes first and the legs follow after. Very much like diving from a diving board into a swimming pool.

I have shown a representation of a trip with the body lurching forward head first. Is this what happened?

Two of the witness statements specifically state that my son fell feet first, namely Witness 2, Charleston, and Witness 3, Los Angeles.

Witness 2, Charleston, states -

> *"I looked back to the direction again a few seconds later, and I saw the same guy in white clothes falling from a troop transport boat. He was flailing his arms, and* **he was falling feet first.**"

Witness 3, Los Angeles, states -

> *"He initially fell with* **his legs under him pointing towards the water,** *but his momentum caused his legs to point towards the bow of OCEAN."*

As my son did not fall head first over the side of the LCVP, we can therefore quite logically state that he did not trip.

## DID HE RECEIVE A HUGE FORCE FROM BEHIND?

We have to consider whether my son received **the impact of** a huge and unexpected **force** from behind?

Witness 3, Los Angeles, is very clear in his statements that he sees my son walking carefully and calmly towards the port edge of the LCVP. He also notices that he is holding onto the rail around the wheelhouse.

*"He appeared to be comfortable doing what he was doing he was not tentative in his actions or motions"*

Suddenly he sees my son's body swing and rotate round.

What has caused this sudden and forcible change of direction? What has caused my son to be thrown off balance?

Witness 3, Los Angeles, is the only witness to see my son thrown off balance. He states –

*"When he swung/rotated his body around to get to the port side, his foot slipped and his hand grip gave way and he fell off of the landing craft"*

Let us consider the analogy of an open door that is hinged on the right hand side.
When a force is applied from behind it swings and rotates. These are the very words that Witness 3, Los Angeles, has used in describing the strange and unexpected movement of my son, Joshua's, body.

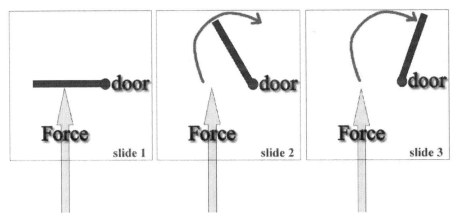

**This figure shows the direction of motion when a single force is applied to a door. The door rotates and swings round on its hinges.**

Joshua displayed the exact equivalent direction of motion when he was moving carefully towards the port side of the LCVP. His body suddenly was observed to swing and rotate.

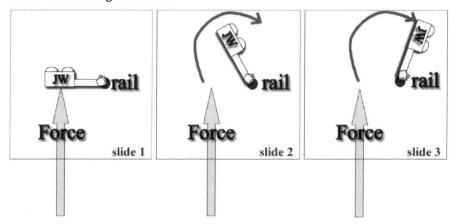

This figure shows the identical direction of motion as a door swinging on its hinges. Joshua swung and rotated around the rail whilst his hand desperately held on as he was fighting for his life.

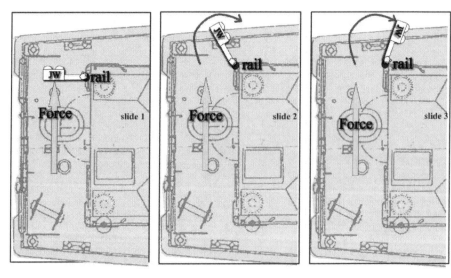

This figure is the same as the previous figure, except also showing the plan of the LCVP to indicate when my son would have lost his footing as he swung over the edge.

We will now try to represent Joshua from a different view point as Witness 3, Los Angeles, would have seen him. We have used photographs of the LCVP that we took whilst at the Royal Marine Base, Poole, in September, 2011. You will notice that the LCVP is in the water. We will have to try to imagine the LCVP in the LCVP Bay.

**Joshua is seen by Witness 3, Los Angeles, making his way carefully to the port side of the LCVP.**

Witness 3, Los Angeles, is the only witness to view Joshua at this moment in time.

**Joshua is seen by Witness 3, Los Angeles, as he starts to suddenly swing and rotate. What caused him to suddenly swing and rotate – a blow from behind?**

**Joshua continues to swing and rotate.**

Joshua continues to swing and rotate.

I have placed Joshua in a sitting position, as I am endeavouring to understand the mystery of the feet seen by Witness1, Phillipines. It was only one week before the Inquest that we found out that the feet were not my son's feet.

**Joshua continues to swing and rotate.**

Witness 3, Los Angeles, states –

> *"When he swung/rotated his body around to get to the port side, his foot slipped and his hand grip gave way and he fell off of the landing craft"*

As Joshua's body is violently swung round to the port side, his foot slips and then his right hand is unable to hold the weight of his whole body and the sudden jerking action as his body drops. He loses his grip and falls.

# Witness 3, Los Angeles – the Fall

Witness 3, Los Angeles, now describes to us in great detail Joshua's fall.

> "He initially fell with his legs under him pointing towards the water, but his momentum caused his legs to point towards the bow of OCEAN. He continued to rotate and when he initially landed on the, what I believe to be the inboard landing craft below, his head and shoulder was the first part of him to hit. His head hit the forward section/edge of the wheelhouse. The impact then caused him to rotate and his legs hitting the stowage box/container on the landing craft; this then rotated him again. I saw him fall in between the wheelhouse and stowage box/container for his third and final impact. During his fall, he hit three separate and distinct times. I did not hear him scream or yell on his way down. I heard all three impacts. They obviously happened very close to each other and if I had not seem them directly I would have assumed that they were all one impact. The final impact made the loudest sound of them all. When I saw the man hit his head, I thought to myself that there is no way anyone could survive that impact. I later told other members of the crew that I believed the man was most likely dead."

This is confirmed by ET Myers, who was on the LCVP below, and, on hearing my son's loud terrified scream, looked up, and saw him fall. Section 12 of the Immediate Ship's Investigation states -

> "ET4 **(ET Myers)** heard a scream and looking up saw a person wearing white overalls falling from the Port Aft LCVP Bay. ET 4 **(ET Myers)** did not know who the casualty was, as he is only a couple of weeks into his first sea draft, but he recognised the white overalls as belonging to an officer. He observed the casualty impact the top of the wheelhouse of NC LCVP (head and shoulders striking the superstructure) before being flipped by the impact and landing on the starboard engine hatch."

Witness 3, Los Angeles, draws my son's fall to aid us in our understanding of his explanation.

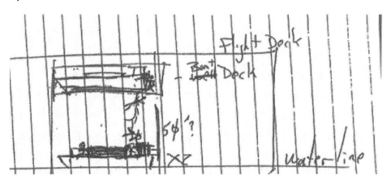

The original diagram by Witness 3 Los Angeles.

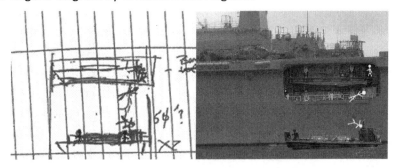

I have added a matching photo of HMS Ocean together with stick men in order to show the accuracy of the statements and descriptions given by Witness 3 Los Angeles.

And despite the detailed explanations of my son's fall and the drawings, Witness 3, Los Angeles, gives us yet more drawings, this time to make it clear to us the three impacts that my son's body made when he hit the LCVP. Witness 3, Los Angeles, has put these three impacts into one drawing, and labelled each impact. I have endeavoured to show the six steps or stages of my son's fall from the time he is seen standing at the back of the LCVP to his fall, and then his three impacts, as recounted and then drawn by Witness 3 Los Angeles.

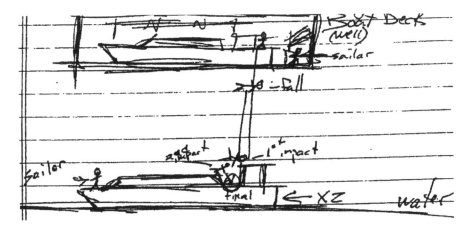

This is the original sketch made by Witness 3, Los Angeles, in order to show us the detail of my son's body hitting the LCVP and how it made a total of three impacts.

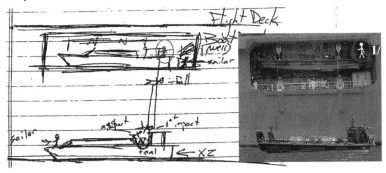

**Step 1**. My son is standing comfortably behind the wheelhouse on the deck of the LCVP.

I have circled his starting position as seen by Witness, 3 Los Angeles, who writes,

*"While I was manning the rails, I noticed a man in a white jumpsuit onboard HMS OCEAN. He stuck out to me because he was wearing all white. I noticed he was standing on one of OCEAN's landing crafts in a well deck. He was on the aft end. I saw him grab a stanchion/part"* (the hand rail) *"of the landing craft, and he appeared to try to proceed to the port side of the craft using the stanchion as leverage/handle. "*
*"He appeared to be comfortable doing what he was doing he was not tentative in his actions or motions. He was only using one hand, and I believe it was his right hand."*

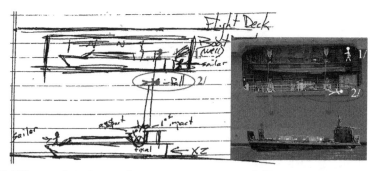

**Step 2**. Witness 3, Los Angeles, now sees my son falling.  He says,

*"When he swung/rotated his body around to get to the port side, his foot slipped and his hand grip gave way and he fell off of the landing craft. He initially fell with his legs under him pointing towards the water, but his momentum caused his legs to point towards the bow of OCEAN."*

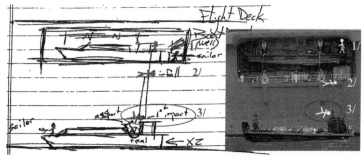

**Step 3**. Witness 3, Los Angeles, shows us the first impact, when Joshua's head hit the metal wheelhouse roof. Witness 3, Los Angeles, says,

*"He continued to rotate and when he initially landed on the, what I believe to be the inboard landing craft below, his head and shoulder was the first part of him to hit.  His head hit the forward section/edge of the wheelhouse."*

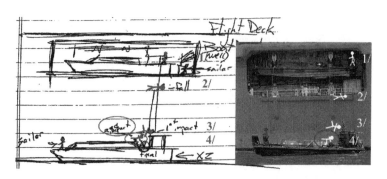

**Step 4.** He draws the second impact, when Joshua's body was flipped over and hit the raised deck of the LCVP. He then says

> *"The impact then caused him to rotate and his legs hitting the stowage box/container on the landing craft; this then rotated him again"*

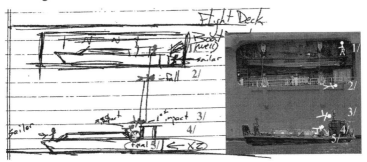

**Step 5**. He draws an arrow to the place of the final impact, when my son's body landed finally on the recessed part of the LCVP. He then draws two arrows, the first one to show how Joshua's body was flipped onto the deck and then second arrow pointing to the word "final" to emphasize that this is where my son's body came to rest. He then says

> *"this then rotated him again. I saw him fall in between the wheelhouse and stowage box/container for his third and final impact. During his fall, he hit three separate and distinct times."*

I quote the full account below -

> *""When he swung/rotated his body around to get to the port side, his foot slipped and his hand grip gave way and he fell off of the landing craft."*
> *"He initially fell with his legs under him pointing towards the water, but his momentum caused his legs to point towards the bow of OCEAN. He continued to rotate and when he initially landed on the, what I believe to be the inboard landing craft below, his head and shoulder was the first part of him to hit. His head hit the forward section/edge of the wheelhouse. The impact then caused him to rotate and his legs hitting the stowage box/container on the landing craft; this then rotated him again. I saw him fall in between the wheelhouse and stowage box/container for his third and final impact. During his fall, he hit three separate and distinct times. "*

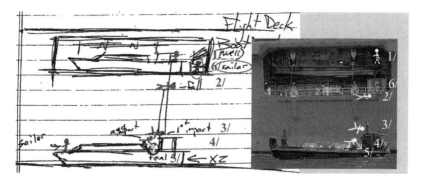

**Step 6.** He now shows us where he saw a man in blue appearing in the well deck. He says,

*"I saw another Royal Navy sailor in dark coveralls in the well deck where the man fell from. He peeked his head out of the well deck and looked down and I think he saw the fallen man. He then ran inside the skin of the ship."*

All these diagrams verify the accuracy and care that he has taken in ensuring that we have understood what he saw.

## Witness 3, Los Angeles – sees PO Fulton

Witness 3, Los Angeles, tells us that he saw ET Myers in the LCVP below go into the wheelhouse to presumably call for help. This is confirmed in the ISI Item 13. (Immediate Ships' Investigation)

*"I then saw another Royal Navy sailor, who was on the outboard landing craft, investigate the sound of the impact. I saw him apparently discovered the man who fell because he went into the wheelhouse of the landing craft to presumably radio for help. I saw another Royal Navy sailor in dark coveralls in the well deck where the man fell from. He peeked his head out of the well deck and looked down and I think he saw the fallen man. He then ran inside the skin of the ship."*

He then sees a man in dark overalls in the well deck where the man fell from. Is this PO Fulton? Is this when PO Fulton finally decides to look for my son in the LCVP bay, and, after not finding him there, decides to look over the side?

## US Navy Witnesses and SIB Wilson Military Police

With such a God send as this, three independent US Navy witnesses, and one who saw the entire episode from start to finish, one would not even have to think about questioning them – it would be a given.

SIB Wilson does not bother interviewing any of them. Instead he bases his criminal investigation on the word of the only man with my son, and so rules out foul play completely.

# Witness 2, Charleston – View from the Bridge

Let us now look at the statements made by Witness 2, Charleston.

STATEMENT

Place : NCISFO Norfolk, VA
Date : August 13, 2010

I make the following free and voluntary statement to whom I know to be a Representative of the United States Naval Criminal Investigative Service. I make this statement of my own free will and without any threats made to me or promises extended. I fully understand that this statement is given concerning my knowledge of the death of a British Royal Navy Sailor.

For identification purposes, I am a white male, 73" tall, 205 lbs, with brown hair and blue eyes. I was born on in Charleston, SC. My social security number is onboard USS MITSCHER (DDG 57).

On 06AUG10, I was onboard USS MITSCHER on the port side of the bridge. We were leaving Naval Station Mayport, FL, and as we sailed past HMS OCEAN, who was tied up to the pier, I noticed a man in white clothes walking along the edge of the flight deck. I looked back to the direction again a few seconds later, and I saw the same guy in white clothes falling from a troop transport boat. He was flailing his arms, and he was falling feet first. I did not see him hit the ground, but I heard a loud "Boom." I heard a few other people onboard MITSCHER gasp when they heard the "boom." I don't know who they were.

When I first saw the guy fall, I thought that the Brits might be playing a practical joke. I thought they might have thrown a dummy overboard. Another reason why I thought it was a dummy was that after the man fell, I saw another sailor onboard HMS OCEAN walking slowly in the vicinity of where the man fell. The sailor was wearing blue and he did not appear to be in any hurry.

I don't think very many people saw the fall because nobody was talking about the man's fall that day.

This statement, consisting of this page and 0 other page(s) was typed for me by as we discussed its contents. I have read and understand the above statement. I have been given the opportunity to make any changes or corrections I desire to make and have placed my initials over the changes or corrections. This statement is the truth to the best of my knowledge and belief.

Signature

Sworn to and subscribed before me this 13 day of AUGUST in the year 2010 at

NCIS FO NORFOLK VA

Witnessed

Representative, Naval Criminal Investigative Service
AUTH: DERIVED FROM ARTICLE 136,
UCMJ (10 U.S.C. 936) AND 5 U.S.C. 303

Page 1 of 1          (Formerly NCISFORM 016/04-81)

NCIS 5580/26 (1/2001)

Witness 2, Charleston, was on the Bridge of USS Mitscher as she slowly passed HMS Ocean. Witness 2, Charleston, noticed a man in white on the deck of HMS Ocean. He says,

*"I noticed a man in white clothes walking along the edge of the flight deck."*

Was this my son? We were to find out just before the Inquest, when Witness 2, Charleston, made one further statement, that the man in white on the flight deck was wearing shorts. Joshua was wearing white overalls; therefore this was not my son that he first saw.

Witness 2, Charleston, then turned away, and when he looked back at HMS Ocean he saw my son fall from the LCVP, which he calls the troop transport boat. Witness 2, Charleston, thought that the man falling was the same man he first saw. Witness 2, Charleston, says

*"I looked back to the direction again a few seconds later, and I saw the same guy in white clothes falling from a troop transport boat. He was flailing his arms, and he was falling feet first. I did not see him hit the ground, but I heard a loud 'Boom'"*

## Witness 2, Charleston – saw a man in blue

Witness 2, Charleston, saw a man walking on the flight deck. He then turned away and a few moments later saw my son falling and assumed that it was the same man he had first seen walking on the flight deck.

Witness 2, Charleston, did not see Joshua actually swing round before he fell.

What is so important about Witness 2, Charleston, is that he says he saw another man in the vicinity of where Joshua fell from. Is this PO Fulton?

*"I saw another sailor onboard HMS OCEAN walking in the vicinity of where the man fell"*

This shows my son standing comfortably at the back of the wheelhouse as seen by Witness 3, Los Angeles. We believe that the facts support that Joshua receives a huge blow from behind. PO Fulton was the only other person with Joshua.

After Joshua fell, Witness 2, Charleston, says –

*"I saw another sailor onboard HMS OCEAN walking slowly in the vicinity of where the man fell. The sailor was wearing blue and he did not appear to be in any hurry."*

But, in my opinion, one of the important parts of the statement by Witness 2, Charleston, is that he says he thought the Brits were playing a practical joke. He thought that they had just thrown a dummy overboard. The reason that he thought it was a dummy was because he saw this man in blue walking around calm as calm could be, as if nothing at all had happened. Who else was in the vicinity of the LCVP when Joshua fell? We are told that PO Fulton was the only man with Joshua. Witness 2, Charleston, has just seen a man fall, and then he sees a man in blue. His statements make you think that you are not talking of a huge passage of time, but just a few seconds.

Was it PO Fulton that Witness 2, Charleston, is describing to us?

It appeared to Witness 2, Charleston, that this man's calm behaviour, walking slowly in the vicinity of where the man fell, signalled that he had not just witnessed a real live human being falling to certain death. This could not be. Just look at this man in blue. He is calmly and slowly walking around as if nothing has happened. Who is this man in blue? Is it PO Fulton, or is it another man?

In PO Fulton's statements we have already noted how unnatural and contrived his behaviour is. The air is full of shouts and loud vocal alarms, not to mention my son's terrified 1.5 second scream, and yet PO Fulton, by his own admission, is slowly walking on the LCVP, wondering where my son is. It does not add up.

Witness 2, Charleston, states -

*"When I first saw the guy fall, I thought that the Brits might be playing a practical joke. I thought they might have thrown a dummy overboard. Another reason why I thought it was a dummy was that after the man fell, I saw another sailor onboard HMS OCEAN walking slowly in the vicinity of where the man fell. The sailor was wearing blue and he did not appear to be in any hurry."*

(see the website for the full statement)

## Witness 2, Charleston – and SIB Wilson Military Police

Now let us see what Lt Cdr Geoff Wilson, Special Investigations Branch Military Police, makes of this witness.

Witness 2, Charleston, says that he saw a man dressed in white fall from a "troop transport boat". This is excellent news. We have another eye witness account of my son's fall. We have another independent, non-interested party who saw my son's fall.

There are so many questions one wants to ask.

Which part of the LCVP did Joshua fall from?  This is very important.

This man in white walking on the flight deck, tell me about him?  What do you mean by flight deck?  Do you mean the flight deck of HMS Ocean, or do you mean the deck of the LCVP/troop transport boat?

This man in blue, where did you see him?  Where was he walking?  What exactly was he doing?  When did you see him?

So many important questions.  Such a God send.  Another independent witness to a fatal fall, another independent witness to a death.

And then we find that Lt Cdr Geoff Wilson, Special Investigations Branch Royal Navy Military Police did not even bother to interview Witness 2, Charleston, let alone any of the other US Navy witnesses.

And things get even worse than not interviewing US Navy Witness 2, Charleston.  What does Lt Cdr Geoff Wilson, Special Investigations Branch Military Police write in his report, the report that sums up his investigation into my son's suspicious death?

SIB Wilson states in Item 34 of his SIB process

*"By the 11 Aug 10, and in the absence of any evidence to suggest the incident had been anything other than an accident, OIC SIB gave approval for PO Fulton to provide a further statement to investigators.  OIC SIB was satisfied that the SIB team had pursued all reasonable lines of enquiry to establish the facts and had concluded that 'foul play' and suicide had not been contributory factors to Lt Woodhouse falling.  **There were no witnesses to the whole incident.***

SIB Wilson then goes on to say in Item 35 -

*"The location of the LCVP and the fact that the incident occurred on the outboard side of the vessel meant that there were no known witnesses external to the ship at the point Lt Woodhouse was heard to fall.  The LCVP deck is not visible from any other upper deck area in HMS OCEAN and there would therefore be no witness evidence from those areas.  Despite this an appeal was made for witnesses to come forward."*

SIB Wilson in Item 37 states –

*"Information was also received on 11 Aug 10 through The United States Naval Criminal Investigation Service (NCIS) that there were potential witnesses to the incident who had been on board the USS Mitscher, which had been departing the naval base at the time of the incident. Statements were obtained which describe how Lt Woodhouse had been seen to slide down from the bridge roof of the LCVP and lose his footing as he reached the next level. He was seen to make a grab for the handrail or stanchion before falling off the landing craft. No one else was seen to be involved."*

We have SIB Wilson in items 34 and 35 saying that there were no witnesses to the whole incident, and then he contradicts himself two paragraphs down in item 37 by saying that there were potential witnesses.

He then goes on to use the adjective 'honestly'.

*"The receipt of the US statements meant that OIC SIB was able to conclude with the honestly held belief, that having established the facts and gathered all available evidence, Lt Woodhouse had not been the victim of an intentional act or suicide. The investigation then concentrated on all other matters relating to the incident which are contained within RNP SIB report 100025/10.*

If SIB Wilson did not interview the three US Navy Witnesses then he did not gather all the evidence, therefore he was in no position to use the word honestly or to state that my son had not been the victim of an intentional act.

## Witness 1, Philippines – at first all I could see was his feet

Let us now look at the statement by Witness 1, Philippines, who was standing on the quarter deck of USS Mitscher as she sailed past HMS Ocean.

STATEMENT

Place : NCISFO Norfolk, VA
Date : August 12, 2010

████████████ make the following free and voluntary statement to ████████████ whom I know to be a Representative of the United States Naval Criminal Investigative Service. I make this statement of my own free will and without any threats made to me or promises extended. I fully understand that this statement is given concerning my knowledge of the Royal Navy sailor who fell while onboard HMS OCEAN.

For identification purposes, I am a Filipino American, 65" tall, 150 lbs, with black hair and brown eyes. I was born on ████████████ n Pangasinan, Philippines. My social security number is ████████████ ████████████ tationed onboard USS MITSCHER (DDG 57)

On 06AUG10, at approximately 0900, the MITSCHER was getting underway from Mayport, FL. I was standing Officer of the Deck Inport on the Sea and Anchor Watchbill. I was stationed on the port side, midships quarterdeck. I was standing watch ████████████ but I don't think he saw the entire incident.

MITSCHER got underway and as we were passing HMS OCEAN, who was tied up pierside, I noticed a man sitting on top an LCAC. He was wearing white clothes. At first, all I could see was his feet. He was by himself. I saw him slide down the LCAC to the next level, but he lost his balance. I saw him attempt to grab something to regain his balance, but he was unsuccessful. I saw him fall off the LCAC, but I did not see him land. I did hear a very loud noise that sounded like a loud "boom." I don't think anybody onboard OCEAN saw him fall, but a few seconds after he fell, I saw another sailor in blue clothes walk to where the sailor in white fell. It appeared to me that the sailor in blue discovered the fallen sailor in white.

When I saw him attempt to slide down to the next level, I noticed he did not have a harness on and I thought to myself that what he was doing was very unsafe. I heard later from someone that MITSCHER contacted OCEAN over bridge-to-bridge to let them know somebody from their ship fell.

This statement, consisting of this page and 1 other page(s) was typed for me by ████████████ as we discussed its contents. I have read and understand the above statement. I have been given the opportunity to make any changes or corrections I desire to make and have placed my initials over the changes or corrections. This statement is the truth to the best of my knowledge and belief.

Signature: _____

Sworn to and subscribed before me this 12 day of August in the year 2010 at

NCIFO NORFOLK VA

Witnesses: _____   _____
                                        Representative, Naval Criminal Investigative Service
                                        AUTH: DERIVED FROM ARTICLE 136,

NCIS 5580/26 (1/2001)          Page 1 of 2          (Formerly NCISFORM 016/04-81)

We found the statement by Witness 1, Philippines, hard to understand. It was very clear that Witness 1, Philippines, wanted to help us by telling us as much as he could. There were so many questions that we wanted to ask. There were so many puzzle pieces.

The style of writing by Witness 1, Philippines, is also different. He tells us a statement, and then he tells us the cause or he tries to explain the events leading to the statement he has just made.

Witness 1, Philippines, tells us that the first thing he saw of my son was his feet.

*"At first, all I could see was his feet."*

Questions, questions, questions. Why did he only see the feet first? What was obstructing his view of my son that he only saw his feet?

We found out later (a few days before the Inquest) that it was not my son's feet that he saw, but the feet of another sailor working on a moveable platform on the side of HMS Ocean, doing painting or maintenance work.

But, on first receiving his statement, we did not know this bit of information. We did not know that there were sailors working on the side of HMS Ocean very close to where my son was standing.

All we had was this strange account of feet from Witness 1, Philippines.

All three US Navy witnesses saw my son fall. We wondered whether any other US Navy witness saw the entire episode from start to finish as US Witness 3, Los Angeles, stated he had done.

We know that Witness 2, Charleston, saw a man on the flight deck, and then he turned away. When he looked again and saw a man falling, he assumed that it was the same man that he had seen on the flight deck.

We believe the same thing happened to Witness 1, Philippines, but, until just the week before my son's Inquest, we did not know that there were other men working on the side of HMS Ocean, near to my son. We did not know that the feet he saw belonged to another person, and not to my son.

Without this information we pondered the mystery of 'the feet'.

## Witness 1, Philippines – I noticed a man sitting

Witness 1, Philippines, tells us that he saw a man sitting on top of a LCAC / LCVP.

Witness 1, Philippines, said

*I noticed a man sitting on top an LCAC. He was wearing white clothes. At first, all I could see was his feet. He was by himself. I saw him slide down the LCAC to the next level, but he lost his balance. I saw him attempt to grab something to regain his balance, but he was unsuccessful. I saw him fall off the LCAC, bit I did not see him land. I did hear a very loud noise that sounded like a loud "boom."*

We did not know that there were workmen on a moving platform in close proximity to where Joshua was standing, so when Witness 1, Philippines, stated that he saw feet first, we made the assumption that he saw Joshua's feet.

Why did he only see the feet first? Why did he say my son was in a sitting position when Witness 3, Los Angeles, clearly saw Joshua standing comfortably on the back of the LCVP?

We shall start with my son comfortably standing at the back of the LCVP watching USS Mitscher sailing past. I have put together this representation of my son's position from a picture of a LCVP we visited. The LCVP on which my son was standing was in the Bay on HMS Ocean, but this picture shows the LCVP in the water. Please use your imagination to place the LCVP in the Bay of HMS Ocean.

**Witness 3, Los Angeles, saw Joshua standing behind the wheelhouse and holding the rail at the back of the wheelhouse.**

Witness 3, Los Angeles, had told us that Joshua is walking comfortably and that he is not tentative in his movements when suddenly he sees Joshua violently swing and rotate round.

Joshua suddenly moves violently round. His body swings and rotates

My son now starts to fall and to lose his grip.

Joshua is in a 'sitting' position, his feet are seen

**Joshua is in a sitting position as he continues to rotate and lose his balance.**

Is this the time that Witness 1, Philippines, first sees Joshua?

*"At first all I could see was his feet."*

It would only be possible for Witness 1, Philippines, to see Joshua's feet if those feet were not touching the ground.

As Joshua has now lost his balance and starts to fall, he is desperately trying to regain his balance. Witness 3, Los Angeles, mentions that *"his foot slipped"*

Joshua continues to rotate
one foot has slipped
& his hand has given way
Joshua is still in a sitting position

**Joshua continues to rotate and now his foot has slipped and his hand has given way. He is still in a sitting position.**

Could this explain how and why Witness 1, Philippines, saw feet first and saw my son sitting? We had so many questions we wanted to ask.

Did SIB Wilson have any questions?

# Witness 1, Philippines – on top of an LCAC

The next puzzling piece of information in the account by Witness 1, Philippines, is that he says he saw my son on top an LCAC.

We only found out the week before my son's Inquest that there was a moving platform on the side of HMS Ocean, and its position was in the middle of the LCVP Bay and at the top of the Bay.

The feet of the man sitting on the moving platform are the feet that Witness 1, Philippines, first saw.

Witness 1, Philippines, made the assumption that the man he saw falling a few moments later was the same man that he first saw sitting on the moving platform.

We did not have this information, and so we pondered and we puzzled. What could Witness 1, Philippines, possibly mean when he said that he saw my son on top an LCAC?

There were so many questions. We would have loved to have had the opportunity to have asked him further questions.

Witness 1, Philippines, said

*I noticed a man sitting on top an LCAC. He was wearing white clothes. At first, all I could see was his feet. He was by himself. I saw him slide down the LCAC to the next level, but he lost his balance. I saw him attempt to grab something to regain his balance, but he was unsuccessful. I saw him fall off the LCAC, bit I did not see him land. I did hear a very loud noise that sounded like a loud "boom."*

So we were back to pondering and questioning this strange account from Witness 1, Philippines. What did Witness 1, Philippines, mean when he said the top of the LCAC? Why did his account appear to be so different from the very accurate and systematic and diagrammed account given to us by Witness 3, Los Angeles?

The top of the LCAC. Could Witness 1, Philippines, be trying to convey to us that to a spectator, there are two places where a man can stand? The first is on top of the LCVP, and the second position is underneath the LCVP, in the Bay. Is this what Witness 1, Philippines, was trying to convey to us?

**Joshua has lost his grip and begins to fall feet first**

It is at around this point that both Witness 2, Charleston, and Witness 1, Philippines, start witnessing my son's fall.

Witness 1, Philippines, states –

*"I saw him slide down the LCAC to the next level, but he lost his balance."*

We see that the word slide is a very good description of how Joshua is falling past the two levels of the LCVP Bay.

Witness 1, Philippines, further states –

*"I saw him attempt to grab something to regain his balance, but was unsuccessful"*

In this picture I have put all the stages of my son's fall as seen by Witness 1, Philippines.

## Witness 1, Philippines – did not see him land

The next puzzling piece of information in the account by Witness 1, Philippines, is that he says he did not see my son land.

Why didn't Witness 1, Philippines, see my son land?

*"I saw him fall off the LCAC, bit I did not see him land. I did hear a very loud noise that sounded like a loud 'boom'."*

He further writes in his statement that he saw a man in blue, which means that he saw the LCVP in the water below. Why didn't he see my son fall?

*"I don't think anybody onboard OCEAN saw him fall, but a few seconds after he fell, I saw another sailor in blue clothes walk to where the sailor in white fell. It appeared to me that the sailor in blue discovered the fallen sailor in white."*

Witness 1, Philippines, tells us that USS MITSCHER immediately contacted HMS Ocean bridge to bridge to tell them that someone had fallen from their ship.

*When I saw him attempt to slide down to the next level, I noticed he did not have a harness on and I thought to myself that what he was doing was very unsafe. I heard later from someone that **MITSCHER contacted OCEAN over bridge-to-bridge to let them know somebody from their ship fell."***

This would be perfectly feasible as Witness 2, Charleston, was on the bridge and he too witnessed my son's fall.

I believe the fact that HMS OCEAN was informed immediately of my son's fall is relevant. Another puzzle piece and a lot more questions.

## Witness 1, Philippines – and SIB Wilson, Military Police

Now let us see what Lt Cdr Geoff Wilson, Special Investigations Branch, Military Police, makes of this witness.

This witness statement is very strange. Feet? Where did they come from? Why could he only see feet? Where did he see a man sitting? What does he mean by top of LCAC? What does he mean by the next level? Why didn't he see my son land?

But he does do something proactive. SIB Wilson tells us with the greatest certainty in item 37 of his document that

*"Information was also received on 11 Aug 10 through The United States Naval Criminal Investigation Service (NCIS) that there were potential witnesses to the incident who had been on board the USS Mitscher, which had been departing the naval base at the time of the incident. Statements were obtained which describe how Lt Woodhouse had been seen to slide down from the bridge roof of the LCVP and lose his footing as he reached the next level. He was seen to make a grab for the handrail or stanchion before falling off the landing craft. No one else was seen to be involved."*

Lt Cdr Geoff Wilson, Special Investigations Branch Military Police, tells us that statements were obtained which describe how my son was seen to slide down from the bridge roof. We have scoured the statements from the three US Navy witnesses and none of them state that they saw my son slide down from the bridge roof, and then SIB Wilson goes on to tell us that

*"No one else was seen to be involved"*
But
*Another reason why I thought it was a dummy was that after the man fell, I saw another sailor onboard HMS OCEAN walking slowly in the vicinity of where the man fell. The sailor was wearing blue and he did not appear to be in any hurry.*

*Witness 2, Charleston.*

Was this investigated as it is at variance with the statement, 'No one else was seen to be involved'?

Further, we know that Lt Cdr Geoff Wilson, Special Investigations Branch Military Police, has read the statement by Witness 3, Los Angeles, because it is this pivotal witness that uses the term 'stanchion', which word SIB Wilson uses in his statement of how my son died.

And yet SIB Wilson creates statements that do not exist, and then sums up his entire investigation in item 39 saying that

*"Any foul play would have been identified. Simply, there was none which could be found."*

## Was PO Fulton Seen?

We have just read the three accounts by the three US Navy Witnesses.

What could possibly have caused my son to swing and rotate violently, and then lose his grip and fall over the side of the LCVP to his ultimate death?

A great force from behind would have caused this huge change of direction, and would have caused this sudden great momentum resulting in his fatal fall. PO Fulton was the only man with my son.

Did anybody see him at this moment in time? We are not sure whether Witness 2, Charleston, saw PO Fulton when he saw a man in blue.

*Another reason why I thought it was a dummy was that after the man fell, I saw another sailor onboard HMS OCEAN walking slowly in the vicinity of where the man fell. The sailor was wearing blue and he did not appear to be in any hurry.*

*Witness 2, Charleston.*

We wandered whether Witness 2, Charleston, saw him?

It was only a few days before the Inquest that we found out it was not Petty Officer Fulton he saw. But we still pondered, we investigated, we asked questions. Could Witness 3, Los Angeles, see him?

## Was it Easy to See PO Fulton?

We then have to ponder how easy it would have been to see  him whilst he stood on the LCVP.

It would have been very easy for him to hide during this time.

## LCVP BAY IN DARKNESS AND SHADOW

In the brightness of the Florida sunshine the recesses of HMS Ocean are very difficult to view and are much darker than if they were viewed in a normal English day.  My son was wearing white and was easily visible.

**this is taken from jacksonville.com showing HMS Ocean when in Mayport, Florida in August, 2010.**

this is also taken from jacksonville.com showing HMS Ocean when in Mayport, Florida in August, 2010.

## PO Fulton Dressed In Dark Overalls

Some force from behind caused my son to swing and rotate suddenly and violently. The only other person on the LCVP was PO Fulton. As the force came from behind, it is reasonable to say that PO Fulton was in all probability behind my son.

It would be quite difficult for someone 80 – 100ft away to pick out PO Fulton as he stood behind my son in the darkness of the LCVP bay as he was wearing dark overalls.

Contrast this with my son who was dressed in white overalls and was easily visible to the eye.

Witness 3, Los Angeles, states –
*"I saw another Royal Navy sailor in dark coveralls in the well deck where the man fell from. He peeked his head out of the well deck and looked down…."*

The only time that Witness 3, Los Angeles, sees PO Fulton is when he peeks over the side of the LCVP Bay.

## Hidden Behind Wheelhouse

Further, after my son's fall, it would take PO Fulton just one or two steps in order to walk behind the wheelhouse, and so be entirely hidden from view. There is no eye that can see him if he were to stand in this position.

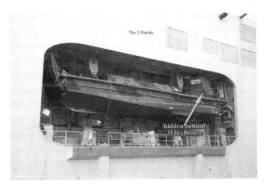

**This figure shows how easy it is for PO Fulton to step behind the wheelhouse and be completely out of view.**

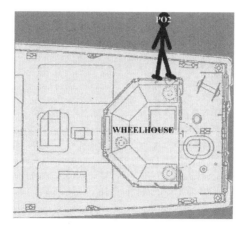

**This figure showing that it is impossible to view anyone if they were standing behind the wheelhouse**

## Human Eye Follows Movement

It is highly likely some force from behind caused my son to swing and rotate suddenly and violently. The only other person on the LCVP was PO Fulton. As the force would have come from behind, it is reasonable to say that PO Fulton was probably behind my son.

The only person that viewed Joshua at the very moment that he suddenly started swinging and rotating was Witness 3, Los Angeles. Why did he not see PO Fulton standing behind my son? For the reasons already stated above, but also because the human eye is always attracted to movement.

My son starts to swing/rotate violently. He starts to lose his balance. He is fighting to regain his balance. He is fighting for his life. His arms are flailing (in the words of Witness 2, Charleston).

In view of this it is not surprising that the human eye is not drawn to a man dressed in 'dark coveralls' in the dark recesses of the LCVP's furthest corner, hidden by the wheelhouse, and shielded by the figure of a man dressed in bright white.

It would also have been extremely easy to step back a pace or two and be completely hidden from view behind the wheelhouse.

# What Happened the Night Before?

The next items we devoured in the bundle of documents that the Coroner sent us were the witness statements by the three lieutenants, who were with my son the night before his fatal fall.

It is to be noted that my son's movements the night before his fall were investigated, and I wonder if the movements and activities of PO Fulton were in like manner also investigated?

I shall commence with the statement by my son's fellow engineer, Lt Jennifer Hayes.

## Lt Jennifer Hayes

Lt Jennifer Hayes tells us that at 5pm the day before my son's fall she, my son, and Lt Pearson decided to go for a meal at Bukkets bar.

We found out later that Bukkets Bar has a beautiful view over the Florida sea and the famous Florida beaches and that these three young people left the ship early in order to enjoy a lovely American meal in a beautiful American setting – Florida.

When we were in Jacksonville whilst my son was dying on his hospital bed we first met Jennifer Hayes, and she told us that she has a very precious last memory of my son as they enjoyed a beautiful meal together in an equally beautiful setting.

Lt Jennifer Hayes goes on to tell us that following the meal, at a time she cannot remember, the three of them went to Ocean Club, where they met up with Lt Lisa Pitman. It appears that later on in the evening the rest of the ships company went ashore for an arranged social time at Ocean Club and then Lynches bar.

Lt Jennifer Hayes tells us that on the following morning, my son knocked on her cabin door to make sure that she was up. Lt Jennifer Hayes tells us that my son was bright and happy, and did not appear dishevelled in any way.

> *At 0755 Lt Woodhouse knocked on my cabin door to make sure I was up. Lt Woodhouse **appeared bright and happy** and was making jokes at my expense. Lt Woodhouse **did not appear dishevelled in any way.***

(see the website for the full account)

## SIB Wilson and Lt Jennifer Hayes

Now let us see what Lt Cdr Geoff Wilson, Special Investigations Branch Military Police, makes of this witness.

Nothing at all.

SIB Wilson ignores this witness in the same way that he ignored the account by Witness 3, Los Angeles.

Why is that? Could it be perhaps because this witness makes it quite clear that my son was bright and happy and did not appear dishevelled in any way? Lt Jennifer Hayes states -

> At 0755 Lt Woodhouse knocked on my cabin door to make sure I was up. Lt Woodhouse **appeared bright and happy** and was making jokes at my expense. Lt Woodhouse **did not appear dishevelled in any way**.

Could it be because this witness does not allow SIB Wilson to prove that my son was drunk?

## Lt Ellis Pearson

Lt Ellis Pearson, together with Lt Jennifer Hayes and my son were the party of three who left the ship at 5pm in the afternoon to go and have a meal on the beautiful Jacks Beach.

He tells us that they walked around Jacks Beach looking for a nice place to eat their meal, when at 6pm they decided on Bukkets bar.

He further goes on to say that they did not leave Bukkets bar till five hours later. They had eaten food, which we found out later was quite a significant amount, together with some Corona beer.

After leaving Bukkets bar at 11pm they went to Oceans Club where he says that they consumed two plastic cups of lager, the size of the cups he thought would be slightly larger than half a pint. So we have my son consuming two plastic cups of lager in two hours.

Lt Ellis Pearson sums up by saying that during the time he was with my son, neither he nor my son were inebriated at any point.

> *During my evening in company with Lt Woodhouse we both consumed alcohol and had an enjoyable, relaxing evening, **but by no means were we inebriated at any point**.*

(see the website for the full account)

## SIB Wilson and Lt Ellis Pearson

Now let us see what SIB Wilson makes of this witness.

He treats this witness statement in the same way as he treated the three US Navy witness statements, and the witness statement by Lt Jennifer Hayes.

He totally ignores them.

These statements do not fit the account of the events that SIB Wilson wants us to believe.

## Lt Lisa Pitman

We then proceeded to read the account by the third Lieutenant who had seen my son the night before his fall. Lt Lisa Pitman met up with the three Lieutenants (my son, Lt Jennifer Hayes, and Lt Pearson) later on that evening as the ship's company went out for a night's socialising.

Her account is not particularly remarkable except where she describes my son's appearance and behaviour the following morning. She writes –

> *When I knocked on Lt Woodhouse cabin door I noticed he was dressed in White overalls and was cleaning his teeth. Lt Woodhouse looked at me and laughed because I did not look too well due to my late night. I noticed Lt Woodhouse **looked slightly shabby, with slightly bloodshot eyes**. He looked as though he had not had a lot of sleep.*
>
> *At approximately 0900 I telephoned Lt Woodhouse from the*

*Boats Workshop on the vehicle deck as I was with an agent who had a breaker for his department. Lt Woodhouse came to the gangway and we spoke about the breaker and joked about the previous night out. Lt Woodhouse had a bottle of water in his hand which is not unusual as he would often carry a bottle of water.*

*Lt Woodhouse was being **his normal self and did not appear to be under the influence of alcohol**. I do not know where Lt Woodhouse went after he had spoken to me on the gangway.*

(see the website for the full account)

What is remarkable is what SIB Wilson does with her account.

## SIB Wilson and Lt Lisa Pitman

We have seen how SIB Wilson from nowhere created a statement from the US Navy witnesses to fit PO Fulton's statement saying that my son was seen to fall from the bridge roof. None of the US witnesses saw my son on the bridge roof and one US witness clearly saw my son standing comfortably at the back of the wheelhouse before he fell.

SIB Wilson states in Item 37 of his RN SIB Investigation process -

*Statements were obtained which describe how Lt Woodhouse **had been seen to slide down from the bridge roof** of the LCVP and lose his footing as he reached the next level. He was seen to make a grab for the handrail or stanchion before falling off the landing craft.*

Let us see what further contortions SIB Wilson performs with this latest witness statement, that of Lt Lisa Pitman.

Why, SIB Wilson does none other than misquote the witness statement, and he is even careful enough to include the quotation marks.

In the Background section of his document Summary of Evidence SIB Wilson writes -

*"It has been established that Lt woodhouse had gone ashore at 1700 on 5th August with colleagues and had been seen by*

*a number of witnesses throughout that night enjoying the evening; he was observed on various occasions consuming alcoholic drinks. It has not been possible to ascertain the quantity of alcoholic liquor consumed by Lt Woodhouse or blood alcohol level at the time of incident as pre-transfusion samples were not secured. Lt Woodhouse returned to HMS OCEAN at 0205 on the 6th August as indicated in the After Midnight Log (Exhibit NS/9). At 07:45 that day Lt Woodhouse was seen by Lt Pitman who describes him as looking **"shabby with blood shot eyes".***

Let us see what Lt Pitman really did write -

*When I knocked on Lt Woodhouse cabin door I noticed he was dressed in White overalls and was cleaning his teeth. Lt Woodhouse looked at me and laughed because I did not look too well due to my late night. I noticed Lt Woodhouse looked **slightly shabby, with slightly bloodshot eyes.** He looked as though he had not had a lot of sleep.*

SIB Wilson has removed the word 'slightly' from the witness statement and then omitted quoting the same word at the start of the statement. Both omissions cast a completely different light on the witness statement.

This is the man that has been entrusted with an investigation into a suspicious death.

Why would he misquote a witness statement? To me the answer is perfectly simple and transparent. To achieve two goals.

- To prove that my son was drunk at the time of his fall, and dear me, it was all the dead man's fault. Dead men can't defend themselves.
- To cover my son's suspicious death.

## What Happened Down Below?

The next items we read in the bundle of documents reluctantly given to us by the Coroner were the accounts of the two men working on LCVP NM and N3, and the account by the Medical Assistant Lorraine Connolly.

I had intentionally put off reading these accounts, as I knew they would be extremely painful to me. PO Dot Cottam went to help my son and cradled his head, his broken head.  Thank you Dot, for your kindness to my son.

Thank you to the Royal Marines and to the US medical personnel, and to all who swiftly ran to help my son and for the practical help you gave him.

Thank you to ET(ME) Darbyshire for holding my son's hand.  Thank you to MA Mace and CPOMA Lorraine Connolly for giving my son medical attention.

From all our family I would like to say thank you to all who did their utmost to help my son in this time of his greatest need.

## The Miracles

Besides the great pain when reading PO Dot Cottam's account of my son's fall, my husband and I marvelled at how swiftly aid came to my son.  There appeared from nowhere Royal Marines who administered first aid.

In addition the harbour helicopter was called which immediately took my son to Shands Jacksonville Hospital in Jacksonville – a distance of about twenty two miles by car.

Another miracle to us was the fact that we were told by a medical doctor that Shands Jacksonville Hospital is rated as one of the best brain damage hospitals in the USA.  This is where my son, with his head split open from ear to ear was taken.  He could not have been taken to a better hospital.

The entire episode of my son's fall had far too many coincidences and as Christians we knew these were no chance events.  There is a God in Heaven, a good God, who rules in the affairs of men.

> *The LORD hath prepared His throne in the heavens;*
> *And His kingdom ruleth over all.*
>
> *Psalm 103:19*
>
> *And all the inhabitants of the earth are reputed as nothing: and he doeth according to his will in the army of heaven, and among the inhabitants of the earth: and none can stay his hand, or say unto him, What doest thou?*
>
> *Daniel 4:35*

How was it possible that there was a US Navy ship sailing past at just that moment in time? More than that, how was it possible that one US sailor saw my son's fall from start to finish? We have calculated that this is a very small time interval of just a few seconds.

How was it possible that all Joshua's family were able to be brought to his bedside for the remaining three days of his life?

How was it possible that the two aircraft bringing two groups of the family from opposite ends of the earth both landed at Jacksonville, Florida, at exactly the same time, at 9:24pm?

How was it possible that my son was not killed instantly?

How was it possible that the Royal British Legion should start an Independent Inquest Advice the month before my son's fall?

How was it possible that top lawyers and a top barrister should come to our aid from nowhere? To come to our aid with no thought of repayment and no possible gain to themselves. This was not possible.

It was not possible that we got the verdict we did get at my son's Inquest. It was not possible that we got this verdict when we had the full weight of the MOD, RN Military Police, Royal Navy, and the Coroner set against us.

There are too many miracles to disregard. This was and is very clearly the good Hand of our dear God on the whole sad episode, and it is all for His glory.

## PO Dot Cottam, ET Myers, and Lorraine Connolly

I shall continue with the account as relayed by the additional documents that the Coroner took over one year to release to us.

I have created a diagram to represent my son's position just before his fall, comfortably standing at the back of the LCVP by the wheelhouse door, probably admiring USS Mitscher as she is sailing past.

I have shown PO Dot Cottam in the engine bay of LCVP N3. I have shown him with his head visible, but he was under the deck and out of sight at that time. ET Myers is on the deck of LCVP N3.

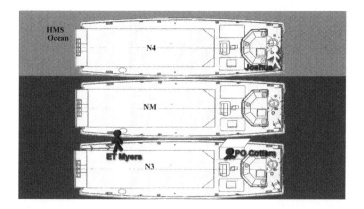

Reading the account by PO Dot Cottam and ET David Myers, one is aware of the shouts, my son's scream, and the alarm calls as they endeavour to get help to my son. The alarm is piped too, so that we have people from inside the recesses of the ship hearing the calls and come running.

But, do not forget, all this time that these shouts and scream are filling the air, PO Fulton is wondering what could possibly have happened to my son.

The full accounts by POET(ME) Dot Cottam, and ET David Myers, and CPOMA Lorraine Connolly can be seen on the website.

## What did PO Fulton Say Now?

Let us resume our study of all the documents that we received from the Coroner, which can be found on my son's website. We now look at PO Fulton's statements.

There were two witness statements that he made, one on the 6th August, 2010, on the day of my son's fatal fall, and the second on the 10th August, 2010, the day my son died.

They contained the same implausible account of the events as those in the ISI. The ISI was none other than PO Fulton's account of what happened up on the LCVP. Who else could have told Lt Cdr Pickles, Lt Cdr Lucocq, and WO Clapham what happened but PO Fulton himself?

However there was an interesting difference in PO Fulton's account of the 6th August, 2010. Here he does not mention that he heard a scream at all. It is completely ignored. He states –

> "As I was climbing down I heard what I thought was Lt Woodhouse jump from the Wheel House roof it sounded to me as though he landed in the area of the Port Engine Hatch, I then heard something like 'whoa, whoa, whoa' this was not excessively loud and I initially thought he had landed unsteadily and fallen over on landing."

Reading the ISI we have quite a noticeable difference. Item 11 of this investigation states –

> 11. "Having completed the task, PO2 (PO FULTON) proceeded to the back of the wheelhouse to climb back down. As he was doing so, he heard a loud thud which he presumed was the sound of Lt Woodhouse jumping down from the front of the wheelhouse onto the deck of the LCVP (although he did not see anything). Almost immediately after the initial thud, he heard Lt Woodhouse's voice say something that sounded like 'Whoa, Whoa, Whoa' (as if he had lost his balance) followed by a scream."

Here we have the scream, but his story seems to have changed in his statement of the 6th August, where he specifically does not mention a scream.

This is just another example of his constant contradictions and weavings.

## PO Fulton and the Safety Number

Another interesting bit of information in PO Fulton's statements of the 6th and 10th August, 2010 was the 'Safety Number.'

This 'Safety Number' is also mentioned in another witness statement by CPI (ETME) Laurence James Lawson who explains to us the concept of a Safety Number when he states that the normal practice when working at height was –

> "There was also another person there with me at all times as a safety number as per the man aloft routine."

Going back to PO Fulton's Witness Statement of the 6th August, 2010, he recounts the events leading to my son's fall, stating –

> *"The requirement of a safety number had been fulfilled because there were two of us out on the LCVP."*

and

> *"When working on the LCVPs safety harnesses are to be worn and a safety number is to be present"*

And in his statement of the 10th August, 2010, he states —

> *"When I am working at height I always have a safety number who remains on the boat deck until I come down."*

So he is telling us that my son was the 'Safety Number' whose primary purpose was to remain on the deck until he, PO Fulton, came down.

PO Fulton might have been a rule breaker, as we shall find out, but my son was not. If my son went up to the LCVP in order to be the Safety Number, then he would do that job, and he would do it well. My son would remain on the deck until PO Fulton came down from the LCVP bridge roof.

In addition it is highly unlikely that my son would have climbed onto the roof for the reasons listed below -

- The roof is **dangerous,** being just a few feet from death.
- The roof is a **small, cramped area.**
- There is just **crouching room on the roof.**
- The roof has **sensitive radar equipment, wires, and obstructions.**
- Climbing on the roof would **jeopardise** the **life** of the **person already on the roof.**
- The job in hand was a mere **eyeball exercise**, certainly not requiring two men. There was no need for my son to go on the roof.

My son's role as Safety Number makes PO Fulton's account even less credible.


## Supplementary Ship's Investigation (SSI)

We now came to the next document in the list of documents from the Coroner, the Supplementary Ship's Investigation. This document is also on my son's web site.

One of the people from Royal Navy HQ on Whale Island found the Immediate Ship's Investigation unsatisfactory. His name was Captain Forsey.

Captain Forsey was asking some of the questions we were asking. Why did my son have to physically check the flexible hoses? Is there not a register in place? Does the Royal Navy not have a spares inventory system? These were just some of our questions.

When we received the ISI, on the 18th December, 2010, recording the events leading up to my son's death, we were struck immediately by two inexplicable items.

### Why Would You Physically Check The Hoses?

Why would a responsible, intelligent, safety conscious Royal Navy Officer, who was so proud to be in the Royal Navy, risk his life in order to physically check whether a hose replacement had been carried out, when there must have existed a system whereby one could obtain this same information safely?

### Why Did PO Fulton Behave So Unnaturally?

Why did PO Fulton behave in such a strange, contrived manner, following my son's fall?

Armed with the new information that the Coroner had seen fit to disclose to us in February, 2012, we felt better able to answer both these questions.

Instead of allaying our concerns that foul play caused our son's death, that my son was unlawfully killed, this new information strengthened our concerns, and in fact showed us that the episode was even darker and more sinister than we had imagined.

It is to be noted, that there is more vital information that the Coroner has not released to us. We would dearly like to see this, as we believe it would shed even more light on my son's suspicious death.

## JOSHUA – "JUMPING TIGGER"

Whilst reading the SSI, I was aware that it was necessary to explain my son's character to my readers so that they would better understand the events leading up to his death.

When on HMS Ocean after Joshua died, we were told that Joshua was known as 'Jumping Tigger', as he was always popping up everywhere, and was always on his way from having just completed one job and onto his next job. He was always working. He was always industrious. He was always happy and caring.

I have put a few comments from the Condolence Book that support why he was called 'Jumping Tigger'. The messages highlight Joshua's hands-on approach, his boundless energy, his total willingness to help, his hard work, and his ability to communicate easily and readily with all the ship's company, irrespective of rank or age.

Even though he was always working, he was nonetheless in control and able to make time for people.

I believe all of this is important when we analyse how Joshua dealt with the dilemma of the missing LCVP davit hoses.

## QUOTATIONS FROM HMS CONDOLENCE BOOK – AUGUST, 2010

*"His **active participation** in pretty much everything meant that he seemed to **appear around every corner**, where one would meet his ready smile and enjoy a warm exchange on some aspect of his busy life." – Captain*

*"His **drive and determination** meant he was highly productive and he set an excellent example for others to follow" Captain*

*"I knew him to be a fun loving but **industrious young man**" Commander*

*"I worked closely with Josh on a daily basis and as such he would always brighten my day. He responded with **such an infectious energy** it was hard to keep up" WO2 Hall*

*"Josh was everything a young engineer should be: bright, enthusiastic and dedicated. **I have never known anybody with his energy.** He was pivotal in the department and he will be sorely missed." Senior Engineer*

*"**He was always running around and never seemed to stop**." – POET Morris*

*"**always willing to help** never afraid to take on a challenge " ASEO Cattis*

*"always smiling and **eager to help others**" – CPOMEA(ML) Griffiths*

*"Josh, **God only knows where you got your energy from**" - Smudge Smyth*

*"Thanks for all the **hard work you put into the ME Department**" - 'China' Fleet*

*"Josh, You were both a friend and a college to me and will miss your cheery face **coming into my workshop**. Take care Big Man" – 'Dot' Cottam*

*"Always willing and **always eager to help others**" – Mac*

*"You always had a kind word **and time for those around you**." – Rob*

*"I will always remember the **energy**, laughter and fun Josh brought to our lives. Behind which sat a **professional** and good man. To the memory of a fellow Engineer and dear Friend" – illegible signature*

## SUPPLEMENTARY SHIP'S INVESTIGATION – WHAT DID HAPPEN?

I read the SSI and pieced together all the events from May, 2010, that led up to my son's death three months later. These events clarify not only my son's actions but also PO Fulton's actions. I shall start in May, 2010.

HMS Ocean was undergoing her maintenance period, called Ship's Maintenance Period (SMP), which was to finish on 10th June when she would be sailing on a very prestigious deployment to the United States of America. This was a dream deployment. HMS Ocean would be stopping off in Florida for four weeks in July/August, during which time half of her crew would each go on a two week holiday.

And there was more excitement. The Queen would be visiting the ship on Thursday, 3rd June, and the following day Friday, 4th June, HMS Ocean opened her doors to the families of her crew and treated them to a Friends and Family Day. All of this before setting sail to America on Thursday, 10th June, 2010.

During the Ship's Maintenance Period it was decided that this would be an excellent time to replace all eight flexible Davit greasing hoses needed by the eight Davits of the four LCVP Bays, as they were due their five year routine replacement. In order to do this, the new replacement hoses were ordered at short notice via Surface Fleet Maintenance (SFM).

Scaffolding was also put up in all four LCVP Bays solely for the purpose of replacing these eight Davit flexible hoses.

Reading the Supplementary Ship's Investigation I noticed that the term Boats Part of Ship or just Boats Part was referred to again and again. I have spoken to a marine engineer about this and the conclusion we have come to is that the Boats Part of Ship was a separate section of the Engineering department that dealt with the maintenance and upkeep of the four LCVPs on HMS Ocean. It would be logical that this Boats Part had their own workshop, stores, and probably office too.

Another interesting item that came from the SSI is that PO Fulton was Head of Boats Section till a few days before my son's fall, when he was demoted and PO Dot Cottam replaced him.

## The Flexible Hose Register

What was my son's involvement with Boats Part of Ship? My son was given, as part of his duties, the job of maintaining oversight of the Flexible Hose Register, which records the upkeep and replacement of fourteen hundred various flexible hoses scattered across the entire ship. The eight Flexible Davit hoses were included in the fourteen hundred hoses.

There were four things that needed to be done with regard to replacing the eight flexible Davit hoses, which had now come up for their five year renewal,

1.  Order eight new Davit hoses.
2.  Receive delivery of the eight new Davit hoses.
3.  Replace the old Davit hoses with the eight new Davit hoses.
4.  Record this replacement in the Hose Register.

Simple.

**Job 1.   Order eight New Davit Hoses.**  Done.
We read that eight new replacement Davit hoses are ordered at short notice from Billy Connelly's office, Surface Fleet Maintenance, in Devonport.

We also see in my son's email to Billy Connelly that my son writes –

> *"I don't know if you remember this, but in the period prior to leaving, I thought you procured eight greasing hoses and put them in the boats workshop for part of ship. If you remember, can you confirm whether that is the case?"*

**Job 2. Receive Delivery of eight New Davit Hoses.** Done.

It appears, however, that nobody knows when these actually arrived, as the person collecting them appears not to have signed for them, or maybe there was not a requirement that they be signed for. The SSI found that my son recorded the delivery date as the day before they sailed, 9th June, and they believe that this can only be an arbitrary date based on the assumption that the hoses had arrived on board sometime previously. Also looking at my son's email above, it appears that Billy Connelly, or his office, put them in the boats workshop.

**Job 3. Replace the old Davit hoses with the eight new Davit hoses.** Done.

This job had been done over the weekend, the Bank Holiday weekend, and PO Fulton, who was Head of Boats Section at the time, was informed that it had been done, though he states he cannot remember which one of his team told him that they had done the job.

It was very good of this man, whoever he was, to work over the Bank Holiday weekend in order to fit the flexible hoses. This man knew that there was an urgency to get the scaffolding down before the Queen's visit, just a few days later, on Thursday, 3rd June. He probably went out of his way to do the job during the Bank Holiday weekend.

When PO Fulton returned from his weekend leave, this man informed him that he had replaced the eight flexible Davit hoses. See Item 9 below

> *"PO Fulton states that he remembers returning from weekend leave and **being informed that the hoses had been changed.** He cannot remember who that person was. Furthermore, he did not pass the information on to Lt Woodhouse at the time because as the Supervisor, **he wanted to check the work had been carried out himself before logging it in the Flexible Hose Register.** PO Fulton does not know who conducted the work and the Investigating Team have been unable to clarify this due to personnel leaving the Ship. PO Fulton, while questioned, **has***

*not offered any specific explanation as to why he didn't check the work between the end of May and, ultimately, the day of the incident."*

**Job 4. Record Job Done in Hose Register.** Why wasn't this done?

Now things start to get strange.

PO Fulton's job is to log the replacement of the Davit hoses in the Hose Register. He does not do so.

What is interesting is that he tells Lt Cdr Pickles and Lt Cdr Lucocq that he didn't do so because he wanted to personally check the work himself, before he logged it in the Hose Register.

I wondered whether it was because these Davit hoses were vital to the entire Davit mechanism, therefore I asked a marine engineer whether the Davit hoses were critical. I was told that this was not critical to the safe operation of the equipment and was further told,

> *"Run an engine without oil and it will seize. Run a piece of machinery without grease and it will, unless highly specialised, continue to run. Therefore greasing hoses are way down the list of critical priorities."*

The questions continued flying. Did Lt Cdr Pickles not think this very strange?

PO Fulton should at the very least have informed my son that the flexible Davit hoses had been replaced, and that he wanted to check the work personally before logging it in the Hose Register.

He did not do this.

Warning bells are starting to ring. If PO Fulton is a perfectionist, then as a perfectionist he would have informed the officer in charge of the Hose Register about the replacement, and his reasons for not logging the work.

Two months later, on 6th August, PO Fulton tells my son that checking the LCVP hoses is an easy job. If this is correct, then why did he not do it and do it immediately? Why did he not do it for two months?

So many questions.

# The Scaffolding is taken Down

The next event is that the scaffolding is taken down.  This is done after the end of the May Bank Holiday and before the Queen's visit of the 3rd June.

We are told that one of the Leading Engineering Technicians (LETs) of HMS Ocean authorised the scaffolding to be taken down.  Could this be the same LET who had replaced the hoses, and therefore knew that the job had been done?

Billy Connelly's email refers

> "The 8 LCVP Davit greasing hoses were manufactured, scaffolding erected, SS U x E, scaffolding taken down.  I am confident that they were exchanged in May this year, **I seem to remember one of your LETs authorising scaffolding to come down.**  They are the hoses at the high point on each davit arm."

Another event occurred during the Ship's Maintenance Period.  An annual survey of all (Category A) Cat A flexible hoses, which included the eight Davit Hoses, happened to be carried out during this time period.  This survey was carried out by Hydrasun, Devonport.  This survey must have been carried out before the hoses had been replaced during their routine five year replacement period.

On the 10th June, 2010, after the Queen's visit, and after the Friends and Family Day, and after the completion of the Ship's Maintenance Period and the Category A Flexible Hose Annual Survey, HMS Ocean set sail for her USA deployment.  My son had been greatly looking forward to this dream deployment.

All was busy on HMS Ocean.  She had her Royal Marines on board too, adding to the interest and excitement of this wonderful deployment.

## Hydrasun Survey Report Received

A month later, in July, the results of the Annual Flexible Hose Hydrasun report arrived on my son's desk.  Four of the Davit flexible hoses were damaged and had to be replaced.

My son knew that in May, replacement Davit hoses had been ordered from Bill Connelly's office Surface Fleet Maintenance (SFM) at short notice for this very purpose.

My son knew that the replacement was scheduled to be done during the Ship's Maintenance Period before HMS Ocean set sail.

My son also knew that the scaffolding had been taken down, meaning that the hoses must have been replaced. However, just to double check my son looked up the Hose Register to ensure that the hoses had in fact been changed.

My son found that there was no entry to show that the eight Davit flexible hoses had been changed. Very strange. Why was this?

My son goes in person to enquire about the hoses. This is my son's nature; this is what he would have done; this is why he was called Jumping Tigger. My son was a hands-on person.

If PO Fulton had completely forgotten to check that the hoses had been replaced to his satisfaction, now was his opportunity to make good, and say to my son,

> *"I'm glad you asked, Sir. The hoses had been changed during the May Bank Holiday weekend but I wanted to just double check them before recording them in the Hoses Register. Thank you for reminding me. I shall do it immediately as it is such an easy job."*

But he does not tell my son that he knew the hoses had been changed. In fact, he tells my son the very opposite.

In his statement of the 6th August, PO Fulton informs us that he tells my son that the hoses have not been changed. He was Head of Boats Section when the hoses had been changed. Therefore it is logical that my son would have approached him in July asking about the hoses.

PO Fulton gives my son false information on the 6th August, when he informs my son that the hoses have not been changed.

> *"I explained to Lt Woodhouse that as far as I was aware **the hoses had not been charge [sic]**, he had been informed that they had been changed."*

PO Fulton's Witness Statement of the 6th August, 2010

When my son enquired in July whether the hoses had been changed, he had been told that they had not been changed. Did Lt Cdr Pickles or Lt Cdr Lucocq find out who it was that told my son in July that the hoses had not been changed? Was it PO Fulton who was once again feeding false information to my son?

Did Lt Cdr Pickles and Lt Cdr Lucocq investigate this further?

## More than one Register

We then find that there are two registers where the replacement of the Flexible Davit Hoses should have been recorded. The first register is the Flexible Hose Register, in which PO Fulton failed to record the Davit hose replacement, until he had checked up on the work himself.

The second register is the TAGOUT log. I shall quote from the letter written by the Assistant Chief of Staff (Ships and Submarines), dated 26th October, 2010.

> Item 3
>
> *"The regulations for working on hydraulic equipment are clearly taught and should be well understood by maintainers in particular including the need for hydraulic systems to be tagged out prior to commencing work and certified correct prior to the service being restored. This must be under the supervision of a senior rating who signs to that effect in the TAGOUT log. From the narrative of both investigation reports, it is not clear why PO Fulton was unaware that work had been carried out in his section as this should have been recorded in the TAGOUT log without necessitating proceeding aloft to check."*

Not only did PO Fulton state that the hoses had been, and then had not been, changed, but if he suffered from temporary memory failure all he had to do was to consult the TAGOUT log. But he chose not to.

## PO Fulton Demoted as Head of Boats Section

We now come to an interesting development. PO Fulton is demoted from Head of Boats Section, and PO Dot Cottam is made the new head. We understand this occurred in July, 2010. This is the month that my son is endeavouring to solve the mystery of the eight Davit hoses. Were they or were they not replaced?

We have seen how PO Fulton has refused to record the replacement of the Davit hoses in the Hose Register.
We have seen how he has misled my son.

And now he has been demoted.

What did PO Fulton do that caused his demotion?

At the Inquest PO Fulton was quizzed on this point and it appears he was demoted for minor administrative failings. I quote from the Inquest tapes which can be found on the website.

Day 1 - Monday 5th November, 2012 - Tape 2 – 01:11:10

> *"It was decided to replace my, ...PO Dot Cottam in the role of Section Head. My,...can't think of the word,... administrative ......paperwork side of it seemed to be lacking."*

It appears, then, that the Royal Navy has exceptionally high standards, and that for minor administrative failings one is demoted.

Who was involved in PO Fulton's demotion? Was an officer involved? Was my son involved?

Our barrister asked PO Fulton at the Inquest

> *"You were being replaced because of problems with paper work. Who else had been chasing you in respect of your administration?"*
>
> (that is in addition to Lt Woodhouse)

To which PO Fulton replied –

> *"The current Assault Section Engineering Officer(ASEO) – Lt Craig Callis? He was my section officer at the time. He was the one who was raising the concerns. "*

01:12:27

An Engineering Officer chasing him for minor administrative failings?

And along comes my son, another Engineering Officer, and he too is chasing

PO Fulton with regard to his administrative duties.

We must not forget the disciplinary records. Why did the Coroner continually refuse to release to us the disciplinary records of HMS Ocean?

Was PO Fulton guilty of something more serious than administrative failings?

Whatever the reasons for PO Fulton's demotion, the fact remains that he was demoted as Head of Boats Section, and it is a public demotion.

But what are the consequences of this public demotion? Is he angry? Could this be the reason that PO Fulton is making a point of not informing my son that the hoses were changed in May? Could this be the reason that he wants to be as unhelpful as possible?

But there is more. Did he receive any warnings with his demotion? Was it a case of two strikes and you're out? Could it be that any other misdemeanour would mean that he loses his job altogether?

Could it be that he cannot possibly afford to let my son know that he was slack yet again, and did not record the replacement in the Hose Register as he should have done, as regulations required?

My son was probing. My son had to find out whether the hoses had been changed. My son had to come to the bottom of the matter. My son knew that if there was no solution, he would have to email John Wedeman and request a concession, until new spares could be obtained and fitted.

## Search of Boats Part Workshop

Let us continue our story. There are four actions that need to occur in order to replace the LCVP Davit hoses .

1. Order eight new Davit hoses.
2. Receive delivery of the eight new Davit hoses.
3. Replace the old Davit hoses with the eight new Davit hoses.
4. Record this replacement in the Hose Register.

In July my son has been told that Step 3, the replacement of the hoses, has not been carried out.

As PO Fulton informed my son, on the 6th August, that the hoses had not been changed, one could therefore guess that it was he, who, as Head of Boat

Section, again gave my son the same information in July that the hoses had not been changed. By his own admission he knew all along that the hoses had been changed.

My son then reasoned that if the damaged hoses have not been replaced then it is logical to assume that the new hoses would still be in the Boats Part workshop stores. The new hoses had been ordered in May, so they must still be around, and must be in the workshop. A logical conclusion to make.

My son therefore orders a search of the Boats Part workshop store room sometime in July in order to find the eight new Davit hoses that had been ordered in May.

It is unlikely that the entire Boats Part Section would not know that a search has been requested for these hoses. We are not told when exactly PO Fulton is demoted from being Head of Boats Section, but we understand it is in July, 2010. But even though he is demoted, PO Fulton is still working in Boats Section.

We ask a question now. Does he know that my son has asked Boats Part Section to do a search of their workshop stores looking for the eight Davit hoses?

Did Lt Cdr Pickles and Lt Cdr Lucocq try to find out?

It is July, 2010. My son has been told, in all probability by PO Fulton, that the hoses have not been replaced. My son then orders a search of the Boats Part Section stores for these eight Davit hoses. How many people are there in the Boats Part Section, four? PO Fulton is still one of the people in the Boats Part section, irrespective if he is or is not the Head of Boats Section at the time of the search. Therefore it is highly likely that he knows that my son has ordered a search of the Boats Part Section.

The next question is, who in Boats Part Section did my son ask to search for the hoses? Did my son ask PO Fulton to get this search done? If so, then we can guess what happened.

The conclusion is that it is highly unlikely that PO Fulton did not know that my son had asked for a search of Boats Part Section looking for the replacement Davit hoses, and yet he keeps strangely quiet.

This is another opportunity PO Fulton had to inform my son that

*"O yes Sir, it has just come to my remembrance that the hoses were changed and it was over the Bank Holiday weekend. Mystery solved, we can all rest satisfied that the job has been done"*

But he did not do this.

## Email to Billy Connelly Surface Fleet Maintenance (SFM)

On the 4th August, my son emails Billy Connelly telling him that Boats Part workshop does not have the replacement hoses that were ordered in May. This means that my son has received the results of the search he requested in Boats Part of Ship.

To recap on the four actions needed in order to replace the LCVP Davit hoses.

1. Order eight new Davit hoses.
2. Receive delivery of the eight new Davit hoses.
3. Replace the old Davit hoses with the eight new Davit hoses.
4. Record this replacement in the Hose Register.

My son found that there was no record in the Hose Register that the hoses had been replaced (item no 4), so he enquired whether the replacement had occurred (item no 3).

As PO Fulton told my son on the 6th August, that the hoses have not been replaced, we can assume that it was also he who again told my son in July that the hoses had not been replaced.

PO Fulton was the Head of Boats Section. He knew exactly what was going on.

As the replacement of the hoses had not occurred, (item no 3) my son then logically concluded that the hoses were still in the Boats Part workshop stores, waiting to be fitted to the Davits. He therefore requested a search of the Boats Section storeroom.

My son has now been told by Boats Part that the eight Davit hoses are not in their Boats Part workshop stores. Therefore my son has to question whether the delivery (item no 2) of the hoses occurred in the first place.

To find out whether they were even delivered, my son emails Billy Connelly, Surface Fleet Maintenance (SFM), in the UK.

Email from Joshua to Bill Connelly on 4<sup>th</sup> August, 2010 16:53d

*"Billy,*
*A quick question – boats part of ship have told me that they do not, in fact, have greasing hoses for the LCVP davits. I don't know if you remember this, but in the period prior to leaving,* **I thought you procured 8 greasing hoses and put them in the boats workshop for part of ship.** *If you remember, can you confirm whether that is the case? It looks like I will have to ask John Wedeman for a concession on these, but if you did provide the hoses I will* **push** *part of ship to do* **another search** *for them. For information, the hoses were L12-MSG-001A through 008A, and as I recall were simple hoses that weren't designed to take much pressure as they were only for greasing.*
*Regards,*
*Josh Woodhouse"*

My son is wondering whether he should get another search done. You will notice that he uses the word 'push'. It sounds very much like it is a hard slog to get Boats Part of ship, called 'part of ship' in the email above, to do anything. Is this my son's experience when dealing with PO Fulton?

Let us now see what the email reply is from Billy Connolly in the UK. You will notice that Billy Connolly's reply is instant, and comes the next day, Thursday, 5<sup>th</sup> August.

Billy Connolly informs my son that he was confident that not only were the hoses delivered, but that they were also fitted in May, before the scaffolding was taken down.

Email from Billy Connelly to Joshua on 5th August, 2010. 08:43

*"Sir,*
*Some questions:*
- *Did you receive the certificates I sent?*
- *Did you receive the box of bellows we sent?*
- *The 8 LCVP Davit greasing hoses were manufactured, scaffolding erected, SS U x E, scaffolding taken down.* **I am confident that they were exchanged in May this year, I seem to remember one of your LETs authorising scaffolding to come down.** *They are the hoses at the high point on*

> *each davit arm.*
> *Regards,*
> *Billy Connelly"*

This is a turn-around for the books.  My son is now told by Billy Connelly that he is confident that the jobs specified in Items 2 and 3 shown below, were successfully completed.  The hoses had been replaced in May.

1. Order eight new Davit hoses.
2. Receive delivery of the eight new Davit hoses.
3. Replace the old Davit hoses with  the eight new Davit hoses.
4. Record this replacement in the Hose Register.

This is totally different to the information that PO Fulton has been providing.

## What Happened Next?

Let us continue the story.

The next day, Friday 6th August, armed with the information from Billy Connelly's email, my son is back in the Boats Part of Ship again.

My son informs PO Fulton that he has been told that the hoses have been replaced.  What is PO Fulton's reaction to this?  This is a wonderful opportunity for him to suddenly say that his memory has been jogged.

> *"O yes, I remember now, way back in May in the Bank Holiday weekend I was told the hoses had been changed.  How wonderful, yes the mystery has been solved.  The hoses have been changed."*

But he did not take this opportunity to inform my son that the hoses had been changed.  He sticks to his story: I quote below

> *"I explained to Lt Woodhouse that as far as I was aware **the hoses had not been charge [sic]**, he had been informed that they had been changed."*

PO Fulton's Witness Statement of the 6th August, 2010.

He persists in informing my son that the hoses have not been replaced.

He suggests that they go up together to check once and for all whether the hoses have been replaced. We must remember that it is such an easy job, in PO Fulton's own words.

There was no need for them to go in person to check the hoses themselves. PO Fulton knew this. There was the TAGOUT log which records all work carried out on hydraulic equipment. The replacement would have been recorded there. He used to be Head of Boats Section, this is something he should have known.

Based on the account by Witness 3 Los Angeles, my son suddenly swings and rotates.

Witness 3, Los Angeles, and Witness 1, Philippines, saw my son trying desperately to hold onto the railing with his right hand. His left hand was too numb from the blow it had just received as it hit the railing to be of much help to him, though he tried hard to hold on.

My son fell over forty six feet and landed on a metal surface on his head, breaking it open from ear to ear.

PO Fulton on the other hand says my son climbed onto the wheelhouse roof. Contradicting this, US Witness 3, Los Angeles, saw my son standing comfortably on the deck of the LCVP behind the wheelhouse, and not on the wheelhouse roof at all.

PO Fulton then said that he was the only one at the back of the wheelhouse. That is strange, for that is exactly where US Witness 3, Los Angeles, saw my son standing comfortably.

PO Fulton further said that he wondered what could possibly have happened to my son. That is strange, as the air was filled with my son's scream, and the emergency shouting from PO Dot Cottam and ET Myers.

PO Fulton said he saw nothing. That is very convenient.

Two men went to do a job and only one came back, and his name is PO Fulton.

## Lt Cdr Pickles and Lt Cdr Lucocq Conducted the Two Ship's Investigations

Immediately following my son's fall, the Royal Navy entrusted Lt Cdr Pickles, Lt Cdr Lucocq, and WO Clapham with the task of investigating my son's death. This is a serious matter. What is more serious than death? The first investigation, the ISI, was completed on the 9ᵗʰ August, 2010, the day before my son died. Due to the inadequacy of the first Investigation, the RN HQ ordered a second investigation.

Therefore, one month later, Lt Cdr Pickles and Lt Cdr Lucocq are tasked with a follow up investigation which was completed on 12ᵗʰ September, 2010. WO Clapham was not involved in the Supplementary Ship's Investigation.

At the Inquest Lt Cdr Pickles admitted that he had limited powers to question PO Fulton more deeply concerning the many discrepancies in his account.

This is the chance for Lt Cdr Pickles and Lt Cdr Lucocq to right the wrongs of their first investigation.

The first investigation should have been coursing through the minds of Lt Cdr Pickles and Lt Cdr Lucocq for over a month now.

In conducting this second investigation Lt Cdr Pickles and Lt Cdr Lucocq find that PO Fulton has made contradictory statements on whether the Davit hoses had been changed.

PO Fulton says that he knew the hoses had been changed, and then he also says that as far as he knew they had not been changed.

Both statements cannot be true.

> *"I explained to Lt Woodhouse that as far as I was aware* **the hoses had not been charge [sic]**, *he had been informed that they had been changed."*
> PO Fulton's Witness Statement of the 6ᵗʰ August, 2010.

> *6. "POET(ME)2" (PO Fulton) "reports that on the morning of Fri 6 Aug he was in 4T LCVP Workshop supervising the painting of the deck. At approximately 0900 Lt Woodhouse (SSEO) arrived to discuss the status of flexible hoses on the LCVP davits. Lt Woodhouse believed that all the hoses had recently been changed,* **whereas PO2 (1)"** (PO Fulton) **"was under the impression that none had been changed.** *In order to clarify the issue, PO2 (1)"* (PO Fulton) *"suggested they go and check the manufacturers label on the hoses.*

Immediate Ship's Investigation of the 9th August, 2010.

> *"PO Fulton states that **he remembers returning from weekend leave and being informed that the hoses had been changed."***

Item 9, Supplementary Ship's Investigation, 12th September.

Not only did PO Fulton know that the hoses had in fact been changed, but he then tells my son that he believed they had not been changed. He maintained this right up to the last day, when my son once again queried him.

Lt Cdr Pickles and Lt Cdr Lucocq do not act on this.

Instead Lt Cdr Pickles and Lt Cdr Lucocq get exasperated with my son and yet not with PO Fulton and comment on his action of emailing Billy Connolly by saying -

> Item 12
> *"As PO Fulton had been informed that the hoses had been changed, it is unclear why Lt Woodhouse was later informed by the Boats Part of Ship that the hoses were not held onboard. However, it should be noted that PO Dot Cottam had taken over as Head of Section by this point and so PO Fulton, although still working Boats Part of Ship, may not have been consulted. **For reasons we shall never** understand, Lt Woodhouse did not consult with PO Fulton or PO Dot Cottam prior to emailing WO1 Connelly. "*

How can Lt Cdr Pickles and Lt Cdr Lucocq say that my son did not consult PO Fulton or PO Dot Cottam? Who told them he hadn't? Was it PO Fulton's word they are relying on?

If Lt Cdr Pickles and Lt Cdr Lucocq had conducted their investigation correctly, then the statements they should have made would have been:-

> *"For reasons we shall never understand PO Fulton told Lt Woodhouse that the hoses had not been changed, when he knew they had been changed."*
> *"For reasons we shall never understand PO Fulton did not make an entry in the hose register that the hoses had been changed."*
> *"For reasons we shall never understand PO Fulton says that he wanted to check the work himself."*
> *"For reasons we shall never understand PO Fulton never checked*

*the hoses for over two months."*

*"For reasons we shall never understand PO Fulton did not inform Lt Woodhouse that the hoses had been changed even when Lt Woodhouse ordered another search of the workshop for the hoses."*

*"For reasons we shall never understand ..........."*

To conclude their investigation, both Lt Cdr Pickles and Lt Cdr Lucocq produce platitudes for my son's suspicious death - the Royal visit, the imminent deployment, the communication breakdown......

This is the Military Justice given to my son by HMS Ocean.

## SIB WILSON CONCLUSION

You could quite rightly point out to me that as SIB Wilson had left the ship a month ago, he would not have any of the information that Lt Cdr Pickles and Lt Cdr Lucocq had just uncovered in their second investigation, the Supplementary Ship's Investigation. And as such, I should not condemn SIB Wilson's conclusions.

But if SIB Wilson had done his job correctly, he would have uncovered everything that Lt Cdr Pickles and Lt Cdr Lucocq uncovered, and far, far more. It would have been part of SIB Wilson's training to investigate, and to find out what led to the strange events of the 6th August, 2010, which led to my son's death.

At the Inquest Lt Cdr Pickles bemoaned his limited powers, but Deputy Provost SIB Wilson RN  Military Police, cannot take this escape route.

SIB Wilson has been given great powers for such an occasion as this; great powers in order to investigate a death, a suspicious death, a death in the workplace, a death on HMS Ocean.

## And now we Read the SIB Investigation Summaries

At the very beginning of this tragic episode, whilst my son lay dying in his hospital bed in Shands Jacksonville, Florida, we were told that the SIB, Royal Navy Military Police, were flown over specially to investigate my son's death.

This brought no small comfort to the entire family.

We thought that my son's death was being investigated correctly. We thought that the Royal Navy was treating my son's death seriously.

We needed to know how my son came to fatally fall. This was very important to us. To show how important it was, one of our party specially made time to speak to Captain Blount in our first full day in Jacksonville. This was whilst my son was still alive. This was precious time that was given up.

We also wanted to find out whether my son had done anything he should not have done, and whether he had omitted to do anything that he should have done.

To both these questions Captain Blount assured the family that my son had not been guilty of either of these actions. Captain Blount assured the family that my son had done this job in exactly the way it was always done.

My son died three days later on the 10th August, 2010, and we buried him in the UK at the end of August, 2010.

We still did not know what caused my son to fall. We were kept in the dark.

At the end of October, 2010, when HMS Ocean returned from her dream deployment, minus my son, my son's fiancée met Captain Blount in Plymouth. It was at this meeting that Captain Blount informed her that the family might not like the conclusions of the Immediate Ship's Investigation (ISI). Captain Blount was trying to prepare us for the shock.

This was our first indication of the treachery of the Royal Navy in their ISI, which we received a week before Christmas, 2010. Following the shock of the ISI, we now had great unease regarding the contents of the SIB Investigation.

It was now February, 2012, one and a half years after my son's death, when we finally received the two summaries of the SIB Criminal Investigation into my son's death.

Due to the treachery of the Royal Navy in their ISI we had an inkling what the SIB summaries would also hold.

But nobody could have warned us or prepared us for these summaries. Nobody at all.

# The SIB Training

The summaries of the SIB Criminal Investigation conducted by Lt Cdr Geoff Wilson consisted of the following two documents, where the first document contains the majority of the investigation.

- RNP SIB Investigation Process – dated 23rd January, 2012 -
- Summary of Evidence – that has no date on it, but we were informed at the Inquest that it was written Nov/Dec 2010

Let us look at the dates of these documents.

We know that the Coroner received the SIB Investigation in December, 2010/ January, 2011. These two documents are, as the name of the second implies, a summary of this initial investigation, and one can only assume that they have been written at the request of the Coroner.

These two documents have been specifically prepared by SIB to explain to us why my son's death was not due to Foul Play.

Let us now study the documents.

We see that SIB Wilson commences with an explanation into the training and qualifications of the SIB personnel, saying that *'The investigation procedures used will be those learned during RN Police training'* Item 10 of SIB Investigation Process, and that they will refer for guidance to such documents as the *Association of Chief Police Officers Murder Investigation Manual 2006.*

SIB Wilson points out that selected investigators complete additional specialised training, like Crime Scene Investigation, Specialist Interview, Cyber Crime etc. He mentioned how they have investigative independence, as well as assessments on their professional competency through inspection by Her Majesty's Inspectorate of Constabulary.

SIB Wilson explains in Item 6 that prior to a team briefing, a discussion is held between the investigators and the RNP SIB management team, to ensure, among other things, that all potential lines of enquiry have been considered.

We were heartened at the vast qualifications, training, and investigative guidelines of this SIB team that were entrusted with investigating my son's death.

# The SIB Conclusion

Item 39 RNP SIB Investigation Process states

> "Police investigated because it was the right and most appropriate thing, amid a range of options. Any foul play would have been identified. **Simply, there was none which could be found.** There was **no difficulty** – and much benefit – in investigating potential criminality, within/alongside a broader factual inquiry. RNP SIB is satisfied that it has followed all reasonable lines of enquiry and there is nothing further of evidential substance to be investigated, regarding the immediate circumstances of death."

This is all well and good.

We all have to make judgments and conclusions based on the facts presented to us.

On reading this, one is heartened and encouraged that people with such great training and experience have been entrusted with this weighty task, the investigation of a suspicious death.

What is also heartening is that SIB Wilson tells us how simple the matter is, and in fact confirms this with his further statement that there was no difficulty in investigating potential criminality.

This is good and we were delighted to be comforted in such a way. According to SIB Wilson, Deputy Provost Royal Navy Police, my son's death was very simple and straightforward, and there was no difficulty in investigating potential criminality, and the conclusion that SIB Wilson came to was that as far as foul play was concerned,

*Simply, there was none which could be found.*

I would rather be told that my son's death was an unfortunate accident, than to know that his violent death under highly suspicious circumstances was due to an unlawful killing.

If the matter is as simple as SIB Wilson assures us it is, then there will be very clear evidence to support his statement.

# The Strength of the Evidence

It is the evidence that determines the conclusion of any Criminal Investigation.

The Royal British Legion explained to us the importance of this Criminal Investigation into my son's death, saying

> *"The Special Investigation Branch of the Royal Military Police will investigate this incident and produce a report **supported by witness statements and exhibits**."*

The evidence that SIB Wilson would have put forward to support his conclusions would have been the strongest material in the case.

One is not always able to include all the material to back the conclusion of a Criminal Investigation, but one has to, by necessity, omit the weaker material, so as to make room primarily for the strongest evidence and material that confirms the findings of the Criminal Investigation.

Therefore in the bundle of documents given to us by the Coroner the strongest evidence has been included that backs the Criminal Investigation carried out by SIB Wilson, Deputy Provost Royal Navy Police (Military Police).

# What is the Evidence?

We will now have a look at the evidence that SIB Wilson has used in the criminal investigation that he carried out into my son's suspicious death, and upon which he has based his conclusions.

Let us look at the strongest and clearest evidence that SIB Wilson puts in front of us to support the conclusions of his criminal investigation.

SIB Wilson's strongest evidence is none other than the witness account given by PO Fulton, the man with my son. This is SIB Wilson's strongest and clearest evidence, on which all his conclusions are based.

PO Fulton's witness account stated that my son was on the wheelhouse roof and jumped off it, thus slipping and falling to his death.

Now we know what the clearest, the simplest, the strongest evidence is according to SIB Wilson, and it is none other than PO Fulton's account of my son's death.

Wait a moment. Two men went to do a job and only one came back, so shouldn't he be the prime suspect?

My son screams loudly for approximately 1.5 seconds. ET Myers and PO Dot Cottam down below then start shouting and continue shouting Loud Vocal Alarms, and PO Fulton wonders where Joshua is.

Isn't this suspicious behaviour from the man whose evidence SIB Wilson has used as the strongest evidence in his investigation?

There is more. PO Fulton openly feeds my son false information regarding the hoses, saying they had not been changed, when he knew that they had been changed. This is the witness that SIB Wilson has elevated to the position of his strongest evidence.

Hmmm. This is not good.

And there is more. US Witness 3, Los Angeles, said that he saw my son comfortably standing behind the wheelhouse on the deck of the LCVP. This is very bad. This contradicts the strongest evidence of SIB Wilson's investigation. This contradicts PO Fulton's account.

In addition my son was seen to fall from the back of the LCVP, and his body moves forwards towards the front of HMS Ocean. If my son had fallen from the front of the wheelhouse, then he would not have landed on the wheelhouse roof of the LCVP directly below him. He would have landed on the deck. Therefore this too contradicts the account of PO Fulton, whom SIB Wilson promoted as his strongest evidence.

We looked at the evidence, the strongest evidence, and we found it wanting.

## Manufacture Evidence and Facts

As the strongest evidence on which SIB Wilson based his entire conclusion is not only flimsy, but positively suspicious, SIB Wilson then resorts to creating evidence, and manufacturing it to fit his conclusion.

SIB Wilson has to somehow change facts to show that my son was sitting on the front of the wheelhouse roof when he, my son, is supposed to have jumped down, slipped, and fallen to his death. SIB Wilson has to do this because his strongest witness, PO Fulton, says so.

But before he manufactures evidence, SIB Wilson tells us that his conclusion was based on an honestly held belief. SIB Wilson informs us that honesty was a part of his Criminal Investigation.

Item 38 states –

*"The receipt of the US statements meant that OIC SIB was able to conclude with the **honestly held belief**, that having established the facts and gathered all available evidence,…"*

SIB Wilson tells us in Item 37 that US Navy witnesses saw my son fall from the wheelhouse roof.

*"Information was also received on 11 Aug 10 through The United States Naval Criminal Investigation Service (NCIS) that there were potential **witnesses** to the incident who had been on board the USS Mitscher, which had been departing the naval base at the time of the incident. **Statements** were obtained which describe how Lt Woodhouse had been seen to slide down from the **bridge roof** of the LCVP and lose his footing as he reached the next level. He was seen to make a grab for the handrail or stanchion before falling off the landing craft. No one else was seen to be involved."*

SIB Wilson has cobbled together a word here and a word there from all three US Navy Witness statements, and he has created a brand new account that does not actually exist.

My husband and I looked and looked and looked long and hard at the three US Navy Witness statements, and nowhere was it written that my son was seen on the bridge roof. Nowhere at all.

However, only one of the US Navy witness accounts, Witness 1, Philippines, writes that he saw a man on top an LCAC.

*"MITSCHER got underway and as we were passing HMS OCEAN, who was tied up pierside, I noticed a man sitting on **top an LCAC**. He was wearing white clothes. At first, all I could see was his feet. He was by himself. I saw him slide down the LCAC to the next level, but he lost his balance. I saw him attempt to grab something to regain his balance, but he was unsuccessful. I saw him fall off the LCAC, bit I did not see him land. I did hear a very loud noise that sounded like a loud "boom."*

On top an LCAC is a totally different matter to sitting on top of the bridge house roof.

We find that SIB Wilson takes the most difficult to understand US Navy witness statement, and manipulates it to fit the account by PO Fulton.

SIB Wilson also told us that the US Navy Witness statements, notice the plural, describe how my son was seen to "*slide down from the bridge roof of the LCVP.* "

As has already been pointed out, none of the three US Navy witnesses said that they saw my son slide down from the bridge roof.

# New Accounts through Handy Omissions

We have seen that Lt Cdr Wilson has created accounts that do not exist.

But there is another side to this and that is by failing to mention relevant events.

We have seen one example of this in SIB Lt Cdr Wilson's failure to mention Lt Jennifer Hayes' witness statement, which said that my son was bright and happy and not at all under the influence of alcohol

> *At 0755 Lt Woodhouse knocked on my cabin door to make sure I was up. Lt Woodhouse appeared **bright and happy** and was making jokes at my expense. Lt Woodhouse did not appear dishevelled in any way.*
> *Lt Woodhouse as the rest of the group did not appear overly intoxicated during the previous evening. He was steady on his feet and was holding **coherent conversations**.*

What a contrast to the statement that Lt Cdr SIB Wilson twisted in order to convey that my son was drunk.

Omitting to mention the full picture and supporting facts is none other than creating a new, a false account of the events.

One has to wonder, where else has SIB Wilson conveniently omitted to mention vital evidence in order to create an account that does not exist?

He has failed to mention the clear, distinct, precise, step by step account by US Navy Witness 3, Los Angeles.

US Witness 3, Los Angeles, goes to great lengths, and detail, in order to give us as much information as he can. He even drew pictures for us.

Witness 3, Los Angeles, says that he saw the entire episode, whereas the other witnesses did not. Witness 3, Los Angeles, tells us that he saw my son standing comfortably on the LCVP deck at the back (aft) of the LCVP, and he drew us a picture that placed him at the back of the wheelhouse.

Witness 3, Los Angeles, tells us that my son was comfortable in what he was doing and not tentative in any of his actions.

Let us come back to SIB Wilson, who tells us that these US Navy witnesses saw my son slide down from the bridge roof.

As has been pointed out, none of the US Navy witnesses saw my son slide down from the bridge roof.

But how can SIB Wilson say that these witness statements (plural) saw my son slide down from the bridge roof, when Witness 2, Charleston, did not say so, and Witness 3, Los Angeles, did not say so?  In fact, Witness 3, Los Angeles, said that he saw my son standing at the back of the LCVP, nowhere near the roof of the wheelhouse.  By omitting to mention the statement by Witness 3, Los Angeles, and by saying that the statements (plural) describe my son sliding down from the bridge roof, we have proved once again that SIB Wilson has manufactured evidence, and has created a brand new account.

In my opinion, this is very serious.  SIB Wilson has manufactured evidence in a Criminal Investigation.

And there are more omissions that completely change the picture that SIB Wilson has painted for us.

SIB Wilson did not inform us that there were sailors carrying out maintenance work a few feet away from my son at the time of his fall.

This is very important information.  We only found out that these men were doing maintenance work a week before my son's Inquest, when we received the further statements from the US Navy witnesses.

In these further statements, Witness 2, Charleston, explained that he saw a man in white on the flight deck giving instructions to workmen on a moving platform, by the LCVP Bay.

We also saw that Witness 1, Philippines, placed the feet at the very top of the LCVP Bay, a place that no feet can be except if they happen to be dangling from a moving platform.

We also then read in the Mayport newspaper that HMS Ocean was occupying their sailors with a lot of maintenance work during their four week stay in Mayport, Florida. We saw pictures of sailors painting the side of the ship from a moving platform.

This was vital information and helped us understand the seemingly obscure and strange account by Witness 1, Philippines.

But SIB Wilson withheld this information from his report. In the same way that he did not mention the account by US Navy Witness 3, Los Angeles, nor did he mention the account by Lt Jennifer Hayes.

By his omissions SIB Wilson has created a brand new account that cannot be substantiated.

# Objectives

In looking at SIB Wilson's Criminal Investigation into my son's death, we were examining the evidence he had presented to back his conclusions. The evidence was so minimal, in fact so suspicious, that all we could see were objectives. We found that objectives were getting in the way of evidence.

It appears the first objective is to show that PO Fulton's account is true.

And yet, in having this objective, to make PO Fulton the prime witness, what is the real underlying objective?

The next objective in SIB Wilson's criminal investigation was his desire to show that my son was drunk, and hence responsible for his own death.

Let us look at SIB Wilson's strongest evidence for proving that my son was drunk. It is the account by Lt Lisa Pitman who said

> *"Lt Woodhouse looked at me and laughed because I did not look too well due to my late night. I noticed Lt Woodhouse **looked***

*slightly shabby, with slightly bloodshot eyes. He looked as though he had not had a lot of sleep."*

There is nothing wrong with that statement, but unfortunately SIB Wilson shows his calibre by misquoting this statement. SIB Wilson even meticulously adds quotation marks to indicate that he is quoting verbatim a witness, and he writes –

*At 0745 that day Lt Woodhouse was seen by Lt Pitman who describes him as looking **"shabby with blood shot eyes"***
See Summary of Evidence – 2nd paragraph.

Further, he would not quote the other witness account (Lt Jennifer Hayes) describing my son's condition on the morning of the 6th August, which stated –

*At 0755 Lt Woodhouse knocked on my cabin door to make sure I was up. Lt Woodhouse **appeared bright and happy** and was making jokes at my expense. Lt Woodhouse **did not appear dishevelled in any way**.*

*Lt Woodhouse as the rest of the group did not appear overly intoxicated during the previous evening. He was steady on his feet and was **holding coherent conversations**.*

I have studied the strongest evidence of SIB Wilson's Criminal Investigation Summary, PO Fulton's witness account, and it is so flimsy that all that can be seen are objectives, objectives, objectives.

We have to ask the question – why are you doing this? SIB Wilson's Summary report states,

Item 6

*"it is common practice to consult with either the OID – (first ranking) or Deputy OIC (second ranking) on any matter that is considered to be contentious, critical or **potentially damaging to the RN**"*

It appears that the good name of the Royal Navy is more important than granting my son an honest criminal investigation into his suspicious death.

# Conflicts, Contradictions, and Many Questions

The Witness Statements of PO Fulton and the three US Navy witnesses highlight serious conflicts in the accounts of my son's last movements.

US Witness 3, Los Angeles, saw my son standing comfortably on the deck of the LCVP behind the wheelhouse, and at the back of the LCVP.

But PO Fulton said my son was sitting on top of the wheelhouse roof, and at the front of the wheelhouse.

This is a huge contradiction. Whose account is correct?

My son fell from the back of the wheelhouse, as proved by his projectory, and by his landing. This fact contradicts PO Fulton's account.

Witness 1, Philippines, said that he first saw feet. Why did he see feet? How could he see just feet? What was hiding the rest of the person?

Witness 2, Charleston, said that he thought it was a practical joke the Brits were playing. Why did he think so? Witness 2, Charleston, saw a man in blue walking slowly in the vicinity of where the man fell. This man did not appear to be in any hurry. Very strange behaviour. It was so strange that he thought it was a dummy that had just been thrown overboard.

What is going on here? Who is the man in blue? Where was he seen? Could this have been PO Fulton?

Witness 1, Philippines, saw a man sitting on 'top an LCAC'? Who is this man? Is it my son? What does he mean by on top an LCAC? Does he mean the deck of the LCVP?

We were to find out the week before my son's Inquest that there were workmen on moving platforms by the LCVP Bay. Witness 1, Philippines, marked the position of the feet at the top of the LCVP Bay, where access would only be via the moving platform. This points very strongly to Witness 1, Philippines, seeing the feet of one of the workers and not my son at all.

However, SIB Wilson tells us that he carried out his investigation with an 'open mind' that took into account all possible explanations, motives, and lines of enquiry.

*Item 22*

*The aim of the investigation was to examine all circumstances that led up to the incident and all circumstances surrounding it. The investigation **was to be conducted with an 'open mind' taking into account all possible explanations motives and lines of inquiry.***

By his actions SIB Wilson has shown us that his Criminal Investigation into my son's death was not carried out with an open mind, nor did he take account of all possible explanations, motives, or lines of enquiry. He didn't even bother to interview the three US Navy witnesses.

# All – Really?

In Item 22 of his Summary, SIB Wilson writes

*The aim of the investigation was to examine **all** circumstances that led up to the incident and **all** circumstances surrounding it. The investigation was to be conducted with an 'open mind' taking into account **all** possible explanations motives and lines of inquiry.*

Item 34 states

*"OIC SIB was satisfied that the SIB team had pursued **all** reasonable lines of enquiry to establish the facts and had concluded that 'foul play' and suicide had not been contributory factors to Lt Woodhouse falling.*

Item 36 states

*"From the outset, **all** available lines of inquiry were followed, including the obtaining of **all** information relating to the LCVP deck."*

Item 38 states

*"The receipt of the US statements meant that OIC SIB was able to conclude with the **honestly held belief**, that having established the facts and gathered **all** available evidence, Lt Woodhouse had not been the victim of an intentional act or suicide. The investigation then concentrated on all other matters relating to the incident which are contained within RNP SIB report 100025/10.*

Item 39 RN SIB Investigation Process states

> *"RNP SIB is satisfied that it has followed **all** reasonable lines of enquiry and there is nothing further of evidential substance to be investigated, regarding the immediate circumstances of death.*

If all lines of enquiry, and all circumstances, and all motives, and all explanations were truly investigated, then there would be no omissions in SIB Wilson's Criminal Investigation, certainly not grave omissions.

However, SIB Wilson

- Failed to interview any of the three US Navy witnesses. These are the only non-interested, independent witnesses. In fact one of these witnesses saw the entire episode from start to finish. A very valuable witness.
- Failed to do a re-enactment. This we found out at the Inquest, where SIB Wilson, on being asked why he didn't do a re-enactment, said
  - *"I'll be honest, Sir. It's not something I actually considered at the time…..um…..I conducted a full CSI scene examination. Once again any evidence I needed, a re-enactment wasn't considered, quite simply."* Tape 1 – 01:28:00
- Failed to look into PO Fulton's records, motives, and history. Perhaps SIB Wilson did do so and omitted to include this information as perhaps it would be damaging to his conclusion?
- Failed to investigate PO Fulton's suspicious actions.
- Failed to question PO Fulton's deliberate falsehoods concerning the flexible hoses over a period of two months.

Reader, I ask you to decide. Can the two coexist? Can SIB Wilson truthfully state that all lines of enquiry were pursued when such grave omissions occurred in his criminal investigation?

I have no doubt that you are saying that this state of affairs could never occur. There are many checks and balances in place. This is the UK.

Firstly, there is his superior, the Provost Marshal, Royal Navy Police. He would never allow such dishonest conduct to occur. Then there is the Coroner. He would certainly examine this investigation, as it is part of his job. Here is another check and balance.

Surely the Coroner would never allow such a dishonest report to come to the light of public scrutiny, let alone use such a dishonest report?

# Checks and Balances

We too thought in the same way. We too thought that our son would get as his basic fundamental human right an honest criminal investigation into his death.

Like a stack of dominoes we watched in horror as investigation after investigation towed the party line, and would rather cover my son's suspicious death than bring disrepute to the good name of the Royal Navy.

An investigation of the calibre of the one carried out by the Deputy Provost of the Royal Navy Military Police into my son's suspicious death made us realise that this must be normal practice.

If a lay person is stunned by this Criminal Investigation, surely SIB Wilson's superiors are also incensed that such an investigation should have been carried out?

Where are the checks and balances? Was the Provost Marshal happy with this Criminal Investigation?

What about HM Coroner?

He had the power and the authority to send the investigation back at the SIB and warn them that reports of this calibre would not be tolerated. But he did not do so.

SIB Wilson, has himself pointed out that the whole investigation process was carried out as a team with continual recourse to other highly trained members of the SIB Royal Navy Military Police. I shall quote Items 6 and 7 of SIB Wilson's report

> *"Prior to any **team briefing**, a discussion between the RNP SIB management team and investigators with relevant experience takes place to ensure that all potential lines of enquiry have been considered. In practice the briefing of the **deploying team** may be conducted personally, by telephone or other method as appropriate."*

> *"Day to day progress and monitoring of individual investigations is **conducted by the Warrant Officer** 1st Class Senior Investigator (Operations) (SI (Ops)) who ranks 3rd in the organisation. Whilst SI (Ops) has the autonomy to provide guidance and direction*

*to teams, it is common practice to* **consult with** *either the OIC – (first ranking) or Deputy OIC (second ranking) on any matter that is considered to be contentious, critical or potentially damaging to the RN."*

Therefor this report is the result of the entire SIB team, and not just SIB Wilson.

Neither do I believe that this charade of a criminal investigation into my son's death stands alone as an aberration.

I believe my son's death is just another in a long line of military deaths which have been conveniently painted as unfortunate accidents or suicides.

# Investigation Disqualified

I have shown why I believe the Criminal Investigation summary conducted by SIB Wilson, is fundamentally and intentionally flawed and therefore has disqualified itself.

If the premises are false, the conclusions are meaningless.

We are now forced to stand in the breach and to conduct our own investigation, using all the evidence put before us in the bundle of documents from the Coroner. These documents are

- The Immediate Ship's Investigation.
- The Supplementary Ship's Investigation.
- Three US Navy Witness statements
- Witness statements of people in the water below – PO Dot Cottam, ET Myers, and Medic.
- Witness statements of lieutenants with Joshua the night before.
- PO Fulton's two statements.
- Post Mortem.

Our first categorisation would have to be on the strength of these statements. Which do I consider strong and why?

I have placed all of the three US Navy witness statements as the strongest evidence. I have done this because they are independent witnesses, they are not 'interested' parties, and one of the witnesses even saw the entire episode from start to finish.

Their accounts have to be examined, but unfortunately, as I have not been vested with the investigative authority that the SIB Military Police has been given, I have to use only what has been given to us.

And which do I consider to be the weakest witness statement? PO Fulton's statements are the weakest because they are inconsistent, contradictory, and unnatural.

I have already mentioned why I consider PO Fulton's statements to be suspicious. The statements by PO Fulton contain so many implausible facts and unnatural behaviour and are made by a man, who, in the Supplementary Ship's Investigation, quite openly persisted in a falsehood. Another reason why his statements have to be treated with suspicion is because 'two men went to do a job and only one came back.'

SIB Wilson gave us the overview of how a Criminal Investigation should be conducted and he says

> Item 22
> The aim of the investigation was to examine all circumstances that led up to the incident and all circumstances surrounding it. The investigation **was to be conducted with an 'open mind' taking into account all possible explanations motives and lines of inquiry**.

Where SIB Wilson has failed we shall endeavour to succeed.

The account by Witness 1, Philippines, is difficult to understand and just does not make sense, especially in view of the fact that Witness 3, Los Angeles, said that he saw my son standing comfortably behind the wheelhouse and on the deck of the LCVP. What is Witness 1, Philippines, talking about when he says he saw my son on the top of the LCVP?

> MITSCHER got underway and as we were passing HMS OCEAN, who was tied up pierside, I noticed a man sitting on top an LCAC. He was wearing white clothes. At first, all I could see was his feet. He was by himself. I saw him slide down the LCAC to the next level, but he lost his balance. I saw him attempt to grab something to regain his balance, but he was unsuccessful. I saw him fall off the LCAC, bit I did not see him land. I did hear a very loud noise that sounded like a loud "boom."

We have to have an open mind.

Feet, feet, why did he see feet first? Was something blocking his line of vision? This has to be investigated.

Unfortunately we did not have the power or the opportunity to interrogate these prize witnesses, so we shall put together a suggested explanation for the strange account of Witness 1, Philippines. Our interpretation demands the necessity for interviewing these pivotal witnesses. They have to be interviewed. We have to find out what happened on the LCVP. PO Fulton says my son was on the wheelhouse roof and that he, PO Fulton, was climbing back down via the back route. US Witness 3, Los Angeles, said that he saw my son standing comfortably at the back of the LCVP on the deck.

Witness 2, Charleston, is another witness that has to be interviewed. Where is the man in blue that he saw? Why was this man in blue behaving so strangely? Was this man in blue PO Fulton?

Why did Witness 3, Los Angeles, say that my son swung and rotated? If I had the resources of the SIB Military Police not only would I interview all of these prize witnesses, I would employ the services of a Kinetics expert. Could this expert tell me by looking at the diagrams made by Witness 3, Los Angeles, what could have possibly caused this sudden and rotational movement? Could this be a gust of wind? Perhaps my son slipped – would this have caused rotation? Perhaps my son tripped – would this have caused rotation and the great velocity? Why didn't my son fall straight downwards? Instead my son fell in a circular motion towards the bow (front) of the ship. Is this a continuation of the sudden rotation and swinging action that occurs when you slam a door violently?

What about the three impacts on the LCVP below? I would again ask the Kinetics expert whether there might be any relevant information in these three distinct impacts that might shed light on how my son came to fall.

What about the bruises? I would have them investigated further.

What about PO Fulton? I would investigate him very closely. What is his history? What is his work record? Why was he demoted? What about the disciplinary records? What was he doing the night before? What dealings did he have with Lt Woodhouse? Had Lt Woodhouse been 'bothering' or rather chasing up PO Fulton for a month now?

# The Bruises

It was only a few weeks after we had received, read, studied, and digested the new documents from the Coroner in February, 2012, that my husband suggested that we look again at the bruises on my son's body as recorded on the post mortem. I have made a diagram, see below, which shows the bruises identified in the post mortem and I have numbered them. There is only one bruise on the back of my son's body, Bruise number 10, which is on his elbow.

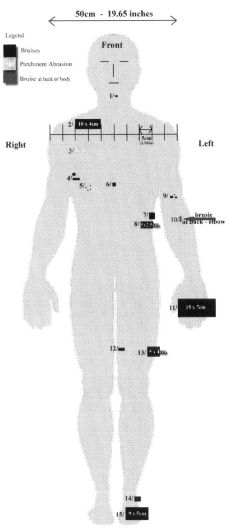

What is striking in the post mortem are two large bruises on my son's left hand and left foot. These are the biggest bruises on my son's body.

My son was not very tall, being about five and a half feet tall, or 1.65 metres. His hands and his feet were also about the same size as his father's hands and feet. I have therefore taken a picture showing the bruises against my husband's left foot and left hand, as they would be very similar to my son's.

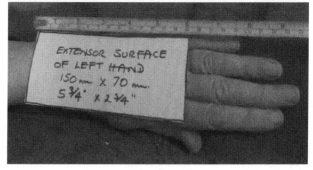

The picture of the bruise on Joshua's hand

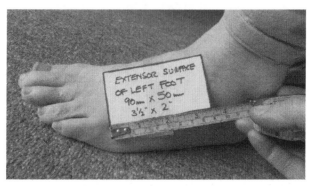

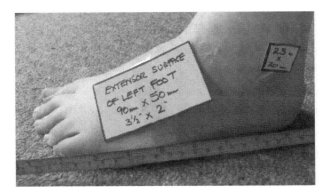

**Joshua's bruise on his left foot.**

Both these bruises are large. What is noteworthy is that my son was wearing the full navy issue protective boots, and the bruise on his left foot occurred despite the fact that his foot was protected by these navy issue boots. It must have been a horrendous blow he received on his left hand and foot to have caused such bruises.

These bruises tally with the description of my son's movements given by US Navy Witness 3, Los Angeles.

US Navy Witness 3, Los Angeles, stated that my son was standing comfortably at the back of the LCVP before he suddenly swung round, desperately tried to keep hold of the railing, and then lost his grip and fell to his ultimate death.

What caused this sudden change from a comfortable position to one of sudden, violent momentum and change of direction?

A violent gust of wind could have caused one who is standing comfortably to suddenly display huge velocity and swing round, lose his grip, and fall forty six feet.

An earth tremor could also have caused this drastic change to a sudden large momentum.

A slippery surface could never have caused this huge momentum.

A slippery surface could not have caused such a sudden huge momentum that the left hand and left foot shoot out and hit the metal railing and metal post of the LCVP.

A slippery surface would not have caused that direction of movement. A slippery surface would have resulted in my son falling backwards and landing on his backside.

My son did not fall backwards. My son was propelled forwards.

What force caused my son to suddenly be propelled forwards?

My son had quick reactions. My son was also safety conscious. My son was holding the railing with his right hand.

My son in all probability stopped his work specifically to enjoy watching that beautiful American warship sail past. What a lovely sight that would have been.

I have put together a representation of my son standing at the back of the LCVP. I used the picture of the LCVP from our trip to the Marine Base in Poole, and it therefore shows the LCVP in the water. We have to imagine that the LCVP is in the body of HMS Ocean.

My son's position would have been identical to the representation I have made. You will notice I have shown my son holding the hand rail around the wheelhouse with his right hand, and that there is a bollard and another rail in front of him.

Below is another picture of the guard rail and the bollard, to show what was in front of my son as he was probably watching USS Mitscher sail past.

But what caused my son to suddenly change direction and swing and rotate?

We have already ascertained that the likely cause of the sudden rotation and increase in momentum could have been caused by a large external force from behind.

But the bruises. What do the bruises tell us?

As my son tightened his grip on the hand rail with his right hand, the result would have been a rotating action, like a door swinging on its hinges. This rotating action could then cause his left hand to swing uncontrollably outwards and hit the railing accounting for the huge bruise on my son's left hand.

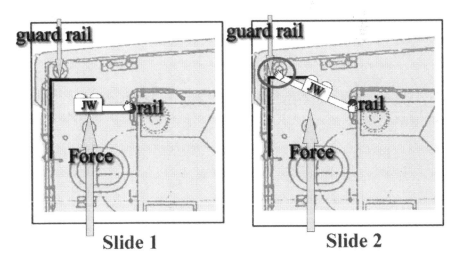

To begin with, my son's left arm and left hand would in all probability have been in the downward position by the side of his body.

After receiving the huge blow from behind, his left arm and his left hand would have swung violently outwards. This motion would have been in proportion to the force he received on his back.

Joshua's left hand would have hit the guard rail with terrific force. This bruise is the largest bruise on his body and measures 15cm x 7 cm   (5.9in x 2.8 in).

In the same way, Joshua's left leg could in like manner have flown outwards. The force with which his left foot hit the bollard must have been extremely large to have caused a bruise of 9cm x 5cm (3.5 inches x 2 inches) through protective Royal Navy safety boots.

I have represented his foot hitting the bollard below −

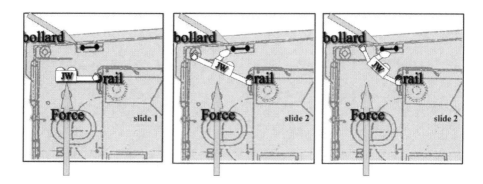

**This figure shows the possible movement of Joshua's body as it was swung violently forward.**

As Joshua's body is swung violently round, his foot could have struck the bollard which was directly in his way, accounting for the massive bruising through the safety boots.

**This figure shows the possible movement of Joshua's body as it was swung violently round and his foot hits the bollard with great force**

This might have been the time that Witness 3, Los Angeles, states that Joshua's foot slipped.

*"When he swung/rotated his body around to get to the port side, his foot slipped and his hand grip gave way and he fell off of the landing craft"*

**This figure shows the possible movement of Joshua's body after his foot hit the bollard with great force, gave way under him, and then his body drops down to a sitting position.**

The size of the bruise on my son's left foot is testimony to the huge force that propelled my son over the side of the LCVP and to his death.

I find it very sad to read the account by Witness 3, Los Angeles, who said that my son tried so hard to grab the railing with his other hand – his left hand. This is the hand that had just received a huge blow as it struck the railing. The hand was stunned, and it was badly hurt. This left hand could not help my son as he tried desperately to hold onto the LCVP with just one hand, his right hand.

My son's attempt to save his life after receiving a huge blow from behind failed, and he fell forty six feet, first hitting the bridge roof of the LCVP in the water below with his head.

## The Bruises and the Legal Team

We put together our thoughts on the bruises and the account by US Navy Witness 3, Los Angeles, for the legal team.

The legal team immediately pursued this line of thought and found a pathologist who was prepared to investigate this for no charge. The legal team asked him to please confirm whether the bruises were grounds for proving conclusively that my son was pushed.

The answer of course is that they are not grounds, as my son fell forty six feet, violently landed on a metal surface, and received a blow to the head which cracked his skull open from ear to ear.

The bruises might not by themselves prove that my son was pushed, but the bruises do support the account of US Navy Witness 3, Los Angeles.

## Checks and Balances

I have to go back to the checks and balances.

When one check fails, then there is another one further up the ladder.

These checks and balances are evident in the procedures laid down in the Royal Navy and the UK military.

**Check 1.  Initial Ship's Investigation.  Lt Cdr Pickles, Lt Cdr Lucocq, and WO**

## Clapham

Lt Cdr Pickles, Lt Cdr Lucocq, and WO Clapham took the word of the prime suspect as the truth. At the Inquest, when asked about PO Fulton's suspicious actions, Lt Cdr Pickles explained he had limited powers. What does that tell us?

Did Lt Cdr Pickles, Lt Cdr Lucocq, and WO Clapham do anything about their limited powers to conduct this investigation?

Check 1 failed.

### Check 2. Initial Ship's Investigation. Captain Blount's approval.

Lt Cdr Pickles, Lt Cdr Lucocq, and WO Clapham were to report to Captain Blount, or the Executive Officer (second in command), regarding their investigation. It is highly unlikely that Lt Cdr Pickles, Lt Cdr Lucocq, and WO Clapham did not discuss this with either Captain Blount and/or the Executive Officer, and relay their concerns. Did they have any concerns? Two men went to do a job and only one came back and his account was highly suspicious.

Whether or not these concerns were relayed, does not take away from the responsibility of Captain Blount and/or the Executive Officer when they read and approved the report.

PO Fulton's account is so implausible that it would be hard for Captain Blount and the Executive Officer not to notice the multitude of suspicious facts throughout his account.

What else did Captain Blount and the Executive Officer know that we did not know?

The Initial Ship's Investigation is approved by the Commanding Officer of HMS Ocean.

Why was it approved?

The second check has failed.

### Check 3. SIB Wilson's Investigation.

We have just recounted the openly flawed summaries of the criminal investigation conducted by SIB Wilson.

This is our third check, and instead of rectifying any failings in the previous checks, this check is getting more and more absurd and ludicrous as it performs the most amazing acrobatics and contortions of facts and the truth, and yet has the audacity to use the word 'honestly' when summarising his report.

As the premises of these summaries of the SIB criminal investigation are false, its conclusions are worthless.

Check 3 has failed miserably.

**Check 4. Supplementary Ship's Investigation. (SSI) RN HQ Request.**

There was another check.

The ISI was sent to Royal Navy HQ in Whale Island, Portsmouth, and landed on the desk of Captain Forsey. He was not satisfied with the minimal information contained in the report.

The ISI raised more questions than it answered. Captain Forsey therefore requested more information, and a Supplementary Ship's Investigation was carried out a month later in September, 2010.

Here we have someone who appears on the surface to have a different character to the men we have come across thus far.

Here is someone who was not content with the information in the ISI, and wanted more information. It might not have been for the same reasons as I would have asked for more information, but here was a man who did something constructive.

So Lt Cdr Pickles and Lt Cdr Lucocq conducted a further investigation, and what do we find? This second investigation heightens our suspicions about my son's death.

Did this second Ship's Investigation not ring any warning bells for Captain Forsey?

It appears that it did, for he stated in the Inquest, when questioned, that the Royal Navy received 'Heavily [sic] Legal Advice' not to conduct a Service Enquiry into my son's death.

Aah. Here we have the mask slipping. If RN HQ received 'Heavily [sic] Legal

Advice' not to conduct a Service Enquiry into my son's death, then you must come to the conclusion that the two Ship's Investigations did send loud alarm bells ringing. Very loud indeed, so loud that they elicited 'Heavily [sic] Legal Advice' to do nothing further.

This SSI involved four people

- Captain Forsey RN HQ, who requested this report.
- Lt Cdr Pickles and Lt Cdr Lucocq, who interviewed PO Fulton again and wrote this second report.
- Captain Blount, HMS Ocean, who approved the report.

All are accountable for their part in the investigation of my son's death.

We have to ask what could possibly be the reason why these four people did nothing concerning the suspicious facts surrounding my son's death.

For whatever reason you choose to select, the outcome is the same.

The 4th check failed.

**Check 5. Coroner David Horsley – Discover the Facts**

The Coroner's duty is to 'discover the facts', and to make diligent search. For what? Primarily to find out whether there was any foul play in the death being investigated by his trained men the SIB, Military Police.

The Coroner's duty is to comb through the report by his men, the SIB, Military Police, and should there be any hint of foul play, his role demands that he immediately hands the investigation of the death to the civilian Police Force.

We have the Criminal Investigation by SIB Wilson landing on the Coroner's desk. This occurred at the latest in January, 2011.

One presumes the Coroner took the time to read the SIB Criminal Investigation.

If he did read the full Criminal Investigation, then you have to ask the same questions previously asked as to why the Coroner, who is trained in searching out a matter, especially a suspicious death, did not notice the glaring faults in the Criminal Investigation before his eyes.

Could he have received orders regarding the desired outcome of the Inquest into my son's death?

The 5th check has failed

# Why did Five Checks Fail?

Checks and balances.

The whole objective of checks and balances is that where one fails, for whatever reason, the others will not fail.

All five checks failed.

We cannot attribute all five checks to stupidity, mental illness, unfitness for the job, or to personal problems. Probability itself testifies that five checks could not all have failed.

There can only be one reason.

This is the Military Justice meted out to my son.

## Legal team's Reaction to Health and Safety

My husband and I are not Health and Safety experts, and we were focused solely on my son's suspicious death; therefore we did not study the numerous documents on Health and Safety.

But the legal team did.

We noted the indignation of the legal team to the Health and Safety aspect of my son's death. The legal team informed us that the Royal Navy had said that the Health and Safety failings at the time of my son's death had all been rectified.

There was no independent body that could query or verify this bold statement.

The Royal Navy had whitewashed the Health and Safety aspects of my son's death in exactly the same way they had whitewashed the suspicious circumstances surrounding my son's death.

## Legal team's Reaction to Documents

We were interested to know what the reaction of the legal team was to all the documents that the Coroner had released to us: to these documents which shed more light on the events surrounding my son's suspicious death. Instead of just one document, we now had multiple documents; but what did the legal team make of them?

The legal team pushed even harder to have Foul Play investigated at the Inquest. Why did they do this? The additional documents showed up how false the Coroner's statement was that -

> "*I have no evidence* before me to give me reasonable grounds to suspect that either Lt Woodhouse was unlawfully killed or took his own life."

The additional documents also show how false the MOD barrister's statement was that

> "*No evidence whatsoever* has emerged from any of the investigations undertaken to date to suggest that foul play is a possibility in this case."

And, of course, we cannot exclude the SIB Criminal Investigation Summaries which sum up their conclusion with the equally sweeping and false words –

> "*Any foul play would have been identified.* **Simply, there was none which could be found.**"

Yet, armed with these additional documents, the list of suspicious circumstances has only increased.

For over a year, the Coroner had been sitting on this vital information and did not hand this suspicious death to the Police to investigate, as his role demands. Instead, he sat as an immovable mountain on the path of justice, impeding all attempts to uncover my son's suspicious death.

What could the legal team do? They fought even harder to have a Full Middleton Inquiry into my son's death, to have Foul Play investigated at the Inquest.

Yet there were problems. The legal team had to tread very carefully. Before them was the might of the MOD. Before them was the might of HM Coroner. Both stated that they were independent, both pleaded that they only desired that the truth would be revealed. But their actions speak otherwise.

The legal team was skating on thin ice. That the Coroner and the MOD did not want my son's suspicious death investigated was obvious to all, despite their statements that there were no suspicious circumstances in my son's death.

What could the legal team do? The Coroner's demeanour was evident from the first pre-Inquest hearing. The legal team had to tread very carefully. This man must not be provoked else all hope would be lost of even the smallest chance of getting 'justice' in my son's Inquest.

## Legal Team Fights for Foul Play to be Investigated

The Coroner had set another pre-Inquest hearing for the 15th March, 2012.

After receiving the additional documents, the legal team wrote to the Coroner on the 12th March, 2012, with their requests following this disclosure. This was done in preparation for the next pre-Inquest. (see letter on the website)

Their paramount request was the necessity to have Foul Play investigated at my son's Inquest. These requests are listed in items 2, 3, and 4 below -

> _The circumstances in which Lt. WOODHOUSE came to fall and the **possibility of foul play**_
>
> 2) _The family are concerned to ensure that the **precise circumstances** in which Lt. WOODHOUSE ("JW") came to fall are **examined fully.** They identify **apparent inconsistencies** as between the account of PO Fulton and other sources of evidence, for example:_
>
>> a. _As to PO Fulton's knowledge of the maintenance history of the hoses: In his statement PO Fulton says that he told JW that as far as **he was aware they had not been changed.** The Supplementary Ship's Investigation report (wit. 12, Lt Cdr Pickles) makes it clear that **PO Fulton had been told the hoses had been changed** (para. 9)._
>>
>> b. _As to where Lt. WOODHOUSE was at the time he fell/must have fallen: **PO Fulton says JW was/must have been at the front of the wheelhouse** (since PO Fulton says he climbed down at the rear); **the USN**_

**sailor** (identified as born in Los Angeles) who says "nobody saw the fall as clearly as I did" **states that JW was on the aft end of the landing craft**, trying to proceed to the port side, was comfortable and not tentative in his actions and when he swung/ rotated his body round to get to the port side he slipped. This is itself inconsistent with the account of the first USN sailor (identified as born in the Philippines) who saw a man slide down the landing craft.

3) The family remain anxious to ensure that **there is no possibility of foul play. These inconsistencies in PO Fulton's account have served to heighten their concern.** At present the USN witnesses are to be read rather than called and are therefore not going to be questioned on whether there might have been any person standing near/behind JW before he fell, or whether they would have seen any such person given any shadow/dark areas in the landing craft bay. They therefore respectfully invite HM Coroner to consider calling for:

a) **any disciplinary records** in which JW features either as a person lodging a complaint or a person complained against, so as to allow the **possibility of any bad blood/foul play** to be eliminated from this inquiry;

b) a clearer picture of **PO Fulton's background** and any concerns about him including, but not restricted to, his **disciplinary record,** his actions/ whereabouts in the day or so before the fall, and his training in relevant safety measures.

4) The family are also anxious to know **whether the pattern of bruising on JW's body is or might be consistent with his having received a blow from behind,** causing him to lose his balance. They are hoping to obtain some medical opinion on the subject (see para.12 below) and if it is of relevance they will of course be content to make that available to HM Coroner to consider.

And the legal team wanted to pursue my son's bruises, as they pointed to his having received a blow from behind. In item 12 of their letter they stated –

**E) Is Expert evidence necessary?**

12) *The family hope to obtain medical opinion re:* **patterns of bruising** *and will happily make that available to HM Coroner to consider. It must be stressed that all representation and assistance is currently being provided on a pro bono basis and as such they cannot be confident of obtaining such opinion.*

The Coroner has it again pointed out to him that my son's death is suspicious. Will the Coroner still persist in his statement that –

> *"I have no evidence before me to give me reasonable grounds to suspect that either Lt Woodhouse was unlawfully killed or took his own life."*

# Legal Team Fights for US Navy Witnesses to be Interviewed

As the SIB Military Police would not do their job and investigate my son's suspicious death by, at the very least, interviewing the US Navy Witnesses, and as the Coroner also refused to do his job and demand that these witnesses be interviewed, it was left to the legal team to stand in the breach.

In this same letter to the Coroner, of the 12th March, 2012, the legal team requested that these vital independent witnesses be interviewed –

**B) Witnesses (live/r.37)**

6) *13 witnesses have been identified as live witnesses for the inquest.*

7) *A further 11 have been provided under r.37.*

8) *The three anonymous USN witnesses (r.37 item 1) are* **the only witnesses who saw JW fall.** *It is submitted that they are* **important witnesses** *and* **all the more so given the apparent**

*inconsistencies identified at para. 2(b) above. HM Coroner is respectfully asked to consider whether a **TV link might be used for the USN witnesses**. Either in conjunction with that or as an alternative, for the **reasons identified at para. 2(b) above**, we submit it would be helpful for clear plans/diagrams to be **sent to these witnesses to ask each to mark** (with as much clarity as possible) where they saw JW at each stage they describe, (e.g. for the sailor identified as born in the Philippines: where did he first see JW's feet etc) and where they saw the other sailor in dark coveralls. It is noted that one of the USN sailors (identified as born in Los Angeles) has attempted this but he has drawn his own diagrams which are very rough. In relation to this, we submit that proper and accurate diagrams of the LCVP should be obtained (see submissions: "photographs/plans" below) and used for all witnesses, to ensure consistency.*

*9) See observations re disclosure below: if HM Coroner is of the view that further disclosure should be made, he is respectfully asked to consider whether the witness concerned, if presently a r.37 witness, should then become a live a witness in these proceedings.*

What will be the Coroner's response to this request? We shall see at the pre-Inquest.

## Legal Team Fights for Independent Health and Safety Assessment

The legal team took the Health and Safety abuses of the Royal Navy very seriously. They saw that the Royal Navy was compliant in name only.

They therefore put in their letter to the Coroner of the 12th March, 2012, the following requests –

### E) Is Expert evidence necessary?

13) *In relation to the **adequacy of/compliance with safety procedures**, we express concern that there is at the moment **no independent witness who deals with this topic**. Mr Wheeler (wit. 8) deals with this aspect of the case - he is a Naval employee. As things stand the Navy, whose systems are susceptible to criticism as part of this inquiry, provides the **sole evidence** as to standards at the time and subsequent compliance. It is submitted that in **workplace death** inquiries, it is desirable (and commonplace) for an **independent** (usually HSE) witness to assist the inquiry with **independent** evidence on such topics. No such **independent** witness is involved in these proceedings. HM Coroner is respectfully invited to consider the need for such **independent** evidence.*

14) *It is submitted that this point becomes all the more important as it would appear that concerns have been voiced that some shortcomings may be fleet-wide (See CRF/3 para.6 and Lt Cdr Hewitt para. 10c).*

15) *The family hope to obtain independent opinion on this topic, and if they are able to do so (within the constraints of their pro bono representation), they will make that opinion available to HM Coroner to consider.*

16) *In relation to this topic we respectfully inquire whether **there has been any referral of this matter to HSE** by the Royal Navy and indeed whether HM Coroner would be assisted at this stage by such a referral.*

All rested on one man.

# Legal Team Fights for Further Disclosure

The legal team was not content with just the summary of the criminal investigation into my son's death. They needed to see the actual criminal investigation itself that is referred to in SIB Wilson's summary Item 38

> *"The receipt of the US statements meant that OIC SIB was able to conclude with the honestly held belief, that having established the facts and gathered all available evidence, Lt Woodhouse had not been the victim of an intentional act or suicide. The investigation then concentrated on all other matters relating to the incident* **which are contained within RNP SIB report 100025/10.**

The legal team then asked once again for the Disciplinary Records that involved my son in any way. This is a stuck record.

The legal team further requested Health and Safety documents so as to be better able to check on the veracity of the bold statements made by the Royal Navy regarding their Health and Safety compliance, and my son's supposed guilt.

The Royal Navy are now having to substantiate their bold claims.

My husband and I do not believe my son was ever on the wheelhouse roof at all: but let us continue with the Health and Safety charade. If someone was to climb onto the wheelhouse roof, what could they possibly attach their harness to? Are there any places that have been approved as anchor points on the LCVP? Are there any places that are strong enough to bear a man's weight should he slip and fall?

This was another reason that we needed photographs and plans of the LCVP and the LCVP in the Bay.

I quote from the legal team's letter –

### F) Any outstanding disclosure issues

> 17) *HM Coroner is respectfully asked to consider the following areas for further inquiry/disclosure:*

> *a)* ***Disciplinary records*** *relating to JW (for the reasons*

*mentioned at paras. 2-4 above);*

b) *Lt. Col. Wilson:*

i) *(first document "summary of evidence"): have the* **photographs** *and SGO's mentioned been considered for disclosure (to assist in understanding layout and safety measures)?;*

ii) *(second document ("Investigation process", para. 27): has JW's black diary been considered for disclosure? (para. 27 "notably, a black diary was found on a ledge...[it] was identified as belonging to [JW]....it contained details of flexible hoses, the item he had apparently ascended into the LCVP to gain detail of". It is submitted that this document is likely to contain the most reliable insight into JW's actions in the immediate build up to the fall, and the relevance of this is demonstrated by the mention of (earlier ) emails on this topic in the supplementary ship's investigation (Lt Cdr Pickles, wit.12);*

iii) *(second document para. 38):* **has the SIB report** *mentioned at para. 38 been considered for disclosure?*

c) *Capt. Forsey: CRF/2 where is the evidence that JW had recently read SGOs (see ISI para. 27)?*

d) *Mr Wheeler:*

i) *at present he is the* **sole SHE witness** *in the case. He makes references to guidance BRd 167 and JSP 375, sometimes quoting from them but on other occasions summarising their contents. It is submitted that these documents should be made available to* **allow this inquiry to assess the extent to which the procedures at the time were adequate** *and/or were complied with;*

ii) *the index to DP/1 (an exhibit to which he refers)*

mentions a series of risk assessments with A1 prefixes, yet the 2008 risk assessments which follow have A2 prefixes. Are these A1 documents older risk assessments, and if so have they been considered for disclosure? If they reveal deficiencies prior to 2008 it is submitted this may be relevant to the adequacy of /compliance with the procedures at the time.

e) Lt. Cdr. Harris: what is the SHIPHAZ procedure as it applies **to working aloft** (see p.1 of his statement, final lines)?

f) Lt. Cdr. Hewitt: have all the "references" to which he refers (see his report 15 Jan 2012) been considered for disclosure? It would appear only items B, E-G and possibly C and M are within the disclosure. For the reasons set out at para. 5 above we invite HM Coroner to obtain and disclose the 2011 SHE audit (see footnote to para.12 of the report).

g) Lt. Reynolds: can a copy of the task books he refers to on the first and second pages of his statement be made available?

h) PO Sykes-Gelder: can records of the **issuing of harnesses** be obtained and cross matched with landing craft maintenance? This would allow proper scrutiny of the extent to which departures from the claimed approach were tolerated.

## H) Photographs/plans etc

19) We respectfully submit that **photographs and plans will be vital to understand the layout, and how JW came to fall.** We submit this is all the **more important given the apparent inconsistencies in accounts as set out at para. 2(b) above.** In any event, in relation **to safety measures, such documents will assist in assessing whether the claimed measures would**

*be adequate in the circumstances – for example whether a harness could be attached in a safe way or at all, when a landing craft was in a bay.*

20) *To assist with this, the family have obtained their own photographs and diagrams, but these are not official documents. Their plans, for example, have come from the internet and contain estimated measurements; further the family has had to "rotate" images taken on the starboard side so as to show how the port side would look. Examples of these documents are sent with this note.*

# Pre-Inquest Hearing 15th March  2012

We were unable to attend my son's second pre-Inquest hearing, but we had a phone conference with the legal team, who informed us of the proceedings and the decisions that were made, which I shall discuss under the appropriate headings below.

# Pre-Inquest Hearing 15th March – Foul Play Investigation

I venture to repeat, as it is a cause for gratitude and wonder, that it is only due to the large legal team that fought on behalf of my son that we had any disclosure, and that we were now even granted a second pre-Inquest hearing. Without the work of the Royal British Legion, and the London Barrister, and the London legal firm, we would be lost, and my son's cause would also be totally lost.

The Coroner is a servant of the public and paid to uphold this responsible and honourable position. I quote from the Hampshire Coroner's Charter, items 2 and 4 which state that it is the duty of Coroners to -

*"investigate deaths, which are reported to them and which appear to be due to violence, or are unnatural, or are sudden and of unknown cause, or which occur in legal custody, and to carry out certain related responsibilities."*

*"Duties will be discharged impartially, with a view to **ascertaining the facts** surrounding a death for the purpose of the Coroner's statutory responsibilities."*

At the March pre-Inquest Hearing, 15th March, 2012, the Coroner promised our legal team that although he had not granted a Full Middleton Inquiry, he would allow our legal team to question PO Fulton at the Inquest regarding Foul Play.

He did not keep his word. I do not believe that anybody was surprised. At the Inquest, the legal team were forbidden from asking any questions on Foul Play.

# Pre-Inquest Hearing 15th March 2012 – Board of Inquiry / Service Inquiry

I shall now relate some of the other items discussed at this second pre-Inquest hearing.

At this second pre-Inquest hearing it appears that the Coroner became aggressive with the MOD, asking them why they did not conduct a Board of Inquiry. I quote from Commodore Mansergh's letter to us of the 24th November, 2010, which gives information on the legal requirement for a Board of Inquiry/Service Inquiry into a service death.

*"The concurrent investigation being undertaken by the Royal Navy's Special Investigation Branch (SIB) for HM Coroner has yet to conclude but is expected to do so shortly. In the light of this report and the completed Ship's Investigation report, the Royal Navy will then consider whether it is right or necessary to convene a follow on **Service Inquiry (SI)**, which used to be known as a **Board of Inquiry.***

*Under the Armed Forces Act 2006, which came into effect on 1 October 2008, it is **mandatory** for the Royal Navy to consider holding a Service Inquiry into the deaths of all its serving members. The key objective of such an inquiry is to determine the facts of a particular matter and, where applicable, to make recommendations aimed at preventing a recurrence. However, if it is considered unlikely that such an inquiry would establish any new relevant facts, or identify any further recommendations or lessons to be learned over and above those which may have already been identified through the other investigations, arrangements exist for a senior Naval Officer (at*

*Rear Admiral level or above) to dispense with the need to hold such an inquiry.*

*Once a decision has been taken on whether to hold a Service Inquiry, you will be informed as soon as possible, as Joshua's Next of Kin. In the event that a Service Inquiry is convened, you would be provided with a copy of the Inquiry's Terms of Reference, given the opportunity to meet with the President of the Board before he/she starts their work, be given periodic updates on the progress of the Board's deliberations and be provided with a copy of the Inquiry's report once it has concluded its work. This is the procedure that is summarised on the Ministry of Defence's website, and which you allude to in your letter. The process above is not intended to apply to the management of a Ship's Investigation which is aimed primarily at establishing the facts of an incident as soon as possible and learning any immediate lessons. Unlike a Service Inquiry, a Ship's Investigation is **not underpinned by Service Law.**"*

During the Inquest, whilst Captain Forsey was being questioned, he let slip that the Royal Navy had received "heavily [*sic*] legal advice" not to hold a Service Inquiry.

The MOD Barrister, Mr Collins, during the Inquest, wanted this statement eradicated from the records.

Nonetheless, let us return to the pre-Inquest hearing and the Coroner.

He ordered the MOD to explain why no Board of Inquiry had been conducted into my son's death, and required that this submission be sent to him in the next fourteen days.

# Pre-Inquest 15ᵗʰ March 2012 – Other Matters

Our legal team requested that either a TV link be set up with the US Navy witnesses, or that plans or diagrams be sent to them, so that they could mark where they saw my son on HMS Ocean.

The Coroner ordered the MOD to contact the US Navy witnesses in order to ask them to explain their statements with the use of diagrams.

Our legal team also requested photographs, plans, and a glossary. It appears that the Coroner put our photographs, plans, and glossary before the

MOD and demanded that they provide him with a better glossary, better photographs, and better plans.

Our legal team had also requested a visit to HMS Ocean, and the Coroner ordered the MOD to organise it.

These should all have been done by the Coroner over a year before, when he first received the SIB criminal investigation into my son's death.

It took the legal team to request these fundamental and vital items before the Coroner would request them himself, and such a long time after my son's death. The credit of course will go to him. Let him take whatever credit he wishes; we were grateful for small mercies.

## Pre-Inquest 15th March Hearing 2012 – Extend Inquest to 2 Weeks

Our legal team requested that the Inquest be extended from one week to two weeks as the one week that the Coroner had apportioned for the Inquest would not be enough time to investigate all the matters in hand. The Coroner therefore agreed, and extended the Inquest to two weeks.

This request would impact directly on the legal team who were working pro-Bono – without pay. They had by this request voluntarily given even more of their precious time to represent my son.

This act speaks for itself.

## The Legal Team Fights On

After another attempt to get a Full Middleton Inquiry, the legal team is again beaten back. But they kept on fighting. One has to marvel at their resilience. They fought for every tiny little scrap that they could get from the Coroner's sumptuous table.

Despite this enormous setback once again, the legal team would not give up, and continued to fight hard for every inch of ground in my son's Inquest. Their request for a visit to HMS Ocean, their request for official photographs and pictures, their request for further contact with the US Navy Witnesses, are testimony to their determination and fighting spirit.

Their repeated requests and dealings with the Coroner also testify to how unaffected they were by the man's rudeness and ridicule.

Without the legal team, our son's death would have been just another death on the refuse heap of all bothersome military deaths. All to be labelled suicides, accidents, or just the fault of the 'unfortunate individual'.

But the Royal British Legion and our full legal team picked up this one death, my son's death, precious to us, and ceaselessly fought the Coroner and the MOD for the rights of this fallen Royal Navy officer.

Is it not the right of every citizen of the UK to expect a fair investigation into their suspicious death? It appears this right is waived if the death is a military death.

Those fighting for their country are not granted a fair investigation into their suspicious deaths. These heroes who are happy to die for their country are treated like refuse by the MOD and the Coronial system.

It was evident how hard the legal team had to fight to get very little, and all the time I was conscious that without them we, the family, would have received less than nothing. We would have received fables, fables, and more fables, for we had no champion.

## Coroner's Letter 5<sup>th</sup> April, 2012 – Foul Play Ignored

The Coroner's letter of the 5<sup>th</sup> April, 2012 arrived, and it was essentially a summation of the items requested by our legal team for the pre-Inquest hearing of the 15<sup>th</sup> March, 2012.

The main request by our legal team was for Foul Play to be investigated through a Full Middleton Inquiry. This request was not just refused, but, in this letter, ignored.

Another core item that the legal team requested is the actual criminal investigation itself that is referred to in SIB Wilson's summary item 38 -

> "The receipt of the US statements meant that OIC SIB was able to conclude with the honestly held belief, that having established the facts and gathered all available evidence, Lt Woodhouse had not been the victim of an intentional act or suicide. The investigation then concentrated on all other matters relating to the incident **which are contained within RNP SIB report**

**100025/10.**

Let us see how the Coroner deals with this request –

> *"I shall be meeting with the Navy Police to ask them to supply me with a number of the documents mentioned at the pre-Inquest meeting* **with a view to my considering which of them should be treated as Inquest documents.** *I will let you know my decision on this issue."*

We are once again confronted with a great mountain standing and blockading the path of justice.

Like the Disciplinary Records, the original SIB Criminal Investigation was never given to us.

## Coroner's Letter 5th April, 2012 – Other Matters
(see the website)

The Coroner, to put on a façade that he is doing his job, lists the fact that he is asking for more photographs, that he is still waiting for the Royal Navy response regarding the Service Inquiry, and that he will make the Inquest two weeks. He tells us that the Inquest dates are made complicated by the fact that he has to juggle with the availability of the pathologist.

Note also that these secondary details should have been done by his own volition one year previously, without needing our legal team to ask him to do them.

## Visit to HMS Ocean Arranged

The legal team fought long and hard in respectfully asking the Coroner to arrange a visit to HMS Ocean. Is it unreasonable to ask to see the scene of my son's suspicious death? This is yet another job that the Coroner should have seen to when he first received my son's case, and did not.

On the 12th May, 2012 we received news that a visit to HMS Ocean had been arranged for Friday, 15th June, 2012.

The legal team also respectfully requested from the Coroner that photographs be taken during this visit to HMS Ocean.

This visit to HMS Ocean was very important. There were still many things that we did not know.

The SIB Investigation Summary contained no photographs, plans, or information regarding the scene of my son's fall.

We needed to have photographs of the LCVP in position in the LCVP Bay. We had no idea how a man would get onto the LCVP from the Bay.

We had no idea of the head room should a man get onto the wheelhouse roof. We also had no idea where exactly the flexible davit hoses were. Was there any overhang of the LCVP when it was in position in the LCVP Bay? We needed a photograph of this too.

We could only glean a certain amount of information from the internet and from the model makers of HMS Ocean and from our very important visit to a LCVP in September, 2011.

We were very grateful that this visit to HMS Ocean was finally occurring nearly two years after my son's fall, and at the same time amazed that the Coroner had actually allowed it to occur.

The London barrister had a court appearance on that very date, but as he deemed this visit so important he arranged for a colleague to act on his behalf, so that he could personally visit the scene of my son's suspicious death. In the same way, the other members of the legal team did not delegate this visit to HMS Ocean to junior staff, but went in person themselves. They gave of their own time and their expertise, wholeheartedly. Their offer to help my son, to represent him at his Inquest, was not a hollow offer. They gave of their best.

## 15<sup>th</sup> June, 2012 Visit to HMS Ocean

The day arrived, and the full legal team, consisting of the Royal British Legion, the London Barrister and the London legal firm, went to Plymouth to view HMS Ocean. They met the Coroner in Plymouth and met the captain, the second in command, an engineer and some of the Royal Marines. The MOD legal team were also present.

To sum up, the visit took about three hours and the legal team, together with the Coroner, were allowed to inspect the LCVP, see it 'in bed' in the LCVP Bay, see how to access it in that position, see how to climb onto the wheelhouse roof, watch it being lowered, and see the hoses.

This visit was invaluable, as it helped fill the huge gaps in our knowledge, as we tried to make sense of the account given by PO Fulton.

## 15ᵗʰ June, 2012 Visit to HMS Ocean – the Flexible Davit Hoses

Now we come to some of the interesting details of this visit.

A RN Engineering Officer was tasked with helping the legal team understand the Davits and the Davit hoses. This Engineering Officer pointed to two six foot long metal rods, informing the legal team that these were the flexible Davit hoses that Joshua and PO Fulton had come to check.

This was very interesting information. Item 5 and 6 of the Supplementary Ship's Investigation mentioned that my son was in charge of the Flexible Hose Register.

> Item 5
> *"Maintaining **flexible hoses** is an ongoing issue in all ships and HMS OCEAN has over 1400 on its **register.** The ship considers best practice to be for a single officer, working across all Marine Engineering Sub departments, to maintain oversight of both the register and the upkeep and replacement of hoses. Lt Woodhouse had held this responsibility throughout his time on board."*

> Item 6
> *"There is a requirement to conduct an annual survey of all CAT A **flexible hoses**, which includes the 8 LCVP Davit Greasing Hoses, in accordance with the guidelines detailed at the Reference. The most recent survey was carried out by HYDRASUN in Devonport during the SMP, between 24 May and 9 Jun"*

I suppose the Royal Navy Engineer could have thought that the legal team, not being engineers, would not know the difference between flexible hoses and six foot long inflexible metal rods.

Therefore, unfortunately, following the visit to HMS Ocean, the legal team were none the wiser as to what the flexible Davit hoses looked like and where on the Davit arm these flexible hoses were positioned. This was sad, as this information would have been very helpful to us, as the focus of the entire episode rested on checking the flexible Davit hoses.

## 15th June, 2012 Visit to HMS Ocean – Coroner Refuses Photographs

This latest episode was with regard to photographs requested during this visit to HMS Ocean. It appears that a person other than the Coroner made the grave error of asking for these photographs, instead of allowing the Coroner to be the one to ask for the photographs.

The offending person was treated to a public dressing down and humiliation by the Coroner in front of the Royal Navy officers and the Royal Marines.

After this, the Coroner would not allow any photographs to be taken during this visit to HMS Ocean, because he personally had not been the one verbally initiating this request for photographs.

It was not as if the photographs had not been requested, in writing and verbally, for this site visit. I shall quote from the letter to the Coroner by our legal team on 12th March, 2012 -

> **J) Site visit**
> 22) *"It is submitted that such a visit will enable the parties to gain a better understanding of the layout of the relevant areas and the specific safety needs. Any such visit would be with representatives of the MOD. At **such a visit, photographs and video footage** could be taken to further assist."*

This letter was also preparatory for the pre-Inquest of the 15th March, 2012, where the pictures at the site visit were discussed further.

We found this, too, very sad. We had lost a very good opportunity to take photographs during this important visit to HMS Ocean. Power wielding was more important than ascertaining how my son came to die.

## 15th June, 2012 Visit to HMS Ocean – Jumping onto the Wheelhouse Roof

From the documents received from the Coroner in his partial disclosure of the 22nd February, 2012, we were informed in the Royal Navy reports that all the Health and Safety faults and glitches at the time of my son's death had been rectified. They would never happen again.

It must be stressed that after analysing PO Fulton's statement, we doubted that my son had ever climbed onto the wheelhouse roof.

Nevertheless, the Royal Navy wanted to prove that my son was the maverick. My son was the one not obeying Health and Safety. All personnel climbing onto the roof of the LCVP had to have a harness and wear a hard hat. After my son's death, the Royal Navy report by Lt Cdr Hewitt stated that all had been rectified, all lessons learnt, all personnel would always wear a harness and all personnel would always wear a hard hat when climbing onto the wheelhouse roof.

Let us see how Lt Cdr Hewitt assures us that the above recommendations have been implemented -

> *"**I am satisfied that all recommendation**s from HMS Ocean's ISI* (Immediate Ship's Investigation) ***have been implemented."*** – paragraph 12

> *"DCINC's letter directs Commanding Officers to improve safety culture within their own units. DCINC writing to each CO, **gives further evidence** to the level of attention that is being given to a safety culture within the Fleet HQ and front line units ".* – paragraph 16

> *"Post the incident in HMS Ocean a significant amount of work has been commissioned and produced to identify shortfalls both within HMS Ocean and the Royal Navy as a whole. ... **I am satisfied** that their (the Immediate Ship's Investigation & SIB) **recommendations and observations have been taken accordingly."** – paragraph 17

> *"**I am satisfied** that this report has reviewed all recommendations for follow up action, and that those of greatest immediate importance **have been implemented".** – paragraph 20

Let us now return to the visit on HMS Ocean. The legal team enquired from a crew member how one would climb onto the wheelhouse roof.

The crew member promptly climbed onto the roof without a hard hat and without a harness and at the same time stating that that was how they did it all the time.

Ah, here we have the rub. Lt Cdr Hewitt's report stated that all was perfect, that lessons had been learnt, and that the mistakes and oversights of the past had been sorted. It had taken a death for them to sort it, but according to Lt Cdr Hewitt, sort it they had. According to Lt Cdr Hewitt, they had taken my son's death very seriously. According to Lt Cdr Hewitt the Royal Navy had not just tightened their Health and Safety, they had ensured this would never happen again.

We now saw before us that Lt Cdr Hewitt's report was just another Royal Navy fabrication.

## 15ᵗʰ June, 2012    Visit to HMS Ocean – the Forty Six foot drop

The legal team were able to see the sheer drop down the side of HMS Ocean to the water, possibly forty six feet (14 metres) below.

No one in his right mind would jump down from the LCVP wheelhouse roof onto the deck of the LCVP right by this sheer forty six foot drop at the edge of HMS Ocean.

In addition there was no need for my son to climb onto the wheelhouse roof to check the Davit hoses, as PO Fulton was doing the job.

The wheelhouse roof had a radar dome at the very front, and there would not have been room for two men to be on the front of the roof at the same time.

My son was the safety number whose job was to stand on the deck whilst the other man climbed the roof.

Not only would my son not climb onto the wheelhouse roof, but, according to PO Fulton, my son must have then jumped back down onto the deck right by this sheer forty six foot drop. How unlikely is this story from PO Fulton. My son would not have jumped so close to a forty six foot drop.

## 27ᵗʰ June, 2012.    Letter to Coroner – Request Photographs and Davit Hose Information

(see letter of 27th June, 2012, on the website)

Following the visit to HMS Ocean of the 15th June, 2012, and the Coroner's refusal to allow photographs, we were left with no photographs.

On the 27th June, 2012, the legal team again requested these important photographs that were vital to the Inquest.

My husband and I were spectators. We watched as the legal team, always respectful, requested information from the Coroner, never knowing how he would react. The legal team did their utmost not to anger the Coroner in their valiant efforts to unravel the mysterious circumstances of my son's death.

- The legal team requested photographs of the LCVP 'in bed', i.e. in the LCVP Bay.
- The legal team requested photographs of the LCVP in the bay taken from the dock side.
- The legal team requested photographs that would show the height between the LCVP wheelhouse roof and the top of the LCVP Bay. This is where PO Fulton said that he and my son positioned themselves. Could a man stand on the roof? Was there room to kneel?
- The legal team requested photographs of the access route to get to the LCVP. Apparently this was done via two ladders.
- The legal team requested photographs of the Davit hoses. We still did not know what they looked like, nor where they were on the Davit arm.

Why had not the Coroner requested these photographs when my son's case first landed on his desk, one and a half years earlier?

# 27th June, 2012. Letter to Coroner – Royal Navy Health and Safety Hypocrisy

(see letter of 27th June, 2012 on the website)

The visit to HMS Ocean was profitable. Amongst other things it showed once again the hypocrisy of the Royal Navy in their dealings with us.

The legal team, in their letter to the Coroner of the 27th June, 2012, pointed out their grave concern at the assertions by the Royal Navy in the Hewitt review that the recommendations made following my son's death had now been implemented.

What happened during the visit to HMS Ocean? I shall quote from the legal team's letter, page 2, under the heading *Use of safety equipment* –

*"We made a careful note of the statements that were made during the tour. One of the marines giving the tour was asked by our Counsel, in the presence of yourself and the Ministry of Defence legal team, how he would now gain access to the LCVP when it was 'in bed'. He said that he would climb up the ladder/s (squeezing through the metal hoops on one of the ladders) and, when asked about the use of a harness, he said he would do it without a harness because a harness was 'more a hindrance than a help'."*

Had not the Royal Navy told us that since my son's death all crew on HMS Ocean would always wear a hard hat and a safety harness?

What is interesting is that, following the crew member's statement, he then promptly climbed onto the wheelhouse roof without a hard hat or a safety harness.

The legal team in their letter to the Coroner point out how the crew member's action contradicts the Royal Navy's assertion that steps have been taken that a similar action would never occur again. Let me quote from their letter to the Coroner –

*"This seems to us to contradict some of the evidence that has been supplied to you. This evidence is to the effect that, **since the accident**, steps have been taken to ensure that procedures are now in place to seek to **prevent a similar accident in the future**. The evidence currently before you records that a harness and a hard hat should have been worn (Lt Cdr Brewer Aug 2010). The report of the ISI (Sept 2010: para(1)) recorded that recommendations have been implemented to avoid a repetition of the accident. You may also want to consider the Lt Cdr Hewitt review (dated 15 January 2012: paras 6, 12, 16, 17-20) which suggests that the necessary safety measures **have now been implemented**."*

Here are some of the statements made by the Royal Navy which the legal team referred to –

Lt Cdr Brewer states that my son should have worn a hard hat and a safety harness, in the last page of his report dated August, 2010 –

*"In my opinion as SHEO (Safety Health and Environment Officer) for HMS Ocean …. They were working at height and therefore **should have had a safety harness and hard hat**."*

We now come to Lt Cdr Hewitt, who firstly lists the recommendations that have been made following my son's death in paragraph 6 of his report -

> *"Aims and conclusions of the Ship's Investigation ...* **key recommendations** *that were identified within the report that required follow up action are:*
> a. *A whole ship brief should be conducted to re-educate personnel on the risks associated with working aloft and the regulations regarding the* **wearing of safety equipment.**
> b. *The requirement to* **wear a safety harness** *when working on housed LCVPs should be referred to as a specific example in SGOs (Ship's General Orders)*
> c. *A warning sign should be placed at the bottom of all ladders that provide access to workspaces greater than 2m above the deck, or lower if a risk of significant injury exists, to remind personnel of the* **requirement to wear safety harnesses** *when working aloft."*

Then we see how Lt Cdr Hewitt assures us that the above recommendations have been implemented -

> *"I am satisfied that all recommendations from HMS Ocean's ISI (Immediate Ship's Investigation) have been implemented."* – paragraph 12

> *"DCINC's letter directs Commanding Officers to improve safety culture within their own units. DCINC writing to each CO,* **gives further evidence** *to the level of attention that is being given to a safety culture within the Fleet HQ and front line units ".* – paragraph 16

> *"Post the incident in HMS Ocean a significant amount of work has been commissioned and produced to identify shortfalls both within HMS Ocean and the Royal Navy as a whole. ... I am satisfied that their (the Immediate Ship's Investigation and SIB) recommendations and observations have been taken accordingly."* – paragraph 17

> *"I am satisfied that this report has reviewed all recommendations for follow up action, and that those of greatest immediate importance* **have been implemented".** – paragraph 20

The legal team have pointed out to the Coroner the false assertions by the Royal Navy, that all the recommendations made regarding wearing a hard hat and a harness when boarding the LCVP and its wheelhouse roof have been

implemented, writing –

> *"We were concerned that, despite these statements, and the content of the Lt Cdr Hewitt review, the marine's description of how he would carry out the task, given in front of HM Coroner, the Ministry of Defence legal team and our team, suggests **little if anything has changed** in relation to working aloft on landing craft when 'in bed'."*

## RN Health and Safety – the 'Perfect' Photograph

PO Fulton had stated that both he and my son climbed onto the wheelhouse roof. It was therefore very important that we knew how much room there was between the wheelhouse roof and the top of the LCVP Bay. Could a man stand on the roof, or was there crouching room only? How much crouching room?

Our legal team requested a photograph that would show this distance. It was very important to have this photograph for my son's Inquest.

We did receive this photograph, and it was very hard not to smile at this 'perfect' Health and Safety Inquest photograph.

This photograph depicted one man crouching on the roof, and a second man standing on the deck. Both men are wearing safety harnesses. The man standing on the deck has a hard hat which he is holding under his hand. The man crouching on the roof is not wearing a hard hat. And there is the photographer to think of; is he wearing a hard hat and a safety harness?

This perfect Inquest photograph is what the Royal Navy considers to be proof positive that it has, since my son's death, implemented all the recommendations of their investigations.

Let us take a step back. What is the point of a hard hat if you are not wearing one? Let us also look at where the safety harness has been attached by the man on the roof. It has been attached on the 'ceiling' of the LCVP Bay. That means that whilst the man was climbing onto the roof and before he attached it to this position, there would be a moment in time when he was unprotected. He would have needed two attachment hooks.

And then, we must not forget the visit to HMS Ocean where the crew member climbed onto the wheelhouse roof without a hard hat and without a safety harness. And yet the Royal Navy Hewitt Review item 12 states -

*"I am satisfied that all recommendations from HMS OCEAN's ISI have been implemented"*

But this is far deeper than a 'perfect' photograph and proving that the Royal Navy Health and Safety is as perfect as their photograph. This is a suspicious death that we are dealing with. This is the heart of the matter.

My son lies in a lonely grave and the Royal Navy is only concerned with making a phoney photograph for my son's equally phoney Inquest.

# 27th June, 2012.   Letter to Coroner – Disciplinary Records

(see letter of 27th June, 2012 on the website)

The broken record continues playing. The legal team made yet another request for the Disciplinary Records of HMS Ocean. They asked for these records using a different line of attack, a different line of reasoning. We needed to have these records. I quote from their letter –

*"Records of Lt Woodhouse"*

*"One of the issues that the SIB considered during its enquiry was whether Lt Woodhouse contributed to his own death by drinking the night before he died. We are not sure whether this is an issue that will be investigated at the inquest but, in the event that it is, we would ask you to consider requesting discovery of his **disciplinary and other records**, including any instances of complaints or sanctions that were made by/against him."*

No surprises. The Coroner continued to obstruct the course of justice and denied these important records for my son's Inquest.

This is the Military Justice given to my son in the United Kingdom.

## 27ᵗʰ June, 2012.   Letter to Coroner – Relationship with PO Fulton

(see letter of 27th June, 2012)

The legal team now also asked for the Ship Hierarchy in order to try to find what the relationship was between PO Fulton and my son. Did they work in the same unit? What sort of daily contact would they have normally had?

The legal team wrote –

### Ship Hierarchy/outlay

*"For those members of the legal teams and for the Jury, we think that a description of the hierarchy of the ship at the time of the accident would assist in order to understand the chain of command. This could take the form of an organisational structure chart detailing relevant personnel involved. It could show, in particular, the relationship between Lt Woodhouse and for example PO Fulton."*

## The Precious US Navy Witness Statements

We were left with a Criminal Investigation Summary that ignored the most important, and the only independent eye witnesses - the three US Navy Witnesses.

It was left to us to piece together the last moments of my son's life before his violent fall and to take these scraps of paper and create a re-enactment of my son's last moments, as seen from the US Navy ship, the USS Mitscher, that was passing by.

As we were endeavouring to recreate what each of the different witness saw of HMS Ocean and my son's movements, there was another problem we faced. We needed to visualise sailing past HMS Ocean. We needed to have more photographs of HMS Ocean from different angles.

We received our photographs through an unexpected source. In May, 2012, HMS Ocean went up to London in preparation for the security aspect of the Olympics. Countless amateur and professional photographers took pictures of HMS Ocean from all angles and published them on line. We had our pictures.

And so we set to work putting together animation re-enactments of my son's last movements, based solely on the accounts by each of the three US Witness statements.

Each animation was under five minutes in duration and in mid-June they were sent to the legal team for their viewing and information.

These animations are available on my son's website. You must understand that we made these animations based on the only information that had been given to us by the Coroner, and we faithfully followed the statements made by each witness.

# 27th June, 2012.  Letter to Coroner – US Navy Witness – Live Inquest Conferencing

(see letter of 27th June, 2012 on the website)

On the 27the June, 2012, the legal team sent the US Navy animated re-enactments to the Coroner and to the MOD legal team. I quote below -

> *"You will be aware that Lt Woodhouse's parents have made extensive investigations into the circumstances of his death. They have supplied us with a considerable amount of information. For example, they have recently sent us clips they have made that seek to explain and demonstrate what the three US Navy witnesses saw.* **We attach these** *so you can see the very considerable lengths the family has gone to* **in an**

*effort to understand how their son died."*

And the legal team fought on. They then suggested that the US Navy witnesses be interviewed live at my son's Inquest.

> *"Given the discussion that you had with Counsel for the Ministry of Defence at the pre-inquest hearing, we have taken the liberty of investigating the possibility of the three US Navy witnesses **giving evidence to you in person."***

> *"This firm has offices in the United States and our enquiries have indicated that the US Navy would, in fact, make its personnel available to testify at your inquest given that there is at stake no issue of national security. We appreciate that the witnesses are unlikely to travel to Portsmouth for the inquest but **we would be happy to make video-conference facilities available at an office of this firm in the United States that is convenient to the US Navy and to make video-conferencing equipment available at the inquest."***

It was vital that these prime independent eye witnesses be interviewed live, in person, in order to clarify what they saw.

The legal team offered to make video-conferencing available both at the Inquest and at their offices in the US, just so that these vital witnesses could be 'present' at my son's Inquest.

## Request to Include Live US Navy Witnesses in the Inquest

(see letter of 27<sup>th</sup> June, 2012 on the website)

We take a step backwards for one moment as we think on this request by the legal team to have the three independent US Navy Witnesses interviewed live at my son's Inquest via video conferencing.

As more information was released to us concerning my son's death, the more suspicious it became. My son's investigation should have been handed over to Hampshire Constabulary immediately once the Coroner received it. It was dripping with suspicious facts. Yet the Coroner would not relinquish it.

This request by the legal team to interview the US Navy Witnesses in person is the duty of the Coroner in order to rectify at this late stage the damning omissions of SIB Wilson's investigation.

It should not have been left for the legal team to fight to obtain crucial evidence regarding a suspicious death.

## 4th July, 2012. - Coroner sets Inquest Date and Replies to Requests

Nearly two years after my son's death, the Coroner finally sets the date for my son's Inquest, 5th – 16th November, 2012.

On the same day he wrote another letter, replying to the legal team's requests contained in their letter of the 27th June, 2012.

We will now consider the Coroner's replies to some of the requests of the legal team.

**Disciplinary Records** – once again the answer was 'no'.

> *"I do not think Woodhouse's disciplinary and other records will assist in this regard and I will not be requiring them as Inquest documents."*

Top marks, though, to the legal team, for trying yet again to obtain the Disciplinary Records of HMS Ocean.

**Ship hierarchy/outlay** – the answer was no, again.

**Inquest Date** – The legal team had been informed a few days earlier that the Coroner was making arrangements for the Inquest to be some time at the beginning of November. They asked, if possible, to have the Inquest commence after my son's birthday, which was Saturday, 10th November.

The two weeks of the Inquest hearing fell on either side of my son's birthday, it being in the very middle of the two week Inquest.

The Coroner cleverly pointed out to the legal team that my son's birthday fell on the Saturday.

> *"As the clerk of Counsel for the family has been informed, the Inquest hearing will take place between 5th and 16th November 2012 in the Council Chamber, Portsmouth Guildhall. The Inquest will sit on weekdays only, except for the afternoon of the 13th November when the Council Chamber will not be available. The Inquest will not be in session on 10th November 2012 because that it is a Saturday."*

# Dismissed Animations of Three US Navy Witnesses

(see Animated Witness videos available on website)

The Coroner had been sent the Animated Witness Re-enactments by the legal team. What was the result?

The Coroner has them disqualified, and dismisses these animated re-enactments on two grounds, firstly that they were prepared by interested persons, and secondly that they represent speculation.

I quote from his letter of the 4th July, 2012 -

> *"I am grateful for sight of the DVD prepared by the woodhouse family which you sent with your letter. It may assist me in formulating questions I might want to put to witnesses. However, as it has been prepared by **interested persons** and **represents speculation** on their part about what might have happened, I do not consider it appropriate for it to be used as an Inquest document."*

By these two statements the Coroner condemned himself.

If my son's death had been investigated correctly by his men the SIB Royal Navy Police, and then by him, there would not be left one jot of speculation or suspicion in my son's death.

We then have to turn our gaze to the criminal investigation summary by SIB Royal Navy Police. This has actively and positively created new 'facts' out of thin air, misquoted witness statements, omitted vital evidence, ignored contradictory and implausible statements, and taken us way beyond the realms of speculation.

And then we have to think on Interested Persons. It is very clear that the SIB Criminal Investigation summary has been shoe-horned to fit the account of the one man with my son, PO Fulton. This man towers above them all as being the most interested person.

Yet we, the parents, on seeing that all in authority ignored the US Navy Witness statements, took it upon ourselves to bring them to life and to the attention of the Coroner. For this the animations are disqualified and all information in them is once again placed in obscurity, because we are interested persons.

The legal team sent the animations to the Coroner in order to give him another opportunity to allow a Full Middleton Inquiry into my son's death.

Yet despite being dismissed and this opportunity lost, we believe that it was due to these animated re-enactments that the Coroner changed his Inquest witness list.

# Denied Live Video Conferencing with Three US Navy Witnesses

The legal team placed such great weight on the statements of the three independent US Navy Witnesses that they offered to help provide live video conferencing facilities, both at the Inquest Court room and at whichever US city the witnesses resided in.

Let us now consider the reasons the Coroner gives for denying live video conferencing at my son's Inquest.

### Assistance from the United States Navy:

*"As I have explained on a number of occasions previously, the courtroom I will be using for the Inquest does not have video link facilities and I do not have the resources to provide such facilities. I **would be somewhat uneasy with the prospect of your firm providing such facilities to me,** particularly if the witnesses who might be using them would be doing so from **the US premises of your firm."**

On the surface, these appear such good, sound reasons.

The Coroner sees the need that the US Navy witnesses are not to be influenced in any way. This is correct, and most easy to achieve. The US

Navy had done their utmost to help the UK in all they required. It would have been very easy to request a military 'chaperone', or two, or three, or ten, however many the Coroner thought necessary, to ensure that these live witnesses were under no duress by the law firms of our legal team during the live video conferencing in the Inquest.

We must not forget that the objective of an Inquest is to *'discover the facts of the death'*. I quote below from section 8.1 of Ministry of Justice Guide to Coroner Services

https://www.gov.uk/government/uploads/system/uploads/attachment_data/file/363879/guide-to-coroner-service.pdf

> *"An inquest is different from other types of court hearing because there is no prosecution or defence. **The purpose of the inquest is to discover the facts of the death.** This means that the coroner (or Jury) cannot find a person or organisation criminally responsible for the death. However if evidence is found that suggests someone may be to blame for the death the coroner can pass all the evidence gathered to the police or Crown Prosecution Service."*

We have therefore ascertained that an Inquest is a fact-finding process, where all the parties have a common goal – to uncover the facts and events surrounding the death, and not to apportion blame.

The legal team, in offering vital video conferencing facilities, were doing their utmost to help the Inquest to discover, and to uncover, the facts of my son's death.

## Three US Navy Witnesses - The questionnaires

After dismissing the Animations of the US Navy Witness accounts, the Coroner informs the legal team that he will be asking the MOD to contact the US Navy witnesses in order to put questions to them.

This was a huge breakthrough, though it was nowhere near good enough. Despite this breakthrough, it was still deplorable that it took the presence of a legal team to fight the Coroner in order to obtain some more information.

> *"**As I have explained on a number of occasions** previously, the courtroom I will be using for the Inquest does not have video*

*link facilities and I do not have the resources to provide such facilities. I would be **somewhat uneasy** with the prospect of your firm providing such facilities to me, particularly if the witnesses who might be using them would be doing so from the US premises of your firm.*

*Your knowledge of the procedures of the US Navy **is clearly greater than mine** – and, in the light of what has been provided to me, **greater than that of the Ministry of Defence**. I have not been provided with any report or video from the US Navy. If they exist, I would now expect the Ministry to make enquiries and supply them to me.*

*The Ministry of Defence is making enquiries as to whether the **US Navy personnel can be asked to provide further statements** and this seems to me to be the most practical way of dealing with question of their evidence. I will be providing the Ministry with a list of specific questions I would like them to answer in their statements. If there are any questions you would like to suggest should be put to them, please let me have them at the earliest opportunity for my consideration."*

And so we got to work preparing suggested questions and diagrams for the US Navy witnesses.

## Preparing the Questionnaires

We had this opportunity to put forward suggested questionnaires for the three independent US Navy witnesses.

Formulating the questions was not an easy undertaking, bearing in mind that we could not interview them face to face.

There was the thought that the witnesses might not be alive; they might not even be still serving in the US Navy. What about their memory, their recollection of my son's last movements? It was now July, 2012, nearly two years after they saw the incident.

There were many things we needed to know. We needed to know the position of each witness at the time they saw my son fall. We needed to know the position of my son on the LCVP. What was the distance between USS Mitscher and HMS Ocean? What speed was USS Mitscher travelling?

Were there any obstructions blocking the view of the US Navy witnesses?

We also needed to ask each individual witness further questions regarding their specific accounts. With Witness 1, Philippines, we needed to know where he saw the man in white, and the mystery regarding the feet. What feet? Where were they? Why could he only see the feet?

With Witness 2, Charleston, we needed to know where he saw the man in white walking. Where was the man in blue?

Witness 3 Los Angeles' statement was very clear, he having also provided us diagrams to back his statement, so these questionnaires would be asking him to confirm the position of my son that he drew for us two years previously.

The questionnaires represented an enormous amount of work, of discussion, of thought, by the legal team and us. All parties worked hard to get these right, as the task was very difficult indeed.
The completed questionnaires were sent off to the Coroner at the end of July, 2012.

(see the website)

## 18th August, 2012 – Coroner Amends Questionnaires and Sends Them Off

About three weeks later on the 18th August, 2012, the legal team were informed that the Coroner had finished perusing and amending our questionnaires, and had sent off his version to the MOD to be sent to their counterparts in the USA.

I understand that the US military could not have been more helpful, as they located the concerned parties and arranged for them to answer the questionnaires.

From the family, we would like to say thank you for helping us uncover the many suspicious events surrounding my son's death.

I have placed the Coroner's amended questionnaires in the website for information. I compared the two questionnaires to see what amendments he had made, and I noticed that he just removed questions. On the website I have placed a document of the original questions showing the statements and questions that were removed, highlighted in yellow.

# 12th September, 2012 - Inquest Schedule Witness List Arrives

On the 12th September, 2012, the legal team received the Inquest Schedule Witness List from the Coroner.

This list set out the days that the Coroner would preside at my son's Inquest, and detailed which witnesses would appear in person, and which witnesses would have their statements read out (Rule 37 statements), on each day. See the full schedule on the web site.

Looking at the schedule, I was struck with how little time was set aside to look into the facts surrounding my son's suspicious death.

The Ministry of Justice Guide to Coroner Services points out that the objective of an Inquest is to *'discover the facts of the death'*. I quote below from section 8.1 of Ministry of Justice Guide to Coroner Services

https://www.gov.uk/government/uploads/system/uploads/attachment_data/file/363879/guide-to-coroner-service.pdf

> *"An inquest is different from other types of court hearing because there is no prosecution or defence. **The purpose of the inquest is to discover the facts of the death**. This means that the coroner (or Jury) cannot find a person or organisation criminally responsible for the death. However if evidence is found that suggests someone may be to blame for the death the coroner can pass all the evidence gathered to the police or Crown Prosecution Service."*

Of the six and a half days set aside for the Inquest, only two full days had been set aside to discuss the facts surrounding my son's death, and these two days included medical reports.

Let us examine this Witness Schedule prepared by the Coroner.

### Day 1
There are a total of five witnesses; two are concerning my son's autopsy and wounds, and the third concerns my son's medical history.
That leaves two vital witnesses, the SIB, Military Police witness, and PO Fulton, the man with my son at the time of his fatal fall.

**Day 2**

On this day we have PO Fulton appearing again, and then ten witnesses. Of the ten witnesses, three witnesses were the Lieutenants who were out with my son the night before, three were the vital US Navy witness statements that were to be read out, and three were witnesses on the LCVPs in the water below at the time. The last witness called, MNE Tait, gave information on how a LCVP is supposed to operate.

Then tucked away, on Day 5, we have the live witness, Lt Cdr Pickles, who together with Lt Cdr Lucocq and WO Clapham (who were not witnesses) conducted the ISI (Immediate Ship's Investigation), and then with Lt Cdr Lucocq he conducted the SSI (Supplementary Ship's Investigation).

The rest of the Inquest witnesses concerned Health and Safety matters.

# The Weightier Matters of Law and Justice

The allocation of just two days to discuss the events surrounding my son's death, as opposed to the rest of the days given over to Health and Safety, and then Jury deliberations, showed very clearly the importance placed on my son's suspicious death. It showed very clearly the importance placed on the weightier matters of law and justice. It showed very clearly the contempt that the Coroner placed on the objective of an Inquest, to 'discover the facts'.

But we must not forget, that as far as the Coroner was concerned, there was absolutely no need at all to 'discover the facts', for he himself had already decided that there was nothing suspicious about my son's death. I quote -

> "I have no evidence before me to give me reasonable grounds to suspect that either Lt Woodhouse was unlawfully killed or took his own life."

And we must not forget the equally confident statement of Ben Collins, the MOD barrister, who in like manner said –

> "No evidence whatsoever has emerged from any of the investigations undertaken to date to suggest that foul play is a possibility in this case."

And none can forget Deputy Provost SIB Wilson, who summed up his Criminal Investigation with the statement –

> "Any foul play would have been identified. Simply, there was

*none which could be found."*

United, they denied my son an honest investigation into his death.

## SIB Witness – not the author of the Investigation

Another disturbing item of the Coroner's Witness Schedule was that he had changed the SIB Witness once again. This was the third Inquest Witness list we had received, on the 12th September, 2012, and we noticed that the Coroner had changed this important SIB witness from Lt Cdr Wilson, the author of the investigation, to Lt Cdr Day.

JOSHUA WOODHOUSE – WITNESS SCHEDULE

5th November 2012 – 16th November 2012

(W) = Witness  (S) = Rule 37 Statements

Day 1 (05.11.12)

1)  Lt Cmdr Day (W)

2)  Dr Borek (W)

3)  Aurelian NICOLAESCU (Medical Examiner – Florida) (S)

4)  Surgeon Capt CARNE (S)

5)  PO FULTON (W) **(Also required for Day 2)**

Day 2 (06.11.12)

6)  PO COTTAM (W)

7)  ET MYERS (W)

8)  MNE TAIT (S)

9)  CPO CONNELLY (W)

10) 3 USN PERSONNEL (S)

11) Lt HAYES (W)

12) Lt PITMAN (W)

13) Lt PEARSON (W)

Lt Cdr Day, whom he planned to call to explain the SIB Criminal Investigation into my son's death, was not the author of the SIB Criminal Investigation.

One would have thought that this vital SIB witness should have been the author of the investigation himself, Lt Cdr Wilson, Deputy Provost, SIB Military Police.

Nonetheless, based on our experience of the Coroner's actions to constantly blockade any attempts by the legal team to obtain an honest Inquest for my son, it should not have been a surprise to me.

Let us go through a few imaginary scenarios, where our barrister would be putting the following questions to Lt Cdr Day:

Q   "Was there a re-enactment?"
A   "I don't know, Sir. I did not conduct the investigation. I am sure we can try to find out for you. If it was not done, there must have been a good reason."

Q   "Why were the US Navy Witnesses not interviewed?"
A   "I don't know, Sir. I didn't write the report. There must have been a good reason."

Q   "Did you not find PO Fulton's account full of contradictions and strange?"
A   "I am unable to answer, Sir. I didn't write the report."

Q   "Why was the statement by Lt Lisa Pitman misquoted?"
A   "I don't know, Sir. I didn't write the report."

Q   "Did you not think it strange that PO Fulton said Lt Woodhouse was at the front and yet one US Navy witness saw him clearly at the back?"
A   "I am unable to answer, Sir. I didn't write the report."

And all this time we must remember that the MOD Barrister would be objecting at the absurdity of the questions.

And we must not forget the Coroner. He, too, would interject with the apparent reasonable request "Would the legal team please ask questions that are relevant and that we can get answers for. This is proving to be a waste of counsel's time".

# The Final Pre-Inquest Hearing

There were now just over two months till my son's Inquest. The Coroner set another pre-Inquest hearing for the 25th September, 2012.

There were still outstanding items.

The Legal team continued to ask for the original SIB report, and not just the summary of the report. SIB Wilson mentions this original report

> Item 38 states -
> *"The receipt of the US statements meant that OIC SIB was able to conclude with the honestly held belief, that having established the facts and gathered all available evidence, Lt Woodhouse had not been the victim of an intentional act or suicide. The investigation then concentrated on all other matters relating to the incident which **are contained within RNP SIB report 100025/10.**"*

We never did receive this.

The legal team asked for the references that backed up statements made in important documents, like the reports by Lt Cdr Hewitt, Wheeler, Harris, Sykes-Gelder, and Reynolds. It is all very well making statements without having the records that prove whether or not the conclusions are correct.

The Legal team were asking for supporting plans and pictures of the LCVP, and the ship, HMS Ocean, and 'scene' photographs.

Had the responses been received from the US Navy Witnesses?
We still did not know what a Davit hose looked like, or where it was situated. What Glossary of Terms would the coroner use for the Inquest? The Navy were very good at using acronyms for almost everything, and even the LCVP itself needed to be explained.

What photographs and plans would be available for the Inquest?

(see letter to Coroner on the website)

The following day the legal team attended the last pre-Inquest before my son's Inquest, and discussions were made concerning the points mentioned in the letter to the Coroner. The Coroner and the MOD agreed to supply some further photographs, plans, and the 'scene' photographs mentioned in the SIB document, as well as a Glossary of Terms. As for the other documents requested, these would not be supplied, and cross-examining the witnesses was the only option.

With regard to the US Navy further witness statements, the Legal Team were informed that two of the US sailors were in deployment in a base near Portsmouth, UK, and would be available for questioning by the SIB in person.

Two years too late.

## The Royal British Legion Lawyer Punished

At the first pre-Inquest the Coroner took the RBL lawyer to task, and asked him what he was doing at the Inquest. What was his role; why was he involved? This was new to the Coroner. And truly it was new.

The month before my son died, due to the huge outcry from military families suffering shamefully at the hands of Coroners in the United Kingdom, the Royal British Legion had started an Independent Inquest Advice service.

It was only because of this united legal team, consisting of the Royal British Legion, the London barrister, and the London law firm, that the Coroner had to answer some questions.   It was only because of the enormous amount of work of this united legal team that such headway had been made in trying to obtain any scrap of justice for my son.

What did the Coroner do this time?  For no apparent reason the Coroner banned the RBL lawyer from sitting with the legal team during my son's Inquest.

The RBL lawyer was only allowed to sit alone at my son's Inquest. This was to humiliate the Royal British Legion representative, for he knew that they were the root reason that we had any scrap of a chance at my son's Inquest.

## US Navy Witness Questionnaires Received

The Legal Team were busy with correspondence between the Coroner and their offices, regarding all the important final preparations for the Inquest, which included the selection of the Jury.  How was this to be done; what criteria would be used for selecting the panel, and which persons were going to be involved?

Preparations for travel and accommodation had been finalised, and we were all set to travel to Portsmouth.

Then on the 26th October, 2012, ten days before the start of my son's Inquest, we received three US Navy Supplementary Witness statements.

But there was a surprise waiting for us. The third witness statement was not that of Witness 3, Los Angeles. This must be a brand new witness, which we had never been informed existed. I shall call him US Navy Witness 4. In addition, this fourth US Navy Witness stated that he had made his first witness statement in August, 2010. Where was this original witness statement? Why had we not received this statement in February, 2012, when the Coroner released the 'disclosure' documents?

This raised a great deal of unease.

Where was the supplementary statement from Witness 3, Los Angeles? This is the witness who saw the entire episode from start to finish. This is the witness who saw my son comfortably standing at the back of the LCVP and not jumping from the front of the wheelhouse roof, as PO Fulton states. This is the witness who carefully made sketches for us of my son's position, and of my son's fall. Where was his second set of witness questions and answers?

Had the Coroner and the MOD wished to deceive us again by parading the new Witness 4 as Witness 3, Los Angeles?

The legal team immediately requested the missing Supplementary Witness Statement for Witness 3, Los Angeles. See their letter of the 30th October, 2012 on the website.

The supplementary witness statement of Witness 3, Los Angeles, was given to us lunchtime, on the 5th November, 2012, the day my son's Inquest commenced.

## The US Navy Witness Overview

We were sent three US Navy Witness statements on the 26th October, 2012. On the 31st October, 2012, we were informed that these witness statements had to be recalled, due to the bungling of the MOD, as the documents were unredacted. In the confusion of deleting emails and original documents, and in the confusion of preparing for my son's Inquest in a few days, I have found it hard to locate every detail of each of these prize statements. (see the web site)

| Witnesses | Original Statement | Further Statement |
|---|---|---|
| 1. Witness 1, Phillippines | Date - 12th August, 2010<br>Place - NCIS FO Norfolk, VA<br>(Naval Criminal INvestigation Service) | Date - 27th September, 2012<br>Place - Navy Recruiting District,<br>Minneapolis |
| 2. Witness 2, Charleston | Date - 13th August, 2010<br>Place - NCIS FO Norfolk, VA<br>(Naval Criminal INvestigation Service) | Date - 27th September, 2012<br>Place - NCIS Resident Unit Monterey,<br>Naval Postgraduate School, Building 436<br>-Room 129 |
| 3. Witness 3, Los Angeles | Date - 25th August, 2010<br>Place - NCIS FO Norfolk, VA<br>(Naval Criminal INvestigation Service) | *Only received 5th November, 2012, first day of inquest.*<br>*Date - Unsure?* |
| 4. Witness 4 | | Date - 15th October, 2012<br>Place - The offices of th RNP SIB |

When we finally received the second account by Witness 3, Los Angeles, on the first day of my son's Inquest, we found that there was no new information that changed our understanding of his very clear initial account written on the 25th August, 2010. Witness 3, Los Angeles, confirmed my son's position standing on the deck of the LCVP and behind the wheelhouse.

Reading the account by the new US Navy Witness 4 we noticed that he did not see my son fall but merely heard the sound when my son's head hit the wheelhouse roof.

The original accounts from Witness 1, Philippines, and Witness 2, Charleston, left us asking many questions. Feet, what feet, and where? Why only feet? The man in white, where was he? Was this my son Joshua? The man in blue? Where was the man in blue? Was this PO Fulton?

We now had their second set of statements, which answered these questions, confirmed the account by Witness 3, Los Angeles, and gave us more valuable information. There were men working on a moveable platform in the LCVP Bay area where my son fell from. Why had this information been hidden from us?

## The US Navy Witness Locations

I shall now analyse the further US Navy witness statements and show how they helped us put together the puzzle pieces of my son's last moments. I shall show how they all contradicted the account by PO Fulton, who said that my son fell from the top of the wheelhouse roof, and that he fell from the front of the wheelhouse.

Where was each witness standing on USS Mitscher as she passed HMS Ocean on Friday, 6th August, 2010?

Question 2c of the questionnaire, put to each witness, asked

*"Where were you on USS MITSCHER? - please mark with an X on Diagram 1"*

I have shown the answers to this question in the picture below where I have given each witness a number –

- Witness 1 – Philippines
- Witness 2 – Charleston
- Witness 3 – Los Angeles
- Witness 4 – the new witness

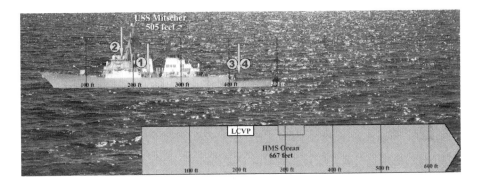

Witnesses 3 and 4 are both placed side by side on the fan tail of USS Mitscher.

USS Mitscher was travelling at about 3 – 5 knots, and in the diagram above I have shown the position of USS Mitscher at the time my son actually fell. Witness 3, Los Angeles, and 4 are directly opposite him when he fell from the back of the LCVP, in the LCVP Bay.

## A Man in White Shorts

Witness 2, Charleston, tells us about the man in white that he saw walking on the flight deck. Was this my son? In his second witness statement he tells us that this man in white is wearing shorts and knee socks. This is not my son. My son was wearing white overalls.

What is interesting is that Witness 2, Charleston, sees this man walking immediately above the LCVP bay, which my son was in.

> *"I looked across the harbour and saw a man in white shorts and knee socks on the flight deck of HMS Ocean."*

Witness 2, Charleston, has drawn the position of the man in white in the figure below. This is another confirmation that the man in white that he saw was not my son.

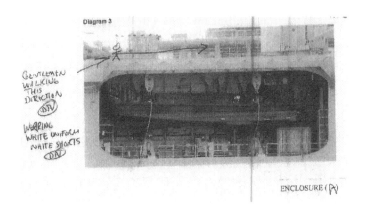

## The Man in Blue

Witness 2, Charleston, tells us that there was a man in blue in the vicinity of where the man fell. We were very interested to hear about this man in blue. Was this PO Fulton? Where did he see this man in blue?

In his first statement he had said

> *"When I first saw the guy fall, I thought that the Brits might be playing a practical joke. I thought they might have thrown a dummy overboard. Another reason why I thought it was a dummy was that after the man fell, I saw another sailor*

*onboard HMS OCEAN walking slowly in the vicinity of where the man fell. The sailor was wearing blue and he did not appear to be in any hurry."*

He tells us in his 2nd statement

*"Sometime after hearing the thud, maybe one or two minutes later, I saw a man in blue nonchalantly **walking on the flight deck** without a safety device. The man appeared to be in no hurry. I have marked the position of the man in blue and the direction he was walking on Diagram 3 of Enclosure B, which has been attached to this statement. I do not remember exactly where the man in blue walked to or where he went next. Around this time, USS MITSCHER was out to sea and I did not observe anything else that occurred about HMS OCEAN."*

This was very important to us, to find out whether this was PO Fulton that he saw. Now we knew that this man in blue, that he saw walking after my son's fall, was not PO Fulton.

## There were Men Working in the LCVP Area

Witness 2, Charleston, tells us a vital bit of information. He tells us that there were men working in the LCVP area, very close to my son's position at the time of his fall.

*"I am not sure exactly which parts of the LCVP bay I could see, but I did see sailors on some platform appearing to be painting or engaging in some other activity. The LCVP bay was*

*approximately the same height as USS MITSCHER's bridge wing (where I was)."*

*"I looked across the harbour and saw a man in white shorts and knee socks on the flight deck of HMS Ocean.* **The man in white appeared to be looking down from the flight deck toward the individuals on the platform (I don't remember if the platform was a boat or scaffolding-like structure).** *The man in white was pointing and waving his hand at the individuals on the platform, appearing to instruct them.* **The main in white seemed to be some kind of supervisor.** *I have marked the path of where the man in white walked on Diagram 3 of Enclosure A"*

I have therefore placed the position of the platform, with the men on it, near to where Witness 2, Charleston, has positioned the man in white on the flight deck, see my diagram below.

As Witness 2, Charleston, mentions more than one sailor, I have taken the liberty to draw two sailors on the platform, both sitting on the platform. I have dressed these men in white, but in all probability they would be ratings who would have been dressed in blue shorts or blue overalls.

**Figure** - showing two sailors working on a platform, whilst the officer on the flight deck is supervising them.

# Witness 1, Philippines – What Feet? Where are the Feet? Why only Feet?

The account by Witness 2, Charleston, of men working on a moveable platform, in the top part of the LCVP Bay, explains the mystery of the feet.

Witness 1, Philippines, was asked -

> Q 3a – Where did you see the man in white clothes sitting? – please mark with an X on diagram 3.

> **Ans 3a - I saw legs hanging top part of the bay, midde portion of the bay. And not physically on top of the LCAC.**

> Q 3b – Why could you only see the feet of the man in white clothes?

> **Ans 3b Because he looks like he/she was sitting and the upper portion of the body is not visible.**

It is also interesting to note what Witness 1, Philippines, confirms this in answer to question 2e –

> Q 2e v) – How clearly could you see the movement of people on the LCVP?

> **Ans 2e (v) I did not see anybody in the LCVP (boat). But I did saw a feet hanging in the upper part of the bay**

We have therefore ascertained that Witness 1, Philippines, has placed feet dangling from the top of the LCVP Bay. It is not possible for any man to be standing or sitting in this position normally.

However, if there is a moveable platform, as that described by Witness 2, Charleston, where sailors were conducting some work, this is the only explanation that accounts for the dangling feet at the top of the LCVP Bay.

# The Men on the Platform

Why were the men on the moveable platform in the LCVP Bay area?

The diagram below (Figure 8), shows the cross section of the LCVP Bay, which we have made, following our observations from the Family Day in June, 2010. What is interesting is that there is a recess below the flight deck, where one is able to walk. In this recess one is able to view the sea below, as the floor of this recess consists of a metal grill. There is also a safety net around the flight deck, so that it is perfectly safe to walk or sit in this recess.

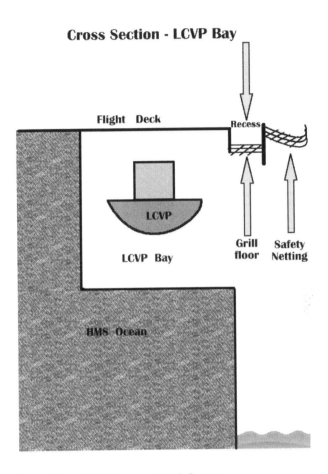

A cross section of the LCVP Bay on HMS Ocean

Picture showing the safety netting and the grill floor of the recess

There is another point to bear in mind. Witness 1, Philippines, tells us that he only saw feet. He did not see the body of the man owning the feet at that moment in time. Therefore the owner of the feet could have been wearing blue or could have been wearing white.

*Q 3b – Why could you only see the feet of the man in white clothes?*

**Ans 3b Because he looks like he/she was sitting and the upper portion of the body is not visible.**

If the sailors who were seen working on the platform were in the Royal Navy, then they would be dressed in blue, if they were ratings, and white, if they were officers. It is probable that these sailors were ratings, and therefore dressed in blue. I have obtained some photographs from a newspaper in Jacksonville showing ratings wearing blue shorts and shirt, blue shorts only, or blue overalls, at the time that HMS Ocean was in Jacksonville in 2010. See url below.

http://photos.jacksonville.com/mycapture/folder.
asp?event=1055628&CategoryID=62882&ListSubAlbums=

# The Man in White Falling

We are all agreed that the man in white falling was my son, and not anyone else.

Witness 1, Philippines, saw a man in white falling. Witness 2, Charleston, saw a man in white falling. Witness 3, Los Angeles, saw a man in white falling.

We have ascertained that Witness 2, Charleston, first saw a completely different man in white shorts and knee socks, walking on the flight deck.

Witness 2, Charleston, looked away and then saw my son falling. Witness 2, Charleston, made the assumption that the man falling was the same man that he had just seen walking on the flight deck, wearing white shorts and knee socks.

We have also ascertained that Witness 1, Philippines, saw feet dangling at the top of the LCVP Bay. This can be none other than the feet of the sailors on the moveable platform.

Witness 1, Philippines, then looks again and sees my son falling. Like Witness 2, Charleston, he also made the assumption that the feet he saw belonged to the man whom he now saw falling.

Also bear in mind that by now USS Mitscher has moved on; both Witness 2, Charleston, and Witness 1, Philippines, are no longer looking straight in front of them, but are looking behind.

At the time of my son's fall, there is only one witness who is looking directly in front at my son, and this is Witness 3, Los Angeles.

## Men Working on the Side of HMS Ocean

There are quite a few interesting points to mention.

This is the first that we had heard that men were working at the side of HMS Ocean at the time of my son's fall. Also, they were not just working at the side of HMS Ocean far, far, away, but in the very vicinity of the LCVP Bay.

Why was this kept so quiet in SIB Wilson's two Investigation summaries? Why was it not mentioned in the ISI and the SSI?

Were any of these men interviewed? Did these men on the moving platform see PO Fulton and my son on the LCVP, as they were inspecting the Davit hoses?

We can see from the timing of the sighting of the moveable platform, to the time of my son's fall, that all these people were in very close contact.

Was anything done to confirm whether PO Fulton's account was true or not? If the men were on the moving platform when, according to PO Fulton, both he and my son were on the wheelhouse roof, then these men would have seen my son, and possibly conversed with him, as they were within a few feet of each other.

It was also very noticeable that during the Inquest, one of the witnesses, Lt Cdr Brewer, let slip that there were men working on HMS Ocean at the time of my son's fall. His reaction after making that statement was a giveaway that he should not have let that slip. It confirmed to me that there had been a concerted effort by all parties to hide the fact that there were workmen in close proximity to my son at the time of his fall.

## No US Navy Witnesses Saw my Son on the Wheelhouse Roof

Having received the three US Navy Supplementary Witness Statements, let us reconsider the conclusion of SIB Wilson.

In Item 37 RN SIB Investigation Process he states -

*"Information was also received on 11 Aug 10 through The United States Naval Criminal Investigation Service (NCIS) that there were potential witnesses to the incident who had been on board the USS Mitscher, which had been departing the naval base at the time of the incident.* **Statements were obtained which describe how Lt Woodhouse had been seen to slide down from the bridge roof of the LCVP** *and lose his footing as he reached the next level. He was seen to make a grab for the handrail or stanchion before falling off the landing craft. No one else was seen to be involved."*

Where did SIB Wilson get this from?  Let us see:

Witness 1, Philippines, said –

**"I noticed a man sitting on top an LCAC.** *He was wearing white clothes. At first, all I could see was his feet. He was by himself. I saw him slide down the LCAC to the next level, but he lost his balance. I saw him attempt to grab something to regain his balance, but he was unsuccessful. I saw him fall off the LCAC, bit I did not see him land. I did hear a very loud noise that sounded like a loud "boom."*

Witness 3, Los Angeles, drew diagrams of my son standing on the deck of the LCVP and behind the wheelhouse.  He stated –

*"I noticed* **he was standing** *on one of OCEAN's landing crafts in a well deck.* **He was on the aft end.** *I saw him grab a stanchion/part"* (the hand rail) *"of the landing craft, and he appeared to try to proceed to the port side of the craft using the stanchion as leverage/handle. "*
**"He appeared to be comfortable doing what he was doing he was not tentative in his actions or motions.** *He was only using one hand, and I believe it was his right hand."*

And then we have Witness 2, Charleston, who said that he saw a man walking on the flight deck

*"I noticed a man in white clothes walking along the edge of the flight deck."*

And from these three US Navy Witness statements, SIB Wilson, authoritatively says *"**Statements were obtained which describe how Lt Woodhouse had been seen to slide down from the bridge roof of the LCVP**"*

There is only one 'witness' who said that my son was on the wheelhouse roof, and that witness was PO Fulton, the only man with my son.

Witness 1, Philippines, mentioned feet, just feet; at first all I could see was feet. This is very strange. Why could he only see feet? Why only feet? Where was the rest of the body? Instead of doing his job and investigating this strange statement, SIB Wilson, used this as a wonderful opportunity to manipulate the statements and say, from his great position of trust and responsibility, that the US Navy witness statements

*"describe how Lt Woodhouse had been seen to slide down from the bridge roof of the LCVP"*

Now we want to see what Witness 1, Philippines, tells us regarding the position of the feet in these additional witness statements -

*Q 3a – Where did you see the man in white clothes sitting? – please mark with an X on diagram 3.*

***Ans 3a - I saw legs hanging top part of the bay, midde portion of the bay. And not physically on top of the LCAC.***

We have also seen where he has drawn the position of these feet. They are positioned where my son could never be. My son was walking comfortably on the deck of the LCVP, and behind the wheelhouse.

PO Fulton is the only 'witness' who says my son was on the wheelhouse roof.

# Where did my Son Land?

The LCVP (NM), on which my son landed, was directly beneath the LCVP on which my son was standing. In addition, the wheelhouses of each of the

LCVPs were exactly aligned.

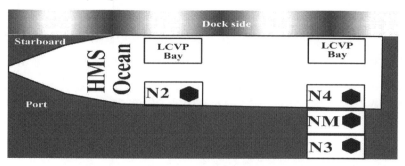

Below is the picture taken at the time of my son's fall to show the exact position of the two wheelhouses in the water below.

We know that my son fell and landed, hitting his head on the front of the wheelhouse NM.

But we have an interesting fact. Both Witness 1, Philippines, and Witness 3, Los Angeles, state that my son did not fall straight downwards. They both state that Joshua's body was propelled forwards, towards the front of HMS Ocean. Due to the swinging motion resulting from his holding onto the hand rail after receiving a blow from behind, Joshua's body was propelled forwards towards the front of HMS Ocean.

Witness 1, Philippines, in answer to Question 3 c draws the path he saw my son fall -

*Q 3c – Please draw the path of the man in white clothes as he slid down the LCAC on Diagram 3*

***Ans 3c He slid down in slight angle from where he is sitting down to the top portion of the LCAC. As marked in the diagram.***

The pictures below show Diagram 3

**Figure 20**: showing the path that Witness 1, Philippines, says he saw Joshua falling

**Figure 21:** this is the same as Figure 20 above, this time with the path highlighted in yellow

You will notice that the path is not straight down. It is at an angle, and to confirm this angle, he writes in Question 3c –

*"He slid down in a **slight angle** from where he is sitting down to the top portion of the LCAC. As marked in the diagram."*

We must not forget that Witness 1, Philippines, believes that the man in white is related to the feet that he saw; therefore the starting position is shown where he saw the feet. In addition, USS Mitscher has moved forward, so that Witness 1, Philippines, is no longer directly in front of the LCVP Bay. Witness 1, Philippines, is looking behind him.

In the same way we see that the path that Witness 3, Los Angeles, shows is not straight downwards, but propelled forwards towards the front of the wheelhouse below, at an angle.

We see the initial drawings that Witness 3, Los Angeles, made, that show my son's body moving forwards.

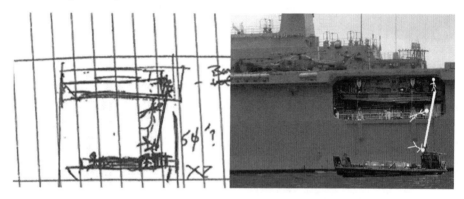

Therefore as both Witness 1, Philippines, and Witness 3, Los Angeles, tell us that my son's body moved forwards at an angle and did not fall straight down, we can calculate his starting position, seeing as we know his end position.

My son's head first hit the front of the wheelhouse of LCVP NM, which was in the water below. As my son did not fall straight down, his starting position can only have been from behind the wheelhouse of LCVP N4.

This confirms the account by Witness 3, Los Angeles, who saw my son standing comfortably on the deck of LCVP N4, and behind the wheelhouse.

This contradicts PO Fulton's account, which states that my son was not only on the top of the wheelhouse roof, but at the front of the wheelhouse of LCVP N4. These statements are not verified by any of the independent US Navy witnesses.

# And the Jury?

As we had analysed these further US Navy Witness statements, and as we were thinking of the approach of my son's Inquest in just a few days, our thoughts turned to the Jury.

What would the Jury make of all the US Navy Witness statements? What could they make of these US Navy Witness statements?

The Coroner had ensured that they were allotted to the category of 'Rule 37 Statements'. Statements that he deemed of such minor importance that he relegated them to 'Rule 37 Statements', that are only to be read out in court.

With these US Navy Witness statements only read out, how could the Jury possibly pick up the great import of what they contained?

We had brought these statements to life. We had dug up drawings, plans, photographs. We had done countless imaginary re-enactments; we had studied and worked hard to bring these statements to life. How could the Jury possibly realise the full import of these statements if they were just read out at the Inquest? Read out like a boring, jumbled, scientific document. How could they imagine what the witnesses saw, and what the witnesses were trying to tell them?

Would the Jury be able to pick up that all these statements contradicted PO Fulton's statements? Would the Jury realise that these statements contradicted the unsubstantiated Criminal Investigation carried out by SIB Wilson?

Add to this the fact that the legal team were forbidden from putting any questions to PO Fulton that at all touched on 'Foul Play'.

# Meeting the Full Legal Team in London

Friday, 2nd November, 2012.

We were invited to meet the entire legal team, in London, on the Friday before my son's Inquest.

We were very conscious of the great amount of time that the legal team had already put towards Joshua's Inquest, all given freely and generously and wholeheartedly. Thank you.

And they were generous in deed, and not just on paper. I do not think we knew the half of the time they gave to my son's Inquest, which they all gave genuinely and not begrudgingly.

We were aware that even giving us this Friday evening was yet another sacrifice that they gladly made. Thank you.

And we were treated as if we were important, which we are not. You would not have known that we were not high flying, paying customers. It was very noticeable that we were not treated as yet another charity case that one manfully endures, in an attempt to win the praise of men. Quite the reverse. The entire legal team treated us as if our son was part of their family, as if they were doing it for their own kith and kin.

And so the meeting began, and we were handed three large files that had been compiled just for the Inquest. An enormous amount of work had gone into preparing these, and they were just the tip of the iceberg.

We shall not forget that first meeting and the huge impression it made on us. We shall not forget.

## The Inquest Statements

I have used the Inquest audio tape recordings to quote the statements made during my son's Inquest.

At times, it has been very difficult to hear every word accurately. I have therefore referenced the origin of the statement on the audio tape, using the format below, and would invite readers to listen to the Inquest themselves. In addition the times can be a few seconds or minutes out due to the electronic variation of the software playing back the Inquest audio tapes.

Tape number - hours : minutes : seconds

e.g. Tape 3 – 01:24:00          refers to Tape 3 on location 1 hour, 24 minutes, and 0 seconds

The Inquest tape recordings and our Inquest Transcripts are located on the web site.

## The Revised Witness List with SIB Wilson as Live Witness

A few days before the Inquest we found out that the Coroner had changed the SIB witness.

The SIB witness was now to be Lt Cdr Geoff Wilson, Deputy Provost SIB Military Police, the very man who had written the two important SIB documents. The very man who had carried out the investigation into my son's death.

This is the way it should have been right from the start. But things are not as they should be when it comes to Military Justice.

## The Inquest     5th – 16th November, 2012.

Finally, two years three months after my son's death, the Inquest commences.

The Coroner chose the Portsmouth Guildhall to hold my son's Inquest. A fine, stately setting.

By the wall with the large windows was the great judgment seat on which the Coroner would sit as he presided over his Inquest.

On the opposite wall were large wooden framed areas recording the names of previous members of the Council holding mayoral office through the years.

Immediately in front of the Coroner's judgment seat was an open area with a table, where the Coroner's Officer controlled the tape recordings of the Inquest, and where the files and paper work relating to the Inquest were located.

Surrounding this open area were seats.

The Jury sat to the left of the Coroner, in line with his judgment seat, facing the wooden panelled wall. Initially no-one sat to the right of the Coroner, but from day two the Royal Navy witnesses were moved there.

Siting directly opposite the Coroner were the two legal teams. The MOD team sat on the right and our legal team on the left.

The RBL lawyer sat solitarily behind our legal team. This was so as not to offend the Coroner, who would probably have thrown him out had he disobeyed his orders not to sit with our legal team.

We sat slightly to the left of the Coroner, looking towards the open area with the table where the Coroner's Officer sat.

In front of us we noticed two men in uniform. These must be none other than PO Fulton and SIB Wilson.

In keeping with this grand setting, the Coroner made his entrance with black legal robes flowing behind him. We assumed this was common practice, but were informed by the legal team that it was not.

## Request for the Missing US Navy Witness Statement

Once the Coroner arrived, he commenced the Inquest by asking the barristers from the two legal teams whether they wished to raise any issues before he brought the Jury in.

Our Barrister was very concerned that we should be given the Supplementary Statement from US Navy Witness 3, Los Angeles. This was the clearest US Navy witness, and the only one who had witnessed the entire episode from start to finish. When the legal team realised that this prime witness supplementary statement had not been included with the others on the 26th October, 2012, they immediately wrote to the Coroner on the 30th October, 2012 (see website) requesting the missing document.

It was now Monday, 5th November, 2012; the Inquest had commenced, but still no supplementary witness statement from US Navy Witness 3, Los Angeles. Our barrister was hoping to question PO Fulton in the afternoon, and needed to see this prime supplementary statement before questioning commenced. He therefore brought his request before the Coroner.

I quote from the Inquest audio tapes -

Day 1 - Monday 5th November, 2012 - Tape 1 – 00:00:40

Our Barrister

> *"We understand that on Friday a statement was provided to you, or your office, from the Los Angeles US Navy Officer or sailor. That has not made its way to us. I think there was an attempt to send it but when it arrived it was not readable"*

Coroner

> *"O that was the one that was illegible because it was on a strange piece of paper that was very grainy."*

Our Barrister

> *"But I am reasonably confident, sir, that from the family's perspective we would like at least to have a few moments to consider that and to identify any....."*

Coroner

> *"We're not going to be getting to it till tomorrow"*

Our Barrister

> *"Indeed. Save that, Sir, of course we understand that Petty Officer Fulton is going to be called and there may be some matters arising from that statement that I'd like to consider before questioning him. Sir, I would like a few moments with it at a convenient point"*

Coroner

> *"I think you will probably get the lunch break with it"*

Our Barrister

> *"Thank you, Sir"*

Coroner

> *"Alright"*

Our Barrister also used this opportunity to make a few enquiries regarding the Jury selection. He also suggested that PO Fulton have his two statements before him when he is questioned, and he lastly enquired about the photographic bundle to be used by the Jury and witnesses.

## Parading as an Angel of Light

It was now time for the Coroner to address the court with his thoughts and concerns before the Jury were brought in.

We were to witness a great transformation of this man when in the public eye.

The Coroner informed us all that he is very concerned that the US Navy Witness Statements will be at a great disadvantage, as, unfortunately, these witnesses could not be live witnesses. He therefore has put great thought into remedying this unfortunate situation. He suggests that the Jury have their own copies of these US Witness Statements when his Officer reads them out. He then explains how valuable these US Navy Witness statements are. I quote from the Inquest transcript below –

Day 1 - Monday 5th November, 2012 - Tape 1 – 00:08:20

Coroner

"The matters I wanted to mention, they are **the statements from the US Navy Witnesses.** We now have quite a lot of them. Given the format they're in I think it would be helpful for the Jury to have copies of those statements before them when they are read by my Coroner's Officer because otherwise **they're going to be very difficult to follow** because of the way they are set out as questions and answers."

"So I am proposing to let the jurors have those statements so they can follow them when they are being read out. Is there any objection to that?"

Our Barrister

"On this side of the room, Sir, we completely agree. It is almost impossible to follow otherwise, thank you."

MOD Collins

"Can I just clarify, Sir. ....I have no difficulty at all with having them in front of them while they are being read out, which I agree that they may well be helpful. **Is it your intention then that they retain them after that?** The only reason that I query that is whether some statements **then take on a greater significance than others** if some of them are held in writing, others only having being heard orally."

"My own preference for them **not to be retained** in writing afterwards given that there is that risk. But the court is in your hands, Sir."

Our Barrister

"Sir, I see the point, it may be the right time to consider this, is once we have reached the stage where we have established how many documents the Jury is in fact going to have, and it may be that's a little early."

Coroner

"My viewpoint on this is that in an ideal world we would have these four US Personnel as witnesses, because *they're the closest we've got to eye witnesses of what actually happened. Therefore I feel their evidence is of significance and the Jury must be aware of that because, it is the best account of what actually happened that we have, because no one else saw things; they heard things. Now if the ... um....It is unusual to let Jury members have Rule 37 Statements but in this case I think that it will be important that if they did retain them unless you've got some overwhelming objection you wish to put to me Mr Collins."*

MOD Collins

*"Certainly not, an overwhelming objection Sir, no. It's a simply the concerns I have expressed already but no difficulty with your..."*

???? mumble mumble, can't hear what is said as Collins and Coroner talking at same time.

Coroner

*"All right then."*

Our Barrister

*"Sir, on that topic with Petty Officer Fulton the diagram drawn by the American sailors have little  Xs marking where they saw certain things happening. I would like to seek some clarity from Petty Officer Fulton about those diagrams. For the Jury to follow that, they would need to have them by the time I question Petty Officer Fulton, Sir. So there is in my submission something for those to be in their hands."*

Coroner

*"That poses a bit of a problem really. I don't want them to have them before they are actually read to them, so you're going to have to manage some other way I think."*

Our Barrister

*"With words, I'll do it that way."*

Coroner

*"Please if you wouldn't mind."*

Before I commence looking at the import of these latest comments by the Coroner, let us first consider his statement that these US Navy Witnesses are *'the closest we've got to eye witnesses of what actually happened'*. The US Navy Witnesses are actual eye witnesses of my son's last movements and not the *'the **closest** we've got to eye witnesses of what actually happened'*

Now we can continue and contemplate the Coroner's proposal that he has just made to both Counsels.

Viewed in isolation, one would think that this is a fine proposal, and one could be taken in with the concern and hand-wringing exhibited by the Coroner that these prime witnesses are not there live at the Inquest.

## The Jury are Brought In

The Jury are brought into the court room.

The Coroner, with a soft, fatherly voice addresses them.

The Jury had no idea that this was the man that had fought our legal team and withheld information from my son's Inquest. The Jury had no idea that this was the man that had used his power and his position to deny my son an honest investigation into his death, and now an honest Inquest into his death.

He also denied my son a Full Middleton Inquiry into his death.

The Jury had no idea that our legal team were forbidden from asking any questions on Foul Play/Unlawful killing.

## The First Witness – SIB Wilson

I was sitting directly opposite SIB Wilson, the first witness. He was to read aloud the two reports he had written, which were summaries of his Criminal Investigation, and which explained why he came to the decision he did, regarding foul play in my son's death, which was -

Item 39 RN SIB Investigation Process

*Any foul play would have been identified.* **Simply, there was none which could be found.**

As SIB Wilson waited for the Coroner to finish his introductory address I was able to consider and watch this man.

He sat there with his documents open in his hand, eagerly waiting to be called to read the two summaries of his investigation.

Here he was, sitting in his fine uniform, with plenty of gold braid. Here he was sitting with the most important documents of the whole court hearing. His word had utmost sway. This was Lt Cdr Wilson, Deputy Provost, Special Investigations Branch of the Royal Navy Military Police.

## The First Witness – the Charade

The Coroner invited SIB Wilson to take the stand and to read out his summary investigations.

We had to listen as SIB Wilson proudly read out the summary of his Criminal Investigation into my son's suspicious death.

We had to sit quietly as we watched the Coroner put on a most attentive, fatherly look, as he listened with great interest to SIB Wilson reading out his summary of his investigation.

O! The charade. It was hard not to be sickened by the play acting.

I found it very hard to sit quietly as I watched this man, Lt Cdr Geoff Wilson, Deputy Provost SIB Military Police, read out the summary of his investigation. Instead of being ashamed of having conducted such an intentionally flawed investigation, we find that the opposite is true. SIB Wilson sat there with his documents in his hand, unmistakably dripping with self-satisfaction and pride.

Our legal team had been silenced, they had no choice; God bless them for their patience and endurance and long suffering.

I could not speak, but I could shake my head. And so, whilst SIB Wilson proudly read out his documents, I sat and shook my head.

To avoid being thrown out, I endured the rest of the Inquest with no more head shaking.

But I had been allowed to shake my head most vigorously whilst SIB Wilson read out his summaries of his Criminal Investigation.

## Which are the Pivotal Documents in the Inquest?

We have to take a step back and ask ourselves, 'Which are the pivotal documents in the Inquest' that investigate the suspicious aspects of my son's death?

The answer has to be the two summaries of the Criminal Investigation into my son's death conducted by the SIB Wilson, Royal Navy Police. (But we must remember that we were denied the actual Criminal Investigation; instead we were given only the two SIB reports called, *'Lt Cdr G J Wilson RN – Summary of Evidence'*, and *'RNP SIB Investigation Process'*.)

Nevertheless, to continue. The Coroner, on being approached on many occasions, from January, 2011, right till the very inquest, would always explain to us that based on the criminal investigation carried out by his men, the Special Investigation Branch of the Royal Navy Police, he was satisfied that there was no foul play in my son's death.

Now we have SIB Wilson in the witness stand before our legal team, before the Jury, before us. As I sat there watching this man, I did wonder if SIB Wilson had ever had to give an account for any conclusions, for any actions, for any investigations he had carried out. We would now watch him give a very small account for his investigation.

## The Coroner Makes another Important Statement

SIB Wilson had just finished reading his two reports, and our barrister pointed out that what he had just read was slightly different from what we had been given, and was asking whether we needed further disclosure. In the discussion that followed, the Coroner made the following profound statement –

Tape 1 – 01:09:22

> *"The witnesses who can help us most are going to be here to fill in the details"*

Hasn't he just told us one hour ago that the best witnesses with the best account of what actually happened are the US Navy Witnesses?

Day 1 - Monday 5th November, 2012 - Tape 1 – 00:09:45

> Coroner
> *"My viewpoint on this is that in an ideal world we would have these four US Personnel as witnesses, because* **they're the closest we've got to eye witnesses of what**

*actually happened. Therefore I feel their evidence is of significance and the Jury must be aware of that because, it is **the best account of what actually happened that we have**, because **no one else saw things**; they heard things. Now if the ... um....It is unusual to let Jury members have Rule 37 Statements but in this case I think that it will be important that if they did retain them unless you've got some overwhelming objection you wish to put to me Mr Collins."*

He appears not to notice that his actions and words continue to contradict each other.

# The Inquest Starts

The questioning of the first witness, SIB Wilson, was just about to commence, marking that the Inquest had started in earnest.

We had been waiting for this for so long. We needed to find out how my son came to die. I had hoped that the Inquest would be like court cases depicted on television where the witness is correctly and persistently questioned till any falsehoods are exposed.

But I was wrong in hoping for this. We were reminded that the legal team was gagged and inhibited by the Coroner. They could ask questions on Health and Safety, but nothing that touched on Foul Play, as this was forbidden.

How could they achieve an open verdict under these constraints? The Ministry of Justice statement says that there is no prosecution or defence in an Inquest and that the aim of both is to discover the facts

*"An inquest is different from other types of court hearing because there is **no prosecution or defence**. The **purpose** of the inquest is to **discover the facts** of the death. This means that the coroner (or Jury) cannot find a person or organisation criminally responsible for the death. However if evidence is found that suggests someone may be to blame for the death the coroner can pass all the evidence gathered to the police or Crown Prosecution Service."*

In reality, there was a prosecution and there was a defence and they were not united in their aims. The objective of the MOD was a verdict of Accidental

Death. The objective of the Coroner was to cover the facts. The objective of our legal team was to discover the facts and open up the events surrounding my son's strange death. How could our legal team achieve this?

Both legal teams were responsible for formulating the questions for the Jury at the end of the Inquest. These questions were vital in steering the Jury to a decision.

And to this end our Barrister did his utmost to work with the MOD barrister, and the MOD legal team, and the Coroner. Our Barrister worked hard not to antagonise a volatile opposition. Our Barrister ignored petty interjections and even open mockery. All this he did in order to achieve that one delicate and rare prize - an open verdict for my son.

And he not only won this prize by his expertise and patient perseverance. He won a second victory.

The Royal Navy did their utmost to paint my son as a Health and Safety renegade who never obeyed the rules, and was therefore responsible for his own death. Our barrister exposed the Royal Navy Health and Safety as a hypocritical shambles, and a Rule 43 was slapped onto the Royal Navy. They were the ones that were the Health and Safety culprits, and not my son.

And there was a third victory that our barrister won. Our son's good name was restored.

We were all about to see how our barrister was to achieve these three great victories.

Watching our barrister hold the court during the Inquest was like watching a master swordsman. He held us all spellbound.

When he stood up, the entire court waited. Our barrister was a gentleman to the last. And he had presence. It was always a pleasure to hear him speak. We still talk of it now. When he spoke, everyone listened. It was a pleasure listening to cogent and clear arguments. It was a pleasure to watch our barrister with one sweep of his sword destroy all false arguments and insinuations.

## The First Witness – SIB Wilson – Setting the Scene

Our barrister was the first to question SIB Wilson. Before he did so he asked permission to set the scene for the sake of the Jury. It was important that the Jury understood the scene of my son's fall, so that they could follow the questioning of the witnesses.

It was important for the Jury to know information about HMS Ocean, its size, its function as a helicopter carrier, its function as a tri-service assault ship, and its crew size.

Our barrister continued to set the scene for the Jury, by explaining that there were Landing Craft housed in Bays on the side of HMS Ocean and showed relevant pictures. He explained the function of the Davits, which were used to not only hold the Landing Craft in position in the Bay, but to also move the Landing Craft into and out of the water. It was the flexible hoses at the top of the Davits that were the reason that my son entered the Bay with PO Fulton.

I now quote where he summarises the entire point of my son's Inquest by saying –

Day 1 - Monday 5th November, 2012 - Tape 1 – 01:15:35

Our Barrister
*"Thank you. And again, just setting the scene. In short the circumstances of this case are that Lt Woodhouse appears to have been on a Landing Craft when it was in the Bay. In other words looking at Photograph 1, the one that's actually housed in the Bay in the side.*
*It appears he was on one of those and somehow, and* **that's what the Jury is going to have to look into,** *he fell from the Landing Craft in the Bay and unfortunately beneath in the water there were two Landing Craft moored side by side. He fell onto one of those and sustained injury leading to death."*

SIB Wilson
*"That's the photographs as they were at the time, Sir."*

Our Barrister
*"Thank you. And that was the premise on which you were conducting your investigation essentially. That sort of factual matrix?"*

SIB Wilson
*"The initial information I received was that the, an officer, or a person, had fallen from height..um.. the exact circumstances were not fully known to me at the time and that's the basis on which a decision was*

*made."*

## SIB Wilson – Questioned – Misquoting Witness Statements

So now that our barrister had explained to the Jury all the background and the scene of my son's fall, he was able to commence questioning Lt Cdr Wilson SIB Royal Navy Police on why he chose to infer that my son was under the influence of alcohol.

SIB Wilson did two things to achieve this goal. He firstly deliberately omitted to include quotations in his report stating specifically that my son was not under the influence of alcohol, and secondly he deliberately misquoted a witness statement, thus painting my son as not fit to be working on that day.

The questioning on SIB Wilson's deliberate manipulation of statements and facts is recorded below -

Day 1  - Monday 5ᵗʰ November, 2012  - Tape 1 – 01:16:00

Our Barrister
> *"You drew the reader's attention to a witness who you say described Lt Woodhouse on the morning of the incident as looking and the quotes were **'shabby with bloodshot eyes'**
> Is there a particular reason why you drew the reader's attention to that feature?"*

SIB Wilson
> *"No particular reason, Sir. I was...um... the purpose of this synopsis ....um.... is to explain as much as possible all of the circumstances surrounding the incident .... um..... at the time it was considered it was pertinent."*

Our Barrister
> *"And that was a part of a statement as you'd seen it from Lt Pitman, is that right, that you are quoting from?"*

SIB Wilson
> *"Yes Sir"*

Our Barrister
> *"And Lt Pitman was an officer who had been out with Lt Woodhouse the night before?"*

SIB Wilson

*"During some stage of the night before Sir, yes, I believe Lt Woodhouse came back alone."*

Our Barrister

*"I'm just going to read the exact quote from that statement, because presumably when you were preparing your report you were basing it on the statement. Is that right?"*

SIB Wilson

*"Yes"*

Our Barrister

*"So what you had quoted was that he was looking Quotes 'shabby with bloodshot eyes' that's the quote you've lifted.*

*"So I am going to the statement of Lisa Jill Pitman in the bundle and it's on the right hand page, if that assists. Reading from that, and by all means ask, we can make a copy available to you. What Lt Pitman says is.."*

**"I noticed Lt Woodhouse looked slightly shabby, with slightly bloodshot eyes"**

*"Is there any reason why you left out the word 'slightly' on two occasions in the report?*

SIB Wilson

*"No Sir"*

Our Barrister

*"Carrying on then it reads*

**'He looked as though he had not had a lot of sleep'**

and then the statement ends by saying

**'Lt Woodhouse was being his normal self and did not appear to be under the influence of alcohol'.**

Is there any reason why you did not include that part in your report?"*

SIB Wilson

*"No reason, Sir ... um... it might be worth explaining the synopsis that is provided **is not part of the evidence package, and should be removed prior to any proceedings going forward"***

Our Barrister

SIB Wilson

*"Just help me to understand what you mean by that please. I am not following."*

Our Barrister

*"It's there as an explanation of the facts in brief. It's not ...um....**it doesn't form part of the evidence**."*

SIB Wilson

*"So, in other words, **your summary doesn't form part of the evidence**"*

Our Barrister

*"Exactly, Sir"*

SIB Wilson

*"It's the evidence that forms part of the evidence. "*

Our Barrister

*"It's the statements which are taken as the evidence."*

SIB Wilson

*"In other words what I've read out rather than your synopsis"*

*"Yes."*

## SIB Wilson – It Doesn't Form Part of the Evidence

SIB Wilson has been called to account for misquoting a witness statement and deliberately omitting to quote another witness statement, as these statements conflict with the conclusions he made following his Criminal Investigation into my son's suspicious death.

It is hard to believe his reason for misquoting a witness statement.

SIB Wilson

*"No reason, Sir ... um... it might be worth explaining the synopsis that is provided **is not part of the evidence package, and should be removed prior to any proceedings going forward**"*

His statement is so hard to believe, that our barrister had to ask him,

*"Just help me to understand what you mean by that please. I am not following."*

SIB Wilson, so pleased that he has such a clever answer, repeats it, stating that his two summary reports are not part of the evidence package, and are not part of the evidence, and therefore he is not answerable for his statements, for his misquotes, or for his unfounded and false conclusions. I quote below.

SIB Wilson

> *"No reason, Sir ... um... it might be worth explaining the synopsis that is provided **is not part of the evidence package, and should be removed prior to any proceedings going forward"***

Our Barrister

> *"Just help me to understand what you mean by that please. I am not following."*

SIB Wilson

> *"It's there as an explanation of the facts in brief. It's not ...um.....**it doesn't form part of the evidence."***

Our Barrister

> *"So, in other words, **your summary doesn't form part of the evidence"***

SIB Wilson

> *"Exactly, Sir"*

It is to be borne in mind that the MOD barrister and the Coroner are both listening to this, and not one of them makes a peep. They are perfectly content with this statement, and their silence gives it credence.

Notice that our barrister was walking a legal tight rope, and his objective was to achieve an open verdict for my son; therefore he left this absurd statement so as not to rile the opposition.

But we, the general public, can use our intelligence, and we can analyse this absurd statement.

SIB Wilson has stated that his summary, his synopsis of his Criminal Investigation into my son's death, is not part of the evidence package, and should be removed prior to any proceedings going forward.

This is exactly what we wanted when we first set our eyes on his intentionally flawed summaries.

It was the Coroner's job, when he first set eyes on these summaries of SIB's Criminal Investigation, to send them back to the SIB and demand a sound investigation into my son's death.

But he did not do so. Instead he sanctioned these summaries and elevated them as the primary evidence at my son's Inquest. To continue the absurdity, one of these summary documents is actually entitled 'Summary of Evidence', but we have just been told this is not evidence.

Now here we come to a very strange set of affairs. On the one hand, the Coroner has set these two summaries by SIB Wilson as the two primary Evidence documents in my son's Inquest.

And now, on the other hand, we have SIB Wilson stating the very opposite, that his summary of his criminal investigation

> *"is not part of the evidence package and should be removed prior to any proceedings going forward"*

and

> *"It doesn't form part of the evidence".*

There are no words to describe this absurdity. It is a comedy Inquest. A comedy-tragedy. This is the Military Justice that was meted out to my son.

## SIB Wilson – Questioned – Omitting to Mention

We have seen how SIB Wilson in his endeavours to portray my son as under the influence of alcohol, has misquoted the witness statement by Lt Lisa Pitman in his Criminal Investigation Summary report.

Our barrister now asks him why he failed to mention the statement by another of the Lieutenants who saw him on the morning of the fall, where she specifically said that -

> *"At 0755 Lt Woodhouse knocked on my cabin door to make sure I was up. Lt Woodhouse appeared bright and happy and was making jokes at my expense. Lt Woodhouse did not appear dishevelled in any way."*

SIB Wilson again hides under his statement that the evidence in his Criminal

Investigation summary reports  is not evidence -

*"It doesn't form part of the evidence"*

See the transcript below, and smile –

Day 1  - Monday 5th November, 2012  -  Tape 1 – 01:19:04

Our Barrister
*"In other words what I've read out rather than your synopsis"*

SIB Wilson
*"Yes."*

Our Barrister
*"All right.   And just one other question on this topic then.  There were other statements available from other crew members who'd been out with Lt Woodhouse the night before weren't there?"*

SIB Wilson
*"Yes, Sir"*

Our Barrister
*"And were those also available to you at the time when you wrote up the report that you read to the Jury?"*

SIB Wilson
*"Yes, Sir."*

Our Barrister
*"And one of those statements is from Lt Jennifer Hayes.  Does that ring a bell?"*

SIB Wilson
*"Er, no Sir, it doesn't but.."*

Our Barrister
*"We can, I'm sure make a copy available to you. Lt Hayes' statement in the bundle immediately precedes Lt Pitman's."*

SIB Wilson
*"I've probably got the statement in this bundle here."*

Our Barrister
*"It's the 11th August, 2010 if it helps you and it's certainly in my bundle and it's in the same section….."*

Coroner

"We're going to have a copy passed to him Mr. R"

Our Barrister

"Thank you, just giving you a moment to familiarise yourself with this. Are you looking at the statement of Jennifer Hayes dated 11ᵗʰ August 2010?"

SIB Wilson

"I am"

Our Barrister

"And from the date can you confirm that you would have had that statement available to you when you were writing your report that you've read to the Jury?"

SIB Wilson

"Yes"

Our Barrister

"And again, looking at what Lt Hayes has to say, summarising, we can see that she too was on shore with Lt Woodhouse the night before. Is that fair?"

SIB Wilson

"Yes"

Our Barrister

"And she then says in the last but one paragraph dealing with the morning of the incident"

**'At 0755 Lt Woodhouse knocked on my cabin door to make sure I was up. Lt Woodhouse appeared bright and happy and was making jokes at my expense. Lt Woodhouse did not appear dishevelled in any way.'**

"And again, just helping the Jury, is there any reason why that didn't feature in your report given that you had chosen to mention shabby with bloodshot eyes as we've seen?"

SIB Wilson

"No reason, Sir."

Our Barrister

"Again, presumably **the same point, that is that the evidence is what the Jury are considering rather than your synopsis.**"

*"Absolutely"*

# SIB Wilson – Questioned – Health and Safety

Having come to a road block concerning the created statements, our barrister then turned to the subject of Health and Safety.

Reading from SIB Wilson's document 'Summary of Evidence', our barrister pointed out the flawed nature of the Royal Navy Health and Safety culture on board HMS Ocean.

- Point 1 mentions that my son on joining HMS Ocean in January, 2010, did not complete familiarisation Health and Safety documentation within 24 hours of joining as it was only instigated later in the same year; therefore he was unable to do so.
- Point 2 mentions that there is a 21 day joining questionnaire to be completed by all new joiners, but that there are no questions on procedures for working aloft.
- Point 3 mentions that the risk assessments conducted for working on LCVPs and Davits in 2008, and 2009, are flawed, and despite an audit, were never rectified.
- Point 4 mentioned that specific orders for conducting work and maintenance on LCVPs is confusing and subject to individual decisions.
- Point 5 mentioned that two Royal Navy personnel went up to the LCVP to photograph the bloody scene below. These personnel were not wearing safety harnesses or hard hats. These Royal Navy personnel were doing what was customary on HMS Ocean at the time of my son's death. They were boarding the LCVP without safety harnesses and without hard hats.

These points confirmed that my son's action in going up to the LCVP without a harness or hard hat was a continuation of the non-existent Health and Safety policy and culture on HMS Ocean.

# SIB Wilson – Questioned – Re-Enactment

Our barrister now asked SIB Wilson whether he did any re-enactment of the suspicious events leading to my son's death

Tape 1 – 01:30:00

282

Our Barrister

*"Finally this from me, did you consider carrying out any kind of re-enactment to assist you in gaining a full understanding in what had happened here?"*

SIB Wilson

*"No, Sir."*

Our Barrister

*"Is there any reason, helping the Jury, why you didn't do that?"*

SIB Wilson

*"I'll be honest, Sir. It's not something I actually considered at the time....um....I conducted a full CSI scene examination. Um.........once again any evidence that I needed, a re-enactment wasn't considered, quite simply."*

I have read that insurance companies will carry out re-enactments, even for claims that don't involve death. Yet here we have a trained, SIB criminal investigator telling us that it didn't even cross his mind. Everything is quite simple to this man.

*"a re-enactment wasn't considered, **quite simply.**"*

In summing up his conclusions into my son's suspicious death, there was another decision that he found very simple too.

*"Any foul play would have been identified. **Simply, there was none which could be found.**"*

## SIB Wilson – Questioned by Collins, MOD Barrister

Tape 1 – 01:33:00

And now MOD Collins rises to question SIB Wilson, and his objective is summed up in his statement –

*"Working at height – all officers would know all about this."*

His objective is to steer the Jury into only one train of thought – it is all my son's fault.

Forget the fact that the Health and Safety culture on HMS Ocean was just a charade. Forget the fact that immediately after my son's death two Royal Navy personnel climbed onto the LCVP to photograph the bloody scene below without safety harnesses and without hard hats. Forget the fact that in June, 2012, after the Royal Navy Hewitt report stated that all the Health and Safety recommendations following my son's death had been implemented, a crew member jumped onto the LCVP roof with no safety harness and no hard hat, saying they always did it this way.

Forget the fact that for the Inquest the Royal Navy produced a phoney photo of men on the LCVP wearing safety harnesses and holding one hard hat.

Here was MOD Collins making my son the one and only rule breaker of the Royal Navy's excellent Health and Safety culture.

And we must not forget the underlying reason behind all these arguments. Health and Safety is just a smokescreen. The Military must have Health and Safety to deflect the Jury from the real motive, the covering up of the suspicious events surrounding my son's suspicious death.

## The Medical Witnesses

Tape 1 – 01:34:00

The inquest then continued with the medical witnesses, listed below. The two latter witnesses had their statements read out, and Dr Borek appeared in person.

Dr Borek
Aurelian NICOLAESCU (Medical Examiner – Florida)
Surgeon Capt CARNE

I was concerned that the MOD might say that my son suffered from a heart attack, therefore our barrister questioned Dr Borek as to whether there was any evidence of heart disease and the answer was emphatically, no.

And so the morning questioning was completed.

## The Second Witness – PO Fulton

Tape 2 – 00:01:00

It is now the afternoon of the first day. SIB Wilson has been questioned, followed by the medical witness, and two medical statements that were read out. We now proceeded to the second witness, PO Fulton, who has since been promoted to Chief Petty Officer.

PO Fulton was about my son's age, if my son had been allowed to live.

Throughout the time of his appearance at the court proceedings, I noticed that he kept looking at the Jury members in a most affable and interested way.

He knew he had a face that appeared open and innocent, and, in my opinion, this is the image he wanted to project to the Jury.

This is the man whose evidence SIB Wilson relied on heavily in his investigation. Instead of treating him as the chief suspect, this is the man that SIB Wilson had elevated to the position of prime witness.

PO Fulton proceeded to read his account of the events.

How can the Inquest discover the facts if the legal team was forbidden from interrogating him with any questions that might touch on foul play?

## PO Fulton – the Questioning Begins

Tape 2  -  00:29:37

Where shall we start? I shall start where our Barrister started. The two opposite statements that the hoses had been changed, and then they had not been changed.

In Item 9 of the Supplementary Ship's Investigation, 12<sup>th</sup> September, 2010, PO Fulton tells us that he was informed that the hoses had been changed –

See Item 9 below

> *"PO Fulton states that he remembers returning from weekend leave and **being informed that the hoses had been changed.**"*

And yet we have the contradictory statement in his Witness Statement of 6ᵗʰ August, 2010, where PO Fulton states the opposite to my son when he informs my son that the hoses have not been changed.

> *"I explained to Lt Woodhouse that as far as I was aware **the hoses had not been charge [sic]**, he had been informed that they had been changed."*

I quote a small part below -

Day 1 - Monday 5ᵗʰ November, 2012 - Tape 2 – 01:07:11

> Our Barrister continues – he is quoting from the Supplementary Ship's Investigation Item 9

> > *"We then go onto the next paragraph, it reads"*

> > > *"PO Fulton states that he remembers returning from weekend leave and **being informed that the hoses had been changed.** He cannot remember who that person was. Furthermore, he did not pass the information on to Lt Woodhouse at the time because as the Supervisor, he wanted to check the work had been carried out himself before logging it in the Flexible Hose Register. PO Fulton does not know who conducted the work and the Investigating Team have been unable to clarify this due to personnel leaving the Ship. PO Fulton, while questioned, has not offered any specific explanation as to why he didn't check the work between the end of May and, ultimately, the day of the incident."*

> > *"Now effectively what is being said is that you'd been told the hoses had been changed, you didn't pass that information on to Lt Woodhouse because you wanted to check yourself but you didn't get around to checking from May until August?"*

PO Fulton
> > *"That's right."*

Our Barrister
> > *"Is that right?"*

PO Fulton
>*"Yes"*

Our Barrister
>*"If someone tells you something has been changed on board this ship, do you generally trust them or would you expect to have to check yourself?"*

PO Fulton
>*"With regard to the flexible hoses log and registers I would check myself."*

Our Barrister
>*"What had you told Lt Woodhouse when he was asking you from May through to August about your plans to check?"*

PO Fulton
>*"I told him as soon as I could get up there and check I would or ...........never, I never had the chance."*

Our Barrister
>*"Did you tell him,*
>>***'I've been told they have been changed. I just want to check for myself'***
>*Did you tell him that?'*

PO Fulton
>*"I didn't tell him. I said .....as far as I was aware I needed to check the hoses have been changed."*

Our Barrister
>*"Do you think that might be a fairly important thing in the chain to be able to say to him -"*
>>***'I've been told they've been changed. I just want to do the final check myself'***

PO Fulton
>*"Well until I can check and confirm that they'd been changed as far as I am aware they hadn't been changed."*

And so he explains away his two opposite, contradictory statements. But this was very important. It was this statement that the hoses had not been changed, that PO Fulton used to get my son onto the LCVP.

## PO Fulton Questioned – his Demotion

Just prior to my son's fall, PO Fulton had been demoted. He had previously held the position Head of Boats Section.

Our legal team were under powerful constraints not to ask any questions involving foul play, and they were also under powerful constraints not to cause any bad humour on the part of the Coroner or the MOD barrister. Should our legal team step out of line, the Coroner would ensure that there would be a total clamp down on the little that had been allowed us.

There would be a further clamp down on any and every question that our legal team asked.
There would be a further clamp down on the verdict allowed at the end of the Inquest.

As a result, our barrister only very gently questioned all the witnesses, PO Fulton included.

Our barrister asked PO Fulton why he had been demoted – see transcript on Tape 2 – 01:11:10 on the website

The answer was, for some petty paper work and administrative failings.

*"administrative ........ paperwork side of it seemed to be lacking."*

This seems a severe consequence for paperwork omissions.

Once again, a piece of the puzzle does not fit.

Here we have a man who has been publically demoted from his position as Head of Boats section, and has been replaced by PO Dot Cottam, one of his team.

We have to ask ourselves this; was PO Fulton in any way affected by being publically demoted and then replaced by one of his team members?

And it was at this time that my son entered the world of PO Fulton.

# PO Fulton – the Questioning Continues

Our Barrister skilfully continued to question PO Fulton.

He had to somehow alert the Jury to the contradictions in PO Fulton's account. He had to somehow bring to the Jury's attention the unnatural behaviour of PO Fulton's account of my son's last movements.

The Jury did not know what our legal team knew.

The Jury did not know that the statement of US Navy Witness 3, Los Angeles, completely contradicted PO Fulton's statements. Would the Jury be able to pick up this contradiction by just having all the US Navy Witness statements read out to them in court?

The Jury did not know that the man in white shorts seen by US Navy Witness 2, Charleston, was not my son. Would the Jury pick up this detail? How could this be brought to the Jury's attention?

The Coroner and SIB Wilson spent over two years to ensure that the US Navy Witness statements remained obscure. The Coroner and SIB Wilson did not want these statements clarified to the Jury, despite the Coroner's maiden speech at the start of the Inquest. MOD Barrister Collins did not even want the Jury members to keep hold of these printed witness statements after they were first given them on Day Two. MOD Collins wanted these US Navy Witness statements instantly taken from them, so as to remain obscure and irrelevant.

In these conditions our Barrister had an impossible task before him. Our Barrister had to somehow prepare the Jury for the evidence of the prime US Navy witness statements that held the key to my son's death. Our Barrister had to alert the Jury to the chief suspect in my son's death, to PO Fulton, who had been elevated by the Coroner to the trusted and honourable position of prime witness.

And this he had to achieve while not angering the Coroner or MOD Collins, who held the seats of power, and whose united objective was to cover the myriad suspicious facts piled on my son's death. Let us watch and see how our Barrister achieved this impossible task.

## It is Highly Unlikely my Son Climbed onto the Roof

How could our barrister alert the Jury to the implausibility of my son ever being on the wheelhouse roof?

Day 1 - Monday 5th November, 2012 - Tape 2 – 01:37:13

> Our Barrister
> *"So, I was asking you about who it was that spotted it.*

You said both of you did. Is that right?"

PO Fulton

"We both looked at the hose when we were, as we got up there"

Our Barrister

"What position were you in perhaps we'll use Photograph 23 for a moment. Can you help us with where you both were **given the limited amount of space** up on the wheelhouse roof?"

PO Fulton

"We were in front of the radar dome ... slightly..." mumble mumble

Our Barrister

"So, standing in front of the dome, is that right?"

PO Fulton

"Crouched in front"

Our Barrister

"Crouched – of course – thank you, you are absolutely right. And by that means the two of you were able to look at the hose?"

PO Fulton

"Yeah, that's how we knew the hose was changed."

Our Barrister

"How much space was there for the two of you to move around given the **cramped** conditions that we've seen? How tight was it up there for the two of you?"

PO Fulton

"It was....we were close together. Side by side while looking at the hose."

Our Barrister

**"Are you sure both of you were up there?"**

PO Fulton

"Yes"

Had the Jury noticed the implausible points he was drawing their attention to? Had the Jury noticed the doubt in that question -

**"Are you sure both of you were up there?"**

# It is Highly Unlikely PO Fulton Climbed down the more difficult Back Route

How could our barrister alert the Jury to the implausibility of PO Fulton taking the back route?

Apart from unusual circumstances, which we shall hear later on in the inquest with PO Dot Cottam, it is natural to ascend and descend the wheelhouse roof by the front route.

Day 1 - Monday 5ᵗʰ November, 2012 - Tape 2 – 01:38:43

> Our Barrister
> *"Now you say that the two of you then came down. You've told our Jury that you came down at the **back** of the wheelhouse?"*
> PO Fulton
> *"Yes"*
> Our Barrister
> *"You climbed up by the front. Climbing up as we can see and you've explained using the handrail in Photograph 23. Why did you decide to go down at the back as you've come up by the front?"*
> PO Fulton
> *"just as …. Lt Woodhouse came down the front. I was …just….for…just to come back to……easier that way both of us to climb down at the same time. …..instead of waiting on top of the wheelhouse…. I just moved to the back and down"*
> Our Barrister
> *"In order to climb down over the back you've got to scramble over the radio mast, haven't you?"*
> PO Fulton
> *"The radio mast was down. It was just, I was crouched, I just had to step over it."*
> Our Barrister
> *"So you've got to navigate a route past the equipment on the roof, get over the radio mast, with the various bits sticking up, and then climb down?"*
> PO Fulton
> *"It wasn't that hard, really. Just stepped over the mast as it was down, and….as you can see on the picture it was just taken from the front, stepping over the mast and climbing down."*
> Our Barrister
> *"There are various prongs which jut out from the top of*

the triangular shape of the mast. How did you get past those?"

PO Fulton

"well you see, they are….. quite spaced in between. No obstacle to get down."

Our Barrister

"Rather trickier than going back down the entirely clear route on the front, isn't it?"

PO Fulton

"It's a little bit, but…"

Our Barrister

"So why didn't you just wait for Lt Woodhouse to climb down and then follow him? i.e. the same way you came up?"

PO Fulton

"Just to get down off the wheelhouse!"

Our Barrister

"Any discussion as between the two of you about the route you'd be taking down from the wheelhouse roof?"

PO Fulton

"No discussion"

Our Barrister

"No?

PO Fulton

"No."

Our Barrister

"What position was Lt Woodhouse when you last saw him?"

PO Fulton

"As I was climbing down the back I'd seen him…… move to the front, had sat down to lower himself down and at that point I then looked down to get my footing."

Our Barrister

"Where was he sitting? Can you help us with where by reference to this photograph?"

PO Fulton

"Front of the wheelhouse"

Our Barrister

"You've got Picture 23 I suspect open. Can you help us with where you recall seeing Lt Woodhouse sitting?"

PO Fulton

"He was sitting between the radar dome and the davit arm. Basically central, I believe"

> Our Barrister
> > *"Central?"*
>
> PO Fulton
> > *"Yes"*
>
> Our Barrister
> > *"So directly in front of the white satellite dome? Is that right?"*
>
> PO Fulton
> > *".... Ah, as far as I can remember, yes ......."*
>
> Our Barrister
> > *"And what was he doing when you saw him there?"*
>
> PO Fulton
> > *"He was,... he moved,.... he had his legs over the front of the wheelhouse then. Sat down, ready to lower himself down I imagine. Then I, that was the last I saw............"*

And so we see from the questioning, he gives no good reason why he took this unnatural, longer, more difficult route. In fact he quite clearly says of the back route with its cables, and its sensitive electronic equipment, and with the mast down, and with protrusions that -

> *"It wasn't that hard, really"*

Not that hard? Really? Not that hard?

And he did give a reason, but it was not a good reason to take the more unnatural back route. He said that *'instead of waiting on top of the wheelhouse,* he just moved to the back and down.

This is very strange.

> *"instead of waiting on top of the wheelhouse"*

How long is he talking about? By this statement he is telling us that waiting for Lt Woodhouse was such a long period of time that he chose instead to take the much longer, much more difficult, and danger-prone back route? Really?

It is highly unlikely that he would have taken the back route to climb back down to the deck of the LCVP, when he supposedly took the front route to climb up to the roof.

This is all very handy. Just so that he will be able to say that he saw nothing.

In the same way that he says there was no discussion between the two men all during this episode, and in the same way that he says he only heard a 'Whoa Whoa, Whoa' and a boot scuffle, but my son's terrified, loud scream isn't mentioned. All very suspicious.

And as the questioning continued, our Barrister asked once again

Day 1 - Monday 5th November, 2012 - Tape 2 – 01:47:17

Our Barrister
*"Are you sure Chief Petty Officer, that you and Lt Woodhouse came down at different places from the wheelhouse roof?"*
PO Fulton
*"YES"*
Our Barrister
*"Is there anything else you can say to this Jury about the circumstances in which Lt Woodhouse fell?"*
PO Fulton
*"No more than I've already said."*

Had the Jury picked this up? Had the Jury been alerted to PO Fulton's weavings and suspicious statements and more weavings?

*"**Are you sure** Chief Petty Officer, that you and Lt Woodhouse came down at different places from the wheelhouse roof?"*

# The Contradiction with the Scream

Here we come to another contradiction in PO Fulton's accounts.

In his statement of the 6th August, 2010, PO Fulton does not mention a scream, only a boot scuffle and 'whoa whoa whoa'. However, in the ISI, of the 9th August, 2010, a scream is mentioned.

Let me quote from his statement of the 6th August, 2010 –

*"As I was climbing down I heard what I thought was Lt Woodhouse jump from the Wheel House roof it sounded to me as though he landed in the area of the Port Engine Hatch, I then heard something like 'whoa, whoa, whoa' this was not excessively loud and I initially thought he had landed unsteadily*

*and fallen over on landing."*

ISI, 9th August, 2010 -

> *11. Having completed the task, PO2 proceeded to the back of the wheelhouse to climb back down. As he was doing so, he heard a loud thud which he presumed was the sound of Lt Woodhouse jumping down from the front of the wheelhouse onto the deck of the LCVP (although he did not see anything). Almost immediately after the initial thud, he heard Lt Woodhouse's voice **say something that sounded like 'Whoa, Whoa, Whoa' (as if he had lost his balance) followed by a scream.***

Could our Barrister come to the bottom of this contradiction with the scream?

## PO Fulton tells us he only heard 'Whooaaa' and a boot scraping/scuffle.

Our Barrister now questions PO Fulton on exactly what he heard.

Day 1 - Monday 5th November, 2012 - Tape 2 – 01:42:20

> Our Barrister
>> *"Now you bend....describe hearing a sound. Can you help us with what that sound was? Just expand a little bit on that"*
>
> PO Fulton
>> *"Just a ... as I came down I heard a 'Whooooaaa' sort of .... sound"*
>
> Our Barrister
>> *"Any other sound proceeding that?"*
>
> PO Fulton
>> *"I didn't hear anything, no. Not that I can think of.*
>
> Our Barrister
>> *"Any sound of him landing on anything which proceeded that?"*
>
> PO Fulton
>> *"Uh.......I heard a boot scraping. That was about it"*
>
> Coroner
>> *"When you say boot scraping because I asked you if you heard a scuffling or a scraping sound and you told me then that you didn't. What do you recall?"*

PO Fulton
> "I..... I recall the .....a sound...his boot scraping and then the 'whoooa' sound."

Coroner
> "Because you said to me before you didn't hear anything. Now you recollect you did is it?

PO Fulton
> "I did hear a sound. I do apologise if I......." mumble mumble

Was the Jury alerted to PO Fulton's inconsistencies? He only heard 'whoa, whoa, whoa' – really?

# Highly Unlikely that my Son Jumped Onto the Port Engine Hatch.

Before I commence I would like to point out that the port side is the side nearest the forty six foot drop down to certain death. The picture below show two views of the Port Engine Hatch which has an emergency life raft always on it.

the Port Engine Hatch

To continue, PO Fulton lets us know that my son landed in the area of the Port Engine Hatch. Our Barrister shows how unlikely this is. Has the Jury noticed?

Day 1 - Monday 5<sup>th</sup> November, 2012 - Tape 2 – 01:43:00

Our Barrister
> "In your first statement Chief Petty Officer you say this -"
> **'As I was climbing down I heard what I thought was Lt Woodhouse jump from the Wheel House**

*roof it sounded to me as though he landed in the area of the Port Engine Hatch. I then heard something like 'whoa, whoa, whoa' this was not excessively loud and I initially thought he had landed unsteadily and fallen over on landing.'*

"Do you see that, first of all?"

PO Fulton

*"I see that, yes"*

Our Barrister

"All right, just going back then to the start of that passage. You say you heard what you thought was Lt Woodhouse jump from the wheelhouse roof."

**'it sounded to me as though he landed in the area of the Port Engine Hatch.'**

"Now, let's just identify the area first of all. If we go to Photograph number 3 for a moment. We've got there a view looking down on the top of the Landing Craft."

PO Fulton

*"Yes"*

Our Barrister

"Identified a little earlier, the two engine hatches to the left and the right, or port and starboard of the craft there. And is it the left hand one that we're looking at, looking down, which we're speaking about?"

PO Fulton

*"Yeah. The port side would be……."*

Our Barrister

"Now on this photograph, Photograph number 3 there appears to be something attached to the top of the engine hatch?"

PO Fulton

*"Yes"*

Our Barrister

"What is that?"

PO Fulton

**"That is the emergency life raft"**

Our Barrister

"Right. Is that a standard piece of kit that's attached to each and every landing craft?"

PO Fulton

*"It is."*

Our Barrister

> *"So that would have been there on the Landing Craft from which the two of you were climbing down?"*

PO Fulton

> *"Yes"*

Our Barrister

> *"So **not the sort of area that you would aim for** because you're likely to land on that and then injure yourself presumably?"*

PO Fulton

> *"Presumably, yes"*

Our Barrister

> *"All right. So when you say in your statement it sounded as though he landed in the area of the port engine hatch. Why did you say that? Why did it SOUND like he landed there?"*

PO Fulton

> *"It's just what I **imagined** where he would land…. obviously because….from where he went down….I just figured he would have landed in the middle of the.. wheelh….middle of the deck."*

Our Barrister

> *"So you **imagined** he'd be landing somewhere to the right of that life raft packaged up?"*

PO Fulton

> *"Yes, somewhere against… the port deck…it's what I was expecting"*

Our Barrister

> *"**Difficult for him to jump down towards the centre** in between the life raft and the davit hook, because the davit arm is there, isn't it?"*

PO Fulton

> *"It is yeah"*

Our Barrister

> *"We can see that over here again, by looking at Photograph 23. You've got the davit arm attaching to the hook. So quite a tight space there if you're jumping down into that area. That is between the life raft and the davit arm?"*

PO Fulton

> *"It is."*

Day 1 - Monday 5<sup>th</sup> November, 2012 - Tape 2 – 01:47:17

Our Barrister

*"Are you sure Chief Petty Officer, that you and Lt Woodhouse came down at different places from the wheelhouse roof?"*

PO Fulton

*"YES"*

Our Barrister

*"Is there anything else you can say to this Jury about the circumstances in which Lt Woodhouse fell?"*

PO Fulton

*"No more than I've already said."*

Our Barrister summed up his questioning on this topic with the question –

*"**Are you sure** Chief Petty Officer, that you and Lt Woodhouse came down at different places from the wheelhouse roof?"*

Did the Jury notice this? Had the Jury been alerted to the improbability of everything PO Fulton said?

## Didn't Check Over the Side – Really?

Day 1 - Monday 5ᵗʰ November, 2012 - Tape 2 – 01:47:42

Our Barrister

*"After you heard the sound that you described, you said that you thought he landed in the area of the port engine hatch, we've just looked at that in your statement, **you said you went round but you couldn't find him** on the deck of the Landing Craft?"*

PO Fulton

*"Yes"*

Our Barrister

*"Now, when the Landing Craft is on the davits in the bay, the port side **hangs over** or **juts over** the side of the bay itself, doesn't it?"*

PO Fulton

*"It does"*

Our Barrister

*"We can see that in Photograph Number 2. Looking at Photograph 2 we're looking up the side of the HMS Ocean, we've got an image of a Landing Craft in the*

water and one in Bay, and we can see the edge **juts over the side as the photograph shows?**"

PO Fulton

"*Yes*"

Our Barrister

"*So, having heard that sound, and having come down and found that Lt Woodhouse was not there on the Landing Craft deck,* **your first thought must have been** *that he'd fallen all the way down, right off the edge?*"

PO Fulton

"*My first thought was that we'd........managed to keep right round the other side of the wheelhouse and moved back to check, he wasn't there I came back round that's when he....... I started feeling .....fallen over the side.....*"

Our Barrister

"*All right. So, if you'd started to feel that he'd fallen over the side why did you go to check on the floor of the Bay* **first?** *Why did you go down there?*"

PO Fulton

"**I just went down.** *I had to come down the VP Bay. I went down the ladder.*"

Our Barrister

"*Why didn't you just look over the edge of the Landing Craft, which is where you were, once you had established he wasn't on the deck of the Landing Craft?*"

PO Fulton

"*I.....can't say.....I ......... just went down to check the VP Bay.*"

Our Barrister

"**Because the obvious thing if he's not on the deck and he's fallen, is that he has fallen right over the side. Isn't it?**"

PO Fulton

"*Looking at this photograph, yes*"

Our Barrister

"**Not just looking at the photograph, but looking at what you saw, because you were on it?**"

PO Fulton

"*Yes*"

Our Barrister

"*And beneath that Landing Craft in Bay were two other Landing Craft floating in the water below?*"

PO Fulton
> *"That is right"*

Our Barrister
> *"So again, can you help us with **why** you saw fit to come off the Landing Craft and go down to the floor of the Bay to look for him there, given that the obvious.....?"*

PO Fulton
> *"**I just did it.** I came down to look, see....."*

Did the Jury pick up what our Barrister was trying to alert them to? It was totally unnatural and contrived to be looking for my son first at the front of the wheelhouse, then in the Bay, and only afterwards over the side.

This is another strange thing in PO Fulton's account. As the LCVP jutted over the side of HMS Ocean it would be impossible to fall outwards and then somehow swing inwards and land in the Bay area. Did the Jury pick up this point that our Barrister was alerting them to?

Did the Jury notice our Barrister questions?

> *"given that the obvious...?"*
> *"Because the obvious thing....?"*
> *"your first thought must have been...?"*

Did the Jury notice PO Fulton answers?

> *"I just did it."*
> *"I just went down"*
> *"I can't say.....I.... just went down"*

# Man on Flight Deck with White Shorts and Socks

Another impossible task that our Barrister had was to prepare the Jury for the US Navy Witness accounts, which were only going to be read out. We had spent hours, days, and weeks studying these accounts. We had discussed them, compared them with the plans of HMS Ocean, re-enacted them, and puzzled over the different positions of the man in white. It was only when the second set of US Navy Witness statements arrived that we could tell that the three men that were first spotted by these witnesses were three different men. When all these accounts were to be read out, how could the Jury pick up half the things that we had picked up after much study, research, and care?

Our Barrister now started preparing the Jury for the account by Witness 2, Charleston, who saw a man on the flight deck, and only in his second statement this witness describes the man as wearing white shorts and socks.

Day 1 - Monday 5ᵗʰ November, 2012 - Tape 2 – 01:50:31

> Our Barrister
> *"The clothing you were wearing that day.  You've explained that you were wearing blue coveralls or overalls?"*
> PO Fulton
> *"Yes"*
> Our Barrister
> *"Lt Woodhouse was wearing white?"*
> PO Fulton
> *"That's correct"*
> Our Barrister
> ***"White overalls?"***
> PO Fulton
> *"Yes"*

Day 1 - Monday 5ᵗʰ November, 2012 - Tape 2 – 01:54:15

> Our Barrister
> *"Was Lt Woodhouse wearing white shorts or knee socks that day?"*
> PO Fulton
> *"No"*

Would the Jury remember these important details when they had the US Navy Witness statements read out to them?

# Preparing Jury for US Navy Witness 1, Philippines.

In his second statement (received 10 days before the Inquest) Witness 1, Philippines, places the feet hanging in mid-air, in the middle top part of the LCVP Bay.  What a strange place.  What could this mean?  Only on reading the second statement by Witness 2, Charleston, did we read that there was a moveable platform with men on it in the middle of the Bay.  This accounts for the strange sighting of the feet.  We had worked hard to piece this information together. How could our Barrister try to prepare the Jury for this sighting of the feet, the feet that did not belong to my son?

Day 1 - Monday 5<sup>th</sup> November, 2012 - Tape 2 – 01:50:54

Our Barrister

*"Now, just a few more questions from me. At any stage, when the two of you were up on the Landing Craft in Bay did either of you go anywhere else that you have not told us about, when you were on the Landing Craft?"*

PO Fulton

*"I....don't believe so. ....... I can't recollect anywhere......"*

Our Barrister

*"**You were there**, so help us please. You told us you went up the ladder. You had a look at the rear davit. And you then climbed up onto the wheelhouse roof. Yes?"*

PO Fulton

*"Yes, I...."*

Our Barrister

*"Did either of you go forward from there? We have a look at Picture No 1 as an example. Did either of you walk forward from the rear davit? I'm going to hold it up and point at what I mean. So the davit nearest the wheelhouse. Did either of you walk forward to any position towards the front of the Landing Craft?"*

PO Fulton

*"Um.........I don't remember. I don't think so. I don't believe so."*

Our Barrister

*"Well, **you were up there**. Would you have done it, given that the aim was to check....?"*

PO Fulton

*"Um, It's possible that we went to see if I could check that .......before .....I took the decision to climb the wheelhouse"*

Our Barrister

*"**Is there any possibility** that Lt Woodhouse fell from a position forward of the wheelhouse and somewhere closer to the front davit? **Is there any possibility** based on what you saw and heard?"*

PO Fulton

*"What, closer to the front davit arm?"*

Our Barrister

> *"I'm going to hold up and point out an area closer to the front davit – so the left hand davit."*
> PO Fulton
> *"No"*
> Our Barrister
> **"Any possibility at all? ......As far as you are concerned?"**
> PO Fulton
> *"As far as I'm concerned it was from that area."*
> Our Barrister
> **"It was off the roof of the wheelhouse and then immediately a fall from there. As far as you're concerned? Is that right?"**
> PO Fulton
> *"Yes"*

What a difficult job, dealing with the likes of PO Fulton. Constant non-committals. Nonetheless our Barrister did manage to get from him an affirmative statement that my son fell from the wheelhouse area and not from anywhere towards the middle or the front of the LCVP.

Did the Jury wonder why it was very important to remember that my son fell from the wheelhouse area and not the middle or front of the LCVP? Would they pick up that the location of the feet was far from the wheelhouse roof? Would they pick up the fact that the feet were not those of my son?

# He didn't see USS Mitscher Sailing Past

USS Mitscher sailed past HMS Ocean at exactly the time my son fell from the LCVP. The Jury were alerted to this by our Barrister asking PO Fulton whether he noticed this US Navy warship.

PO Fulton has already made two opposite and contradictory statements, which he has expertly explained away. Yet the fact remains that as they cannot both be true, therefore one of these statements is untrue.

Day 1 - Monday 5th November, 2012 - Tape 2 – 01:52:54

> Our Barrister
> *"Were you at any stage aware of an American Naval Vessel sailing past?"*
> PO Fulton
> *"Er, no"*

Our Barrister
*"Didn't notice it at all?"*
PO Fulton
*"Didn't.... .... the front"*

# Preparing Jury for US Witness 2, Charleston

Witness 2, Charleston, saw a man in white shorts and knee socks on the flight deck of HMS Ocean giving commands to men on a moveable platform.

The Jury knew nothing of the US Navy Witnesses, as they had been relegated to the next day. These were the witnesses that should have been introduced first, and should have been live witnesses, and it is their testimony that should have been relied on and not PO Fulton's.

So our Barrister is now preparing the Jury for the account by Witness 2, Charleston. He is trying to alert them to the fact that there was a man in white on the flight deck, but that this man was not my son. He is trying to alert them to the bewildering facts concerning the man in white initially spotted by the three US Navy Witnesses. Our Barrister is trying to alert them to the fact that each of the three US Navy Witnesses did see my son fall, but they did not all see my son before he fell; they each saw a different man. Witness 3, Los Angeles, was the only witness who saw my son from start to finish.

Day 1 - Monday 5th November, 2012 - Tape 2 – 01:53:15

Our Barrister
*"Were you or Lt Woodhouse on the flight deck at any point shortly before he fell?"*
PO Fulton
*"No"*
Our Barrister
*"Just so we're clear, we turn to Photograph Number. 2. This is the view along the side of the HMS Ocean. If we work up from sea level, we've got a Landing Craft in the water, we've then got a Landing Craft in the bay, and if we go up one more level we can see perhaps part of the underside of the flight deck, can't we? I'm just going to hold it up there and show you."*
PO Fulton
*"Yes, the cat walk that runs along the flight deck"*

Our Barrister
"So that's a cat walk along the edge of the flight deck, that's where the helicopters are when they're about to take off or land. Is that right?"
PO Fulton
"Up on the flight deck, yes."
Our Barrister
"Thank you. Were you or Lt Woodhouse at any point the flight deck at all that morning?"
PO Fulton
"No"

Day 1 - Monday 5th November, 2012 - Tape 2 – 01:54:15

Our Barrister
"Was Lt Woodhouse wearing white shorts or knee socks that day?"
PO Fulton
"No"
Our Barrister
"Did you go onto the flight deck immediately after or shortly after he fell?"
PO Fulton
"No"

When the Jury did hear the US Witness statements read out, would they remember that my son was not wearing white shorts and was not on the flight deck?

# Preparing Jury for US Witness 3, Los Angeles – BACK OF WHEELHOUSE

Our Barrister is now trying to prepare the Jury for another great flaw in PO Fulton's account of my son's last moments. PO Fulton said that he never saw anything because he says he took the back route to climb off the wheelhouse roof. He said that when he last saw my son, my son was sitting at the front of the wheelhouse roof, before jumping down. He was at the back of the wheelhouse roof when he heard my son falling. We are not sure whether PO Fulton is climbing down or has just arrived on the deck of the LCVP, but we are agreed that he says that he is at the back of the wheelhouse.

Yet we have US Witness 3, Los Angeles, who tell us that he saw my son standing comfortably on the deck of the LCVP, and at the back of the wheelhouse. This is exactly where PO Fulton says that he, PO Fulton, was standing.

But how can our Barrister alert the Jury to the US Witness statements they will hear tomorrow? How can our Barrister prepare them for this great discrepancy? Added to this, how can our Barrister somehow allow them to notice from the accounts that will be merely read out, that only one of the US Navy Witnesses saw my son before he fell? The other two US Navy Witnesses each saw a different man, turned away, and then looking again at HMS Ocean saw my son falling, thinking it was one and the same man. How will the Jury be able to pick this up?

Day 1 - Monday 5th November, 2012 - Tape 2 – 01:54:42

> Our Barrister
> > *"Was, as far as you are concerned Lt Woodhouse ever on the aft end, that is, behind the wheelhouse, of the Landing Craft before he fell?"*
> PO Fulton
> > *"Er, ..No"*
> Our Barrister
> > **"On your evidence, he couldn't have been because that's where you were. Is that right?"**
> PO Fulton
> > *"When I climbed down, yes"*
> Our Barrister
> > *"And you'd have seen him there if he had been there, **on your evidence?"***
> PO Fulton
> > *"Yes"*

# MOD Collins Questions PO Fulton

It is now time for MOD Collins to question PO Fulton. The questioning can be followed on -

Tape 2 – 02:02:52

MOD Collins can be read like a book. Don't allow any questioning on Foul Play, whatever you do; this must not come to the light of day.

It is now MOD Collins' opportunity to question PO Fulton, and the main thrust of his questioning is to show that an officer should have known to wear a safety harness. It mattered not that the entire culture of HMS Ocean cared not for Health and Safety; it was all my son's fault, and MOD Collins was out to ensure that this is where the blame was fixed.

But, hang on a moment. Isn't MOD Collins missing something? I thought that the Ministry of Justice Guide to Coroner Services said that the purpose of an Inquest is to discover the facts, and that it does not seek to blame anyone or apportion blame.

> *"An inquest is different from other types of court hearing because there is **no prosecution or defence**. The **purpose** of the inquest is to **discover the facts** of the death. This means that the coroner (or Jury) cannot find a person or organisation criminally responsible for the death. However if evidence is found that suggests someone may be to blame for the death the coroner can pass all the evidence gathered to the police or Crown Prosecution Service."*

> *"Inquest" or "inquest hearing" is a **fact-finding inquiry** in court (or alternative premises) conducted by a coroner to establish who has died, and how, when and where the death occurred. It forms part of the coroner's investigation. An inquest does not establish any matter of criminal or civil liability. **It does not seek to blame anyone or apportion blame between people or organisations***

MOD Collins firstly does his utmost to apportion the blame of my son's death on my son, on the officer.

When questioning PO Fulton, the chief suspect in my son's suspicious death, he had an opportunity to *'discover the facts'*. He did not do so.

And thus the first day's proceedings are ended.

# The Perpetrator of Confusion

It was now Day Two of my son's Inquest, and before the Jury was brought in our Barrister raised concern over the bad quality in the questionnaire photographs of US Navy Witness 3, Los Angeles, received only yesterday. Our Barrister asked whether the photographs had been lightened in order for the location of the 'X' to be clearly seen.

Our Barrister

"Yes, we spent some time yesterday putting the statements of the American Naval personnel in order, pretty much the Coroner's Officer helping us with that. Bundles have been assembled but you will recall that one issue which has arisen is that the photographs which were sent along with the Los Angeles Naval Statement have been marked obviously, **but the markings were just about impossible to find** in the statements and with that in mind, we asked yesterday whether better copies could be made available. I understand that some further copies have come in. We have not seen them yet, and I wonder whether we might have a look at those, see what they are like."

Our Barrister also pointed out the great confusion in trying to match the correct US Navy Witness Questionnaire answers with the corresponding photograph for that witness. All we had was an initial by each photograph. It was hard enough for us to match them, let alone the Jury. I quote below.

Day 2 - Tuesday 6th November, 2012 - Tape 3 – 00:03:00

Our Barrister

"So again we have to sound the health warning, which is that this clip again contains firstly initials, secondly the Philippine's photographs are again in this bundle, so one needs to be a bit careful, wherever you see the initials BEL they do not relate to the statement. But the point that does..."

Coroner

**"I don't know about you, but my brain is beginning to hurt with these statements**, if I can sort them out."

MOD Collins

"The Social Security number is back in as well"

Our Barrister

"So, we'll apply the same approach as yesterday. Someone seems very keen for us to know who these people are. We shall try to ignore that, we can edit, but the point that I am driving at is that the photographs, the ones that are reparable, to the Los Angeles Statement have the initials **BT or BTM**. These copies, I'm grateful for the effort that has been made, but we submit that *yet again, **it is well-nigh impossible to work out***

What was so amazing was how the Coroner bemoaned the fact that the photographs, and US Navy witness statements, were so confusing.

Coroner
*"I don't know about you, **but my brain is beginning to hurt** with these statements, **if I can sort them out**."*

Did we really hear what he just said?

The confusion was intentional.

But who does know that the Coroner is the author of the confusion created over the US Navy witness statements?

# PO Fulton Mildly Questioned Again

The Jury were then brought in and the Coroner asked to have PO Fulton back on the witness stand. His questions were in the line of finding out whether the LCVP deck was greasy, and whether the deck had a non-slip surface on it. Could a man slip on it? The answer was no, as previous questioning had shown that the deck of the LCVP was made specifically for Royal Marines to run on and off it under the worst circumstances, with mud, grease, water, and all under fire too. It would be highly unlikely that one would slip on that LCVP deck.

The Coroner asked about my son's physical condition on the morning of the 6th August, about my son's mood on that day, about whether my son was irritated at having to go up, about what my son's reaction was on finding the hoses had been changed. Nothing detrimental to my son resulted from this pointed questioning.

It is interesting to note that no attempt was made to find out about PO Fulton's condition on that day, or his state of mind on that day, or his irritation at being asked about the hoses again, or his over-all attitude after having been recently and publically demoted.

The Coroner now publically appeared to want to know the relations between the two men, between PO Fulton and my son. PO Fulton conveyed that he did not know my son particularly well. We shall never know whether or not this was true as no-one else was asked to verify this.

We do not know whether these two men, who worked in the same Engineering department, had any other line of contact with each other, or dealings with each other. Were they perhaps in the same boxing team? Were they perhaps in the same running team? Were they perhaps in the same volley ball team? Was there any bad blood between the two men? We would never know as the Coroner refused to release the Disciplinary Records of HMS Ocean, and he did not enquire about the relations of the two men from a section head, or the head of department, or from any other person in the department.

## PO Dot Cottam

Tape 3 – 00:20:13

PO Dot Cottam took the witness stand.

PO Dot Cottam had been promoted to Head of Boats Section to replace PO Fulton, who had this position stripped from him a few days before my son's fall.

PO Dot Cottam began by reading his account of the events of that day, and how he had cradled my son's broken head. The account was very moving.

On that beautiful Friday morning of 6th August, 2010, there were two LCVPs positioned in the water immediately below the LCVP Bay, called NM and N3. I understand that these LCVPs were strapped together so that a man could easily walk from one to the other.

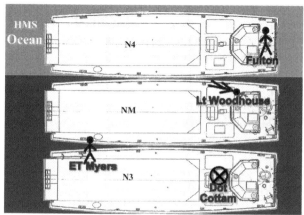

PO Dot Cottam was working in the engine bay of LCVP N3 and therefore saw nothing. He did not see the US Navy ship USS Mitscher sailing past either.

ET Myers was on the deck of one of the two LCVPs and heard a loud scream. On looking up, ET Myers watched as my son was falling from N4, the LCVP in the Bay above them. ET Myers saw my son land on the wheelhouse roof of NM, hitting it with his head.

ET Myers then started shouting the alarm. As PO Dot Cottam was in the engine bay, he did not hear him. ET Myers ran to the wheelhouse, being the entrance to the engine bay, and continued shouting 'Dot! Dot!'

PO Dot Cottam heard a large thud, and then when ET Myers ran to the wheelhouse, PO Dot Cottam heard ET Myers shouting his name, 'Dot! Dot!'. He immediately emerged to find out what all the shouting was about.

PO Dot Cottam saw a man in white on LCVP NM. He immediately ran to help and saw that it was Joshua. Joshua was in a pool of blood.

PO Dot Cottam and ET Myers now both continue shouting to raise an alarm.

Remember in all this time, when the air is filled with shouting and my son's scream, PO Fulton hears nothing, and PO Fulton, who is still on LCVP N4 directly above them, is wondering where my son could possibly have got to. PO Dot Cottam and ET Myers continue shouting 'Casualty, Casualty, Casualty.'

On hearing the shouting, some Royal Marines immediately came on the scene and administered first aid. Three US Medical Personnel arrived onto the LCVP from nowhere. They heard the loud and continuous shouting 'Casualty, Casualty, Casualty' but PO Fulton heard nothing, and was wondering where my son could possibly have got to.

Crew from inside HMS Ocean heard the alarm and came to see what it was about. When they saw Joshua in a pool of blood, they continued shouting and called for the medical officer.

Joshua was taken immediately to the helicopter at the Mayport Naval Base, and was flown to Shands Jacksonville hospital.

Just for information, ET Myers did not appear at my son's Inquest to give any evidence.

## PO Dot Cottam Questioned - What did he Hear?

We have ascertained that PO Dot Cottam heard very little as he was down below in the engine bay. PO Dot Cottam also told us that the entrance to the engine bay was through the wheelhouse. This would explain why ET Myers ran to the wheelhouse in order to alert PO Dot Cottam that there had been a casualty.

Our Barrister wanted to alert the Jury to PO Fulton's very strange behaviour and unlikely account of the events of my son's fall. Therefore our Barrister questioned PO Dot Cottam on what the sounds were at the time that my son fell.

Day 2 - Tape 3 – 00:49:13

PO Dot Cottam was inside the engine bay, which is underneath the wheelhouse, at the time of my son's fall fixing a hydraulic leak, on the OUTER LCVP, N3, the one further away from HMS Ocean.

> Our Barrister
>> *"Were you using any tools, was there any machine running, what sort of sounds were there down there at that time?"*
>
> PO Dot Cottam
>> *"Nothing was running. The power to the boat was on, because it's powered off batteries. The lights were on. There were no fans running, no vent running. **There wasn't really much sound at all,** to be honest. I had a set of spanners, rags, which are like cloths that we use for wiping up oil and that's pretty much it, really."*
>
> Our Barrister
>> *"The other landing craft, the one that was inboard of you and closer to HMS Ocean, was there anything happening on board that at that time?"*
>
> PO Dot Cottam
>> *"No"*
>
> Our Barrister
>> *"Just floating there?"*
>
> PO Dot Cottam
>> *"Yeah"*
>
> Our Barrister
>> *"Engine running, or not running?"*
>
> PO Dot Cottam

"No, not"

Our Barrister

**"Any other noises that you can help the Jury with?** What were the waves like, what sort of sound do they make. Were they loud? Is it a quiet sound?"

PO Dot Cottam

"No, it's just, …… can you imagine it like a trickle of water, like a,…… hard to describe, **just like a bit of a trickle of water almost."**

Our Barrister

"Were you at any time aware of an American Naval ship passing?"

PO Dot Cottam

"No"

Our Barrister

"Didn't notice at all?"

PO Dot Cottam

"No"

Our Barrister

"What were the sea conditions like at this point?"

PO Dot Cottam

"It was, flat calm really"

ET Myers in his testimony, which the Jury had not heard yet, had said that the engine was running at the time. ET Myers did not come to the Inquest, despite being summoned; therefore he could not have been questioned about this. Only his statement was read out.

"I believe I had delayed reactions as I felt as if I was just starring at him for 10 seconds. I then started shouting 'Casualty, Casualty, Casualty.' I did not think PO ET(ME) Dot Cottam heard me as the **engine of N3 was running,** so I went over to the wheelhouse of N3 and shouted 'Dot' which is PO ET(ME) Dot Cottams nick name."

# PO Dot Cottam Always Used the Back Way

This was very strange. When climbing onto the wheelhouse roof PO Dot Cottam told us he always used the back way. We had seen the plans; we had studied these together with the pictures. Why would anyone use the back way to get up or down the wheelhouse roof? When we were at Marine Base, Poole, the Royal Marines told us that they never used the back route as it was too dangerous. It would have been common sense to use the easier and shorter front route.

PO Dot Cottam explained in his own words why he took the back route –

Day 2 - Tape 3 – 00:32:37

> "Because there's a, excuse the way I'm going to explain this, but it's more, it's easier, because the handrail, I don't know if you've seen pictures, is quite high to just get your leg onto, so I've got to step onto the caged winch at the back, there's a little winch at the back of the LCVP. Step onto that, and then step onto the handrail, and then also use the handle for the, one of the windows at the back as well. And then you can also hold onto the mast while you're climbing up as well."

## PO Dot Cottam Never Uses a Safety Harness

It is now two years and three months after my son's death and PO Dot Cottam explains to all present at the Inquest how he does his job on the LCVP, including climbing onto the wheelhouse roof when the need arose. PO Dot Cottam tells us that he never uses a safety harness. (See full transcript on the web site)

Day 2 - Tape 3 – 00:27:30
PO Dot Cottam
> "To bed there's always a laid down, if you're going aloft use the harness procedure, but when we're going aloft **I personally never used it** because we just literally stepped on the LCVP and either go in the engine bay or well deck."

Coroner
> "Have you ever had to climb on the roof of the ..?"

PO Dot Cottam
> "A couple of times"

Coroner
> "Of the wheelhouse?"

PO Dot Cottam
> "Yeah"

Coroner
> "Have you worn a safety harness then?"

PO Dot Cottam

*"No"*
Coroner
*"But you're supposed to?"*
PO Dot Cottam
*"You're supposed to, yeah, but there's also **nowhere to clip on either**"*
Coroner
*"What, up there?"*
PO Dot Cottam
*"Yeah"*

# The Three Royal Navy Lieutenants

It was now time for the three Royal Navy lieutenants to take the stand. Originally these three witnesses had been assigned into the Rule 37 category, where their statements would only be read out.

Then on the 12th September, 2012, our legal team received another updated Inquest Witness List. This was the third one they had received. In this latest Inquest Witness List, the Coroner had changed the status of the three lieutenants from Rule 37 Witnesses to live witnesses.

Why the change? The Coroner had by his continual actions in hiding evidence and in prohibiting a full Middleton Inquiry shown us that all he wanted was to prove that my son was drunk and so responsible for his own death. By calling these three lieutenants as live witnesses, could he achieve this goal? In his questioning of the three lieutenants the Coroner probed hard, trying to prove that my son was drunk from the night before, or at the very least introduce an air of suspicion and doubt regarding my son's state.

What was very sad was that the Coroner had not probed when questioning PO Fulton regarding the myriad suspicious facts surrounding my son's death. Neither had the Coroner probed at all when he received the evidence given in the three US Navy witness statements.

Instead, the Coroner probed my son's drinking from the night before, but his probing backfired on him.

By probing so meticulously the Inquest court obtained a very good idea of my son's character, of my son's behaviour on his last night before his fall, and of my son's kind and generous nature, and of his total control regarding his alcohol consumption during the night's socialising.

This is not what the Coroner was hoping for. I shall now recount the picture that the three Royal Navy lieutenants painted for us of my son's last night before his fatal fall.

# A Dream Deployment in the USA

This was a dream deployment. HMS Ocean was going to the USA, that beautiful country with its rich and diverse peoples, heritage, landscape, and wildlife.

The crew of HMS Ocean were in holiday mood. HMS Ocean was taking the opportunity of stopping in Jacksonville, Florida, to allow the crew to go on leave. Lt Lisa Pitman explained to us –

Day 2 - Tape 3 02:08:34

> Lt Lisa Pitman
> *"Everybody was having a good time. So I wouldn't have said that any of us, I wouldn't have described any of us as being drunk. We'd all had some drinks and we were, there were lots of people around and **we were due to go on leave** in a couple of days' time. Half the ship's company were on leave. We were in Florida, for three weeks. **So half the ship's company were on leave already** and they were due to come back I think the following day, or maybe the day after, and then we were going to swop over and **the rest of us were going on leave.** So, it's kind of like, um, Josh's fiancée was due to come out. **So just having a nice evening** before some people had already come back from their leave. So, it was a just a nice evening to go out, and have a few drinks, something to eat and **before we went on leave for the rest of the time were there."***

In this setting, with half the crew on holiday and the remaining crew about to start their holiday, the ship's company decided to spend a night socialising and celebrating in Jacksonville, Florida, on Thursday, 5th August, 2010.

# A Beautiful Meal in a Beautiful Place

And the three Lieutenants, Lt Hayes, Lt Pearson, and my son, decided to leave the ship at 5pm and have a beautiful meal in a beautiful place, after which they planned to join up with the rest of the ship's company for their night of celebrating and socialising.

It was pointed out that they could have economised and eaten on board HMS Ocean, but these three Lieutenants wanted to enjoy an authentic American meal overlooking the beautiful Florida sea, with its palm trees and balmy beaches. Lt Jennifer Hayes explained to us –

Day 2 - Tape 3 01:34:29

> Coroner
> *"So you went ashore at 1700. So you all changed into civilian clothes and went off together. So you were going ashore to eat. What were the longer term plans that evening? Did you plan to do anything else?"*
> Jennifer Hayes
> *"Eat, like, we were probably **the first ashore that night because we were going to eat.** We'd got everyone else's telephone number. So it's usually just a case of people will phone when they've perhaps finished some of the paperwork for the night, or something like that, or they've had more to do onboard and have kind of **or they've eaten on board because they want to save money.** And then we just tend to as a wardroom phone each other up, organise where to meet and that's how we met some of the other people that night."*

My son, Lt Hayes, and Lt Pearson left the ship for their meal at 5pm, and from about 5:30pm until 11pm sat and talked and talked, all the while enjoying the Florida beach. Lt Jennifer Hayes told us that they put the world to rights. I quote below –

Day 2 - Tape 3 01:34:29

> Coroner
> *"What were you going ashore for?"*
> Jennifer Hayes
> *"I hoped food...although the food on board is of an adequate standard it's often nice to go ashore and eat and in a nice surrounding and rather than surrounded by a metal box that you'd been on board for weeks or*

*months. So that was, the aim was 1700, go ashore and have some food."*

*"Jacksonville Beach was a really nice place to sit. **Sit watching the beach, put the world to rights.** Just have some down time on what had, we'd had a really busy schedule up till then. So it's just some nice time off."*

A few minutes later Lt Jennifer Hayes continues –

Day 2 - Tape 3 01:38:00 continued

> Coroner
> > *"Four bottles each. So you were eating for quite a long time, were you?"*
>
> Jennifer Hayes
> > *"It was a nice spot, Sir."*
> > *"It was right on the beach and looking out over the beach."*
> > *"I believe we were **putting the world to rights.** The three of us were all Engineers so got a lot to talk about."*
> >
> > *"**That's the first opportunity you get off ship just as friends to talk** rather than having your hierarchy there or your subordinates there and stuff like that. So, I think we were there for quite a while."*

Lt Pearson, one of the trio enjoying this beautiful location over a long meal also confirmed this and told us –

Day 2 - Tape 3 01:55:59

> Coroner
> > *"Can you recall how long you were actually eating for before the other officers turned up?"*
>
> Lt Pearson
> > *"I don't recall, but we certainly weren't rushing our food. It was, you know, **you're sat in Florida, on a beachfront with people. It was a promenade in front of the bar with people roller blading and the likes, going up and down. So, we were in no rush. We were just sat back, chilling out."***

The three Royal Navy lieutenants sat and ate and enjoyed this setting for about five and a half hours.

# And the Chicken Wings

What about the food? It can't only have been the astounding location; the food must have been good too. Let us listen to what the Lieutenants told us regarding that most memorable last meal with my son. That meal stretched over a five hour period on the Florida beach, as the sun set and whilst they put the world to rights –

Day 2 - Tape 3 01:37:48 continued

> Coroner
> *"You had some food. What did you have to eat? Can you remember?"*
> Jennifer Hayes
> **"Chicken wings, and lots of them, Sir"**
> Coroner
> *"And Joshua Woodhouse had them as well?"*
> Jennifer Hayes
> **"Yeah. They came in sets of twenty four and I think we had a couple of different flavours of chicken wings. A couple of sets of them."**

And this was also confirmed when our Barrister questioned Lt Hayes –

Day 2 - Tape 3 01:46:10 continued

> Our Barrister
> *"Spent a little time looking for a nice place to have some food and some drinks. You find Bukkets Bar and you **have a large quantity of chicken wings there as you've explained, twenty four in a serving, forty eight you thought, it was two lots.** Might it have been a third amount as well, just helping us with how much you as a trio ate?"*
> Jennifer Hayes
> *"It's not, to be honest, there were three of us, so it's not unfeasible that there were three lots."*
> Coroner
> *"I admire your constitution if you can eat that many chicken wings, Lieutenant."*
> Jennifer Hayes

*"They were good chicken wings, Sir."*
Our Barrister
*"But, one of the aims was to have a nice meal out, the three of you?"*
Jennifer Hayes
*"Yeah, It was to eat out. It wasn't to, we wouldn't have started that early if there had been other motives."*

Lt Pearson also told us about the chicken wings –

Day 2 - Tape 3 01:54:48 continued

Coroner
*"And you recollect* **three buckets of chicken wings** *as well, do you?"*
Lt Pearson
*"We probably bought a portion of chicken wings each because we had different flavours, so we could all try them."*
Coroner
*"Quite a lot of them. So, you were consuming quite a lot of food with that alcohol?"*
Lt Pearson
*"Yes"*

All this while the Coroner, with his meticulous probing, had not proved that my son was drunk, or out of control, but instead, with his probing, had allowed the Lieutenants to paint us a picture of my son's character, and the character of the other two lieutenants.

Here we have three lieutenants who are in no hurry to lose this very precious moment in time. They sat enjoying their meal in Bukkets Bar from about 5:30pm until about 11:00pm

These three lieutenants enjoyed in the fullest sense this once in a lifetime opportunity to bask and absorb the sights, smells, flavours, and culture of the United States. And we felt very much that we were there with them.

# And the Drinks?

What about the drinks? All that probing by the Coroner had to have some results. We did find out what they drank. Lt Pearson tells us how much they consumed whilst they were eating their chicken wings –

Day 2 - Tape 3 01:54:48

> Coroner
> *"And did you have these chicken wings as well that we've heard about? Your recollection of how much the three of you had to drink with the chicken wings. Lt Hayes said she thought probably four bottles each?"*
>
> Lt Pearson
> *"With the chicken wings, I don't know. I couldn't break it down. In my statement I said round about seven bottles. I think the buckets came in seven bottles in a bucket. We probably got two buckets each, so we probably did about six or seven bottles. And being half pint bottles **about three and a half pints over the course of five hours."***
>
> Coroner
> *"And you recollect **three buckets of chicken wings** as well do you?"*
>
> Lt Pearson
> ***"We probably bought a portion of chicken wings each because we had different flavours, so we could all try them."***
>
> Coroner
> ***"Quite a lot of them. So, you were consuming quite a lot of food with that alcohol?"***
>
> Lt Pearson
> *"Yes"*

Lt Jennifer Hayes confirmed this when she told us –

Day 2 - Tape 3 01:38:00

> Coroner
> *"And with your food you say that four bottles of Corona. That's beer, isn't it?"*
>
> Jennifer Hayes
> *"It is, Sir."*
>
> Coroner
> *"And was that four bottles each or?"*
>
> Jennifer Hayes
> *"It was, I couldn't actually tell you Sir, whether it was*

*four bottles each, I assume it was probably four bottles each."*

Coroner

**"Four bottles each. So you were eating for quite a long time, were you?"**

Jennifer Hayes

*"It was a nice spot, Sir. It was right on the beach and looking out over the beach. I believe we were putting the world to rights. The three of us were all Engineers so got a lot to talk about. That's the first opportunity you get off ship just as friends to talk rather than having your hierarchy there or your subordinates there and stuff like that. So, I think we were there for quite a while."*

Coroner

*"So when you say you had four bottles of beer, would Joshua have had the same amount?"*

Jennifer Hayes

**"They were served in buckets. They came as a, like a bucket, and you put however many dollars, and the bucket was full of ice, and that's why it was called Bukkets Bar. The bucket is full of ice and then you had I think it was about six or seven beers in the bucket."**

Coroner

*"So while you were eating you got through about four each?"*

Jennifer Hayes

*"Yeah."*

## Two Cups of Warm Beer

After the meal, at about 11pm, Lt Jennifer Hayes, Lt Pearson, and my son, then joined the rest of the ship's company at Ocean's Bar.

What did my son drink whilst socialising at Ocean's Bar? According to Lt Pearson, my son drank two more beers, which were served in small white plastic cups. And we were further told that these were not particularly appetising, as they were warm, contrasting sharply with the chilled beers kept in ice buckets at Bukkets Bar.

Lt Pearson told us -

Day 2 - Tape 3 - 02:01:18 continued

Coroner
> "So, did you get the impression that you were all getting a bit drunk or not?"

Lt Pearson
> "No. To be honest, that's **a very sort of relaxed and easy pace for the evening. Three and a half pints over five hours**, and **a couple of beers after that.** And it certainly wasn't a huge amount of consumption for me. I can't state what Joshua's tolerance is for alcohol, **but I would say generally that if somebody is not going at the same pace as you, you can spot it. If somebody is getting drunk quicker than you, their behaviour alters. If you're both going at the same time then your behaviour seems natural to each other. I certainly didn't see any shows or tells that Joshua's....**"

Lt Jennifer Hayes also told us how she too had the plastic cups of warm beer, and how they were not particularly nice.

Day 2 - Tape 3 - 01:40:58

Coroner
> "And you say there that you drank two cups of larger?"

Jennifer Hayes
> "Yeah. They were like plastic cups"

Coroner
> "And they were smaller than half pints? Sort of American half-pints?"

When questioned a little while later by our Barrister, Lt Jennifer Hayes told us —

Day 2 - Tape 3 - 01:47:41

Our Barrister
> "And then you go onto the Ocean Club where you had two small plastic cups of beer. **Probably warm as well?**"

Jennifer Hayes
> "**It wasn't very nice.**"

Our Barrister
> "And you are not aware of what Josh was drinking at

that time?"

Day 2 - Tape 3 - 02:01:50 continued

Coroner
*"So nobody was sort of staggering about or being sick or anything like that?"*
Lt Pearson
**"No. It wasn't a heavy night or a mad night, or anything like that. Very sort of relaxed and chilled out"**

And so we find that after their meal my son only consumed two small cups of warm beer, and who is to say that he did not chuck them away as they were so unappetising on that hot Florida night. In total, as Lt Pearson told us, my son only had –

**"Three and a half pints over five hours, and a couple of beers after that."**

# Shark Watch

The Coroner would not let this one go. He kept on probing. He needed at the very least to cast some doubt on my son's state as a result of the evening of socialising.

Lt Pearson had just informed us what a relaxed evening they had had together, and how they had only consumed three and a half pints over five hours, and a couple of beers after that.

Let us listen to the continued probing -

Day 2 - Tape 3 - 02:01:50

Coroner
*"He didn't' seem to be any worse for wear than you in any way?"*
Lt Pearson
*"No"*
Coroner
*"And you felt you were okay and in control?"*
Lt Pearson
*"Yeah"*

Coroner
> *"So nobody was sort of staggering about or being sick or anything like that?"*

Lt Pearson
> **"No. It wasn't a heavy night or a mad night, or anything like that. Very sort of relaxed and chilled out"**

And when our Barrister questioned Lt Hayes, we heard for the first time the term 'Shark Watch'. Lt Hayes explained to us –

Day 2 - Tape 3 - 01:48:25

Our Barrister
> *"When you last saw him that evening, so still on the night out, you were at Ocean Club when you last saw him?"*

Jennifer Hayes
> *"Yes"*

Our Barrister
> *"What sort of state was he in then?"*

Jennifer Hayes
> *"We were all still.. making coherent conversations. We were **putting the world to rights** as you do when you're ashore, **that's the whole purpose.** You go, you chew the fat and you talk about things."*
> *"He was, the last thing I remember of him, we were still **having coherent conversations, if animated**, but nothing that made me think,......"*
> *"We've got this kind of thing called **Shark Watch,** where if someone is becoming too intoxicated or anything like that, and that hadn't kicked in, we're made very wary of people being too drunk and incapable. **And I'd had none of those concerns."***

Our Barrister
> **"So, coherent, steady on his feet, having a conversation which was followable, coherent, and sensible? Yes?"**

Jennifer Hayes
> *"Yes, Sir."*

And Lt Lisa Pitman, who met the three lieutenants after their meal, also confirms that my son was not inebriated. She tells us –

Day 2 - Tape 3 - 02:17:20

Our Barrister

> *"Just putting all that together."*
>
> *"On the 5<sup>th</sup> August, then, you went ashore around 7 o'clock in the evening. You met up with other officers and you had something to eat and some cocktails at a hotel with them. But you were aware that Josh and others were going to be meeting up elsewhere later, and you planned to meet them. You went to the Oceans Bar or Oceans Club, around 10:30 or 11 o'clock. So, you hadn't seen Josh or any of the others in his group up to that point that evening. You spent some time at the Oceans Bar, or club, with Josh and others?"*

Lt Lisa Pitman

> *"Uhum"*

Our Barrister

> *"And as far as you could see Josh at that stage **was in control, being his normal self, effectively. And his normal self is upbeat, lively and positive.** Yes?"*

Lt Lisa Pitman

> *"**Absolutely.**"*

The Coroner's endeavours to bring disrepute or at the very least suspicion on my son's physical state had failed miserably despite his constant probing.

It was this very probing that backfired on the Coroner and instead revealed to the Jury and all present at the Inquest not only that my son was not in the slightest under the influence of alcohol, but this probing also revealed my son's character. As one of the legal team said afterwards, he was one of the nice crowd.

Let us move on to the events of the next morning, the one hour before my son's fatal fall.

# What was he like the Next Day?

Day 2 - Tape 3 - 02:13:08

Coroner

> *"And you say that he looked at you and laughed because you didn't look too well, due to your late night. **A bit wrecked, were you?**"*

Lt Lisa Pitman
*"**No. I wouldn't say I was drunk**, but you know we'd only had, I didn't get back on board until probably half 2, 3 o'clock. So only we'd only had four, four and a half hours sleep"*

Day 2 - Tape 3 - 02:16:06

Coroner
*"He did, there's nothing, there wasn't anything unusual? And you said you had another joke about the previous night?"*
Lt Lisa Pitman
*"Yes"*
Coroner
*"What?"*
Lt Lisa Pitman
*"Just that we'd had a good night out and ..."*
Coroner
*"**Not comments like we're feeling wrecked** or tired this morning or anything like that?"*
Lt Lisa Pitman
*"No, nothing."*
Coroner
*"**He still seemed to be his normal, cheery self?**"*
Lt Lisa Pitman
*"Yes."*

Our Barrister then questioned Lisa Pitman and confirmed that my son was definitely not suffering any effects of any alcohol overindulgence.

Day 2 - Tape 3 - 02:18:30

Our Barrister
*"You move onto 7:45 the next morning. You knock on his cabin door, because that's the sort of supportive relationship that the officers have to make sure everyone is up?"*
Lt Lisa Pitman
*"Yep"*
Our Barrister
*"He was already up when you knocked on his door.*

*Somehow the door came to be open, and when opened he was already dressed?"*

Lt Lisa Pitman

*"Yes"*

Our Barrister

*"And he was cleaning his teeth. A bit of banter between the two of you. **The banter is not because either of you is hung over,** but because you're a bit short on sleep from the previous night?"*

Lt Lisa Pitman

*"Yes."*

We then move on to what Lt Jennifer Hayes tells us about her meeting with my son the morning of his fall.

Day 2 - Tape 3 - 01:49:26

Our Barrister

*"And at five to eight it was Josh who actually came to your cabin?"*

Jennifer Hayes

*"Yes, Josh came to my cabin."*

Our Barrister

*"Alright. And he was already dressed as you told us, and all set to go for the day?"*

Jennifer Hayes

*"Yes"*

Our Barrister

*"A bit of banter, you told us, between the two of you. The Cousin It joke, etc, but certainly nothing about him that **gave you any cause for concern about his state?"***

Jennifer Hayes

*"No. **He was just usual Josh. He was bright, he was bouncy, he was making jokes. He just, he was just being Josh."***

Our Barrister

***"And because you are a good friend to him you would notice if there was anything amiss or whether he was less than 100% presumably?"***

Jennifer Hayes

*"I think so, Sir"*

Our Barrister

> *"And there was nothing about him that caused you to think anything other than that he was 100% that day?"*

Jennifer Hayes
> *"Nothing to make me think he wasn't 100% that day."*

Our Barrister
> *"Thank you very much indeed"*

And so we see that the Coroner had failed in his attempts to prove my son was even slightly under the influence of alcohol. As Lt Jennifer Hayes said, *'Nothing to make me think he wasn't 100% that day.'*

# Bright and Alert the Next Day

The Coroner, seeing that he cannot pin drunkenness on my son, then tries to pin sleep deprivation and exhaustion on my son.

Day 2 - Tape 3 - 02:13:08

Coroner
> *"And you say that he looked at you and laughed because you didn't look too well, due to your late night. A bit wrecked, were you?"*

Lt Lisa Pitman
> *"No. I wouldn't say I was drunk, but you know we'd only had, I didn't get back on board until probably half 2, 3 o'clock. So only we'd only had four, four and a half hours sleep."*

Coroner
> *"So you were feeling the effects of not having slept very much, rather than the effects of the consumption the night before of alcohol and whatever you were eating. I see. So he laughed at you, and you say that you noticed that he also looked slightly shabby with slightly bloodshot eyes. **He looked as though he had not had a lot of sleep?"***

Lt Lisa Pitman
> *"uhum"*

Coroner
> *"So, in the **same sort of state as yourself,** really?"*

Lt Lisa Pitman
> *"But I wouldn't have said that he was drunk the night*

> *before."*
>
> Coroner
>
> *"No, I'm not talking about drunk, **but sort of feeling the effects of not having slept a lot,** rather than hung over. Is that what you 're telling me?"*
>
> Lt Lisa Pitman
>
> ***"Just a bit tired. Yes"***
>
> Coroner
>
> *"So you pulled his leg about that, did you as well? What was his reaction?"*
>
> Lt Lisa Pitman
>
> *"He just laughed."*
>
> Coroner
>
> ***"Did he say he hadn't had much sleep,*** *or anything like that?"*
>
> Lt Lisa Pitman
>
> *"I don't remember. **I don't think so"***
>
> Coroner
>
> *"No. And you say at that stage he was up and dressed and he was wearing white overalls?"*

But we hear from Lt Lisa Pitman that just before 9am that morning she contacted my son about a part that he had wanted her to order over the last few days.

The Coroner in going to such great lengths to prove my son was unfit for work and suffering from sleep deprivation, actually proved the opposite. His questioning revealed that my son was bright, industrious, and alert that morning.

This was my son's normal state.

Firstly we see that my son is easily up on time, bright, happy, dressed for work, and brushing his teeth when Lt Lisa Pitman knocked on his cabin door. He is cheery and making his normal banter at the tired state of Lisa Pitman.

Lisa Pitman then tells us that she called him at 9am that morning to look at a PDF attachment which she cannot open on the ship's computer system, and to check an equipment part that he had requested a few days earlier.

There is no sign of tiredness. There is no sign of 'leave me alone I've had very little sleep.' On the contrary my son is right there to help, firstly trying to sort out the problem with the PDF attachment and then scrutinising the part to see whether it is the one he required. This is not the behaviour of a man who was exhausted from the previous night.

Let us hear how Lt Lisa Pitman describes my son's last moments before his fall –

Day 2 - Tape 3 - 02:14:53

Coroner
> *"But he didn't say anything about feeling hung over. He just looked as though he hadn't had much sleep?"*
> *"But at 9 o'clock you telephoned him from the Boats workshop. What was that about?"*

Lt Lisa Pitman
> *"If I remember rightly, **he needed a part**, and we were trying to get a part from the ship's chandler and the ship's chandler had just come onboard, and he had given us a couple of pages out of a catalogue. And I wanted Josh to come and look and see if we could work out which part it was that we needed to order, and the pages of the catalogue that he'd, the chandler had given us, didn't have the right part on it. And he'd also sent it on an email as well, like a PDF attachment to an email, and **that we couldn't get it to open.** So we, Josh went off to do...."*

Coroner
> *"Can you recall what sort of part it was?"*

Lt Lisa Pitman
> *"No"*

Coroner
> *"It wasn't anything to do with these flexible hoses?"*

Lt Lisa Pitman
> *"I can't remember"*

Coroner
> *"You can't remember? So you met up with him again then, and say that he had a bottle of water with him?"*

Lt Lisa Pitman
> *"He always carried a bottle of water"*

Coroner
> *"He did, there's nothing, there wasn't anything unusual? And you said you had another joke about the previous night?"*

Lt Lisa Pitman

    *"Yes"*
Coroner
    *"What?"*
Lt Lisa Pitman
    *"Just that we'd had a good night out and ..."*
Coroner
    *"Not comments like we're feeling wrecked or tired this morning or anything like that?"*
Lt Lisa Pitman
    *"No, nothing."*
Coroner
    **"He still seemed to be his normal, cheery self?"**
Lt Lisa Pitman
    *"Yes."*

And Lisa Pitman finished by telling us –

Day 2 - Tape 3 - 02:16:23

Coroner
    *"So when you met him there on the gangway, that conversation lasted how long?"*
Lt Lisa Pitman
    *"Just literally a couple of minutes. Long enough for us **to try and open up the attachment** to the email and to have a **look through a couple of pages and realise that they weren't the right ones.** And I said I would contact the chandler again and try to get him to either bring a copy of the catalogue. And Josh went off to do whatever it was that he was going to do"*

Our Barrister questioned Lisa Pitman on this. I recount it below –

Day 2 - Tape 3 - 02:19:10

Our Barrister
    *"You then see him a little later, around 9 o'clock that morning, and you have a conversation with him about a particular part. And just help us with that. Is it a part that he's trying to find?"*
Lt Lisa Pitman
    *"Yes. One of my, basically my role on board was to get all of the stores and everything, as a Logistics Officer,*

to get the stores that the engineers needed. And **he was after a particular part**, and I can't for the life of me remember what it was. But he wanted this part and the chandler was trying to source it for us. So he kept bringing us bits of catalogues from ... Merchants Engineering Companies.. to see if we could find the exact bit that it was that Josh needed."

Our Barrister

"That had all happened that morning?"

Lt Lisa Pitman

"That morning.... it had been on-going for sort of two of three days."

Our Barrister

"All right"

Lt Lisa Pitman

"But the chandler had sent me an email overnight which had got this PDF document attached to it which we couldn't get to open on the ship's system."

Our Barrister

"Had Josh had access to that email before he came back to see you at 9 o'clock?"

Lt Lisa Pitman

"No he hadn't. It had come in to my email account and I'd called Josh to come and have a look and see if we could work out which piece, which part it was that we couldn't get the attachment to open."

Our Barrister

**"Certainly, so far as you could work out, he was by 9 o'clock properly up and into the detail of his job?"**

Lt Lisa Pitman

"Yes"

Our Barrister

"And when you last saw him at that point around 9 o'clock again **he was being his normal self?"**

Lt Lisa Pitman

"Yes."

Our Barrister

**"And his normal self is lively, upbeat, and positive?"**

Lt Lisa Pitman

**"Definitely."**

Our Barrister

**"Nothing to give you any cause for concern about his state or his... nothing at all?"**

Lt Lisa Pitman
*""No, not at all."*

And so we see that the Coroner could not even lay the hint or suspicion of intoxication or sleep deprivation on my son, try as he might. On the contrary, his probing revealed my son as alert, active, and diligent.

It was interesting to note that one of the legal team, after hearing the three lieutenants' accounts, described my son as *'industrious, diligent, and intelligent'*.

This was an accurate appraisal of my son, and this is how we found him behaving right to the very last.

## What was he really like?

What was my son like? What type of person was he, and why is this important?

Let us hear how Lt Jennifer Hayes describes my son –

Day 2 - Tape 3 - 01:33:12

> Jennifer Hayes
> > *"I joined before Joshua Woodhouse."*
> Coroner
> > *"Right. Was he someone you were particularly friendly with?"*
> Jennifer Hayes
> > *"I was the Propulsion Engineering Officer, and he was the Ship's Services Engineer. Therefore, as Lieutenants we were kind of each other's opposite number. We were both pre-charge, which means that we hadn't achieved our Marine Engineer Charge qualifications yet, which is what we were both working towards. As well as having our departmental responsibilities . And so I did, I know Joshua very well, and worked with him in the same office all the time."*
> Coroner
> > *"I see, did you also see him socially as well? He was one of your friends?"*
> Jennifer Hayes
> > *"Yes. He was one of my closest friends on board."*

Day 2 - Tape 3 - 01:43:01 continued

Coroner
*"Why did he come to your cabin?"*
Jennifer Hayes
*"8 o'clock is Turn To. It's good practice to make sure that your friends, especially if you haven't seen them, especially if you've left at different times, stuff like that. It's good practice, and Joshua was a **very good friend** to come and just make sure they're up. 8 o'clock is Turn To. If you're not up at 8 o'clock and Turn To to work then there's administrative and disciplinary procedures that could be put in place. And so he was just, because he hadn't seen me, **he just came down** to knock on my door and just make sure that I was there and alright. **Just being a good friend.** "*

Now let us hear what Lt Lisa Pitman says of her relations with my son –

Day 2 - Tape 3 - 02:05:20

Coroner
*"But you were on board for just over a year by the time that Josh died? Did you get to know him when he first joined the crew?"*
Lt Lisa Pitman
*"Yeah. I would say that **he was a good friend of mine** who lived in the cabin next door to me. So we saw each other first thing in the mornings and when you are going to bed in the evenings, and stuff like that. And go out when we are ashore together and things."*

And then she confirms his character as a lively, upbeat, and positive person –

Day 2 - Tape 3 - 02:20:47

Our Barrister
*"And when you last saw him at that point around 9 o'clock again **he was being his normal self?**"*
Lt Lisa Pitman
*"Yes."*
Our Barrister
***"And his normal self is lively, upbeat, and positive?"***

Lt Lisa Pitman
**_"Definitely."_**

We have just heard how Lt Lisa Pitman and Lt Jennifer Hayes describe my son, and as friends it is quite understandable that they would speak well of their lost friend.

But let us hear how Lt Pearson describes my son. Lt Pearson was new to HMS Ocean, having arrived just over one month previously. Being new to the ship it would be very telling to hear how he views my son.

Day 2 - Tape 3 - 01:52:06

Coroner
*"Now, Lt Pearson you gave a statement to the Service Police back on the 11th August, 2010, and I'd like to run through what you said in that statement as I've just done with Lt Hayes. At the time of this incident how long had you been on Ocean?"*
Lt Pearson
*"I'd been on Ocean since 1st July, Sir, little over a month"*
Coroner
*"You were quite new to the ship?"*
Lt Pearson
*"Yes"*
Coroner
*"So Joshua was already on board when you arrived?"*
Lt Pearson
*"Yes he was, Sir"*
Coroner
*"Had he become a friend of yours by the time you...?"*
Lt Pearson
**_"He was a very likeable character. I was still getting to know the people in the Wardroom but there were a couple of characters that stand out that you sort of get on with very quickly, and Joshua was one of those."_**

We have had a small opportunity to look into the relationships between my son and the three lieutenants present at the Inquest. They confirmed this view. My son was one of that breed of kind, likeable, caring people.

Could this have any bearing on the suspicious events surrounding my son's death?

## These Troublesome US Navy Personnel Statements

Day 2 - Tuesday 6<sup>th</sup> November, 2012 – 02:24:37

Coroner
> *"And that leaves us this afternoon with **these troublesome US Navy personnel statements**. They're a cumbersome set of documents."*

What did I just hear the Coroner say?

And here we have the heart of the Coroner, telling us what he really thinks of the US Navy witness statements.

Day 2 - Tuesday 6<sup>th</sup> November, 2012 - Tape 3 – 00:03:00

Coroner
> *"I don't know about you, but **my brain is beginning to hurt** with these statements, **if I can sort them out.**"*

The Coroner may call the statements of these dream witnesses '**these troublesome US Navy personnel statements**', but I have a different message that I wish to convey to these US Navy Witnesses, and to all in the US who did their utmost to help us.

My message is 'Thank you'.


# The Radio Play

After bemoaning the fact that the US Navy Personnel statements are so troublesome and cumbersome, the Coroner asks the two Barristers for any suggestions as how to best present these statements to the Jury.

In answer, our Barrister suggested that the Jury first be given an introduction, explaining why two sets of documents exist for each of the US Navy Witnesses. With regard to reading out the answers to the questionnaires, our Barrister suggested that perhaps the Jury could be directed to the question first, before the answer is read out.

Surprisingly, MOD Collins came up with a helpful suggestion. He put forward that perhaps the Coroner could read out the question and his Coroner's Officer read out the answer.

Day 2 - Tape 3 – 02:24:37

> Coroner
> *"So we do it rather like a radio play and I play the part of the SIB man and my Coroner's officer plays the part of the witness."*

and a few minutes later

> Coroner
> *"So shall we try it that way? That the first statement gets read out by Mrs. Hamilton **and then we do a double act** on the questions and answers, and let's just see how it goes."*

This was a big help. The Jury would have a better chance of getting an insight into the gold nuggets of these Rule 37 Witnesses.

## SIB Interviewed US Navy Sailors Immediately – Really?

After discussing the great dilemma concerning the 'troublesome' US Navy Witness statements, the Coroner now brings in the Jury for the afternoon session. He then proceeds to give them an introduction to the history behind the US Navy Witnesses, and why there are two sets of statements for three of the four witnesses.

The Coroner begins –

Day 2 - Tape 3 – 02:39:07

> *"Members of the Jury you will remember yesterday morning I mentioned to you that amongst the statements we were going to have read to us, were statements from four US Navy sailors who'd been on a ship called USS Mitscher that had been sailing past HMS Ocean at the time of the incident. Now **they were interviewed by the Royal Navy Police within days of the incident** and we had statements from them."*

This is the first that we had heard of this. The Royal Navy Police interviewed these US Navy Witnesses?

Let us look at the statement by Witness 1, Philippines, dated 12th August, 2010. We see that it is made to a Representative of the United States Naval Criminal Investigative Service.

*Place: NCISFO Norfolk, VA*
*Date: **August 12, 1010***

*"I xxx make the following free and voluntary statement to **xxx***
***whom I know to be a Representative of the United States***
***Naval Criminal Investigative Service.***

And looking at the statement by Witness 2, Charleston, dated 13th August, 2010, we see this is also made to a Representative of the United States Naval Criminal Investigative Service.

*Place: NCISFO Norfolk, VA*
*Date: **August 13, 2010***

*I, xxx make the following free and voluntary statement to xxx*
*whom I know to be a **Representative of the United States***
***Naval Criminal Investigative Service***

Finally with the statement given by Witness 3, Los Angeles, dated 25th August, 2010, we see this is also made to a Representative of the United States Naval Criminal Investigative Service.

*Place: NCISFO Norfolk, VA*
*Date: August 25, 2010*

*I, xxx make the following free and voluntary statement to xxx*
*whom I know to be a **Representative of the United States***
***Naval Criminal Investigative Service**.*

Are we to believe what the Coroner has just said?

But whichever way you look at it, whether the US Navy Witnesses were interviewed by the SIB, Military Police, and then their statements kept hidden from us, or whether they were ignored and never interviewed, both actions speak for themselves.

## Did the Jury Notice – My son was standing at the back of the wheelhouse?

The Question and Answers Radio play scenario suggested by MOD Collins was starting to make MOD Collins feel very uncomfortable.

The first two US Navy witness statements were read out, each finishing with the Question and Answer Radio play. It appears to have been effective, and have brought their statements somewhat to life.

And now the Inquest proceeded to the most important US Navy Witness: Witness 3, Los Angeles. This is the only US Navy Witness who saw the entire episode from start to finish. This is the only witness who was directly opposite my son at the time he fell. This is the only witness who did not turn away. The man in white he saw at the start was the same man in white that he saw falling.

This is the witness who tells us that my son was walking in a leisurely fashion, in all probability enjoying the sparkling blue sea on a hot Florida summer day, and in all probability watching a magnificent US Navy Warship sail past. This is the stuff dreams are made of.

> *"While I was manning the rails, I noticed a man in a white jumpsuit onboard HMS OCEAN. He stuck out to me because he was wearing all white. I noticed he was standing on one of OCEAN's landing crafts in a well deck.* **He was on the aft end.** *I saw him grab a stanchion/part"* (the hand rail) *"of the landing craft, and he appeared to try to proceed to the port side of the craft using the stanchion as leverage/handle."*

> **"He appeared to be comfortable doing what he was doing he was not tentative in his actions or motions.** *He was only using one hand, and I believe it was his right hand."*

After the Coroner's officer read out the first statement by Witness 3, Los Angeles, it was time for the Coroner to read out the Questions. He had already done it for the previous two witnesses, but it seems that reading out the questions for this witness had suddenly become very difficult. He started fumbling around with the papers in front of him, this mass of confusion that he had manufactured. And the fumbling continued.

As if choreographed, MOD Collins jumped up and tried to undo the good suggestion he had made a short time ago. By having the witness statements read out in the Radio Play fashion, the Jury might just pick up on the glaring inconsistency with PO Fulton's account of my son's position and actions.

Day 2 - Tape 3 – 03:11:00

Coroner fumbling.  More fumbling.  Fumble, fumble, fumble…. More fumbling….fumble, fumble, fumble

MOD Collins jumps up to his rescue.

> Collins
> *"Sir, the matter is for you to see how to best assist the Jury, **it may be that now we've all heard the questions, but, it may be easier to simply read the statement.**"*
> Coroner
> *"Yes. Alright. **I think that's why we are struggling a bit here trying to do it this way.** Carry on reading then that statement."*

The Coroner and MOD Collins were not content with this phoney Inquest. They now wanted to ensure that the statement from Witness 3, Los Angeles, remained in the dark. This witness would not be granted the same privileges as the other witnesses.  This witness would have the answers read out and no-one would know what the questions were.

Mrs Hamilton, the Coroner's Officer, proceeded to read the second statement made by Witness 3, Los Angeles, and, as instructed by the Coroner, just started reading out the answers.  What were the questions?

Day 2 - Tape 3 – 03:17:55

> Mrs Hamilton
> *"Question 2C -  I was in the station on the flight deck of USS Mitscher on the (port) left side approximately half way along the rail."*
>
> *"Question 2D - The Mitscher was passing the HMS Ocean on a port (left side) and was just passing the left half port quarter – last half port quarter. I was even with the second (aft) LCVP well deck at the time of the fall"*
>
> *"Question 5A - He was standing on the Landing Craft aft (rear end) just behind the wheelhouse (control structure.)"*

But, as MOD Collins jumped to attention to try to stop the Jury from understanding the importance and implications of the statement by Witness 3, Los Angeles, our Barrister also jumped to attention to interrupt this double-standard of a mock Inquest.

The Coroner thought he had got away with it; he had to control himself more than he was used to, and so tried to talk over our Barrister, as he did not want to let him finish his statement.

Day 2 - Tape 3 – 03:17:55

> Our Barrister interrupts
>> "Sir, it may be that these questions need to be read out. **VERY VERY IMPORTANT, they are significant"**
> Coroner – not happy, talks over our Barrister and tries to stop him
>> "Alright ....Yes, alright. I'll read them out. Let's start again with 5a) Mrs Hamilton."
> Coroner reads question 5a) – crossly
>> "Where was the man in a white jumpsuit when you first saw him?"
> Mrs Hamilton reading out Los Angeles answer
>> "He was standing on the Landing Craft aft (rear end) just behind the wheelhouse (control structure.)"
> Coroner reads question 5b) – crossly
>> "Where was the stanchion?"
> Mrs Hamilton reading out Los Angeles answer
>> "The stanchion was aft of the wheelhouse control structure."
> Coroner reads question 5c) – crossly
>> "Please draw the path that he was moving in on Diagram3."
> Mrs Hamilton reading out Los Angeles answer
>> "The individual was moving from the aft rear of the Landing Craft to the forehead (front) of the vessel along the port (left side). He appeared to be moving on the outside of the vessel (outside of the stanchion)"
> Coroner reads question 5d)
>> "Where did he swing his body around?"
> Mrs Hamilton reading out Los Angeles answer
>> "It appeared that he was swinging his body from the

> *aft stanchion to the port side of the wheelhouse."*
Coroner reads question 5e) - He does NOT read all of it
> *"Where did he fall from?"*
Mrs Hamilton reading out Los Angeles answer
> *"He fell from the port side by the wheelhouse."*
Coroner
> *"He does not seem to have answered question 5f), so go on to 5g)"*
Coroner reads question 5g) - He does not read all of it
> *"Where did you see the sailor on the outboard landing craft?"*
Mrs Hamilton reading out Los Angeles answer
> *"At the xxx time I cannot recall where on the Landing Craft I observed the second sailor. From what I can recall he appeared to come from below deck (a lower deck of the landing craft)."*
Coroner
> *"And that's the further statement from that witness."*

Would the Jury notice the legal battle that had just taken place before their eyes? More significantly, would they notice the great importance of the statements by Witness 3, Los Angeles?

(see full transcript on the website)

# Day Three – Wednesday, 7ᵗʰ November, 2010.

It was now Day Three of this phoney Inquest. Day Three was a half day. All the people on the witness stand had something or other to do with Health and Safety. The first witness concerned the issuing of Safety Harnesses; the second witness was there to tell us about all the Royal Navy courses my son had attended. Did they teach him to watch his back? Is this what they taught my son at Britannia Royal Navy College? Watch your back? If they did not teach him that, then perhaps they are the ones who are responsible for his death.

Nevertheless, let us continue with the list of witnesses on that third day of my son's Inquest. The second witness told us about all the Royal Navy Health and Safety courses my son attended, given by that most perfect Health and Safety employer, the Royal Navy.

The third witness concerned the maintenance of the LCVPs; again, more

Health and Safety. Will you please stop boring me with Health and Safety. This is a death, a suspicious death; why do we have to listen to this?

The fourth witness was Lt Cdr Brewer, the SHEO (Safety Health and Environment Officer of HMS Ocean). We did not come to the Inquest to be entertained. We had come to 'discover the facts' of my son's suspicious death. Instead, in this comedy-drama, we were entertained, when all some people wanted to do was weep.

Am I allowed to weep for my son in the midst of this shameful cover-up of my son's death?

## Lt Cdr Brewer (SHEO), the Man with Moral Courage

Lt Cdr Brewer was a man always on the defensive. No straight answers from him. And there was more; we were all subjected to unwarranted verbosity, delivered at high velocity. My ears are hurting.

Lt Cdr Brewer told us about 'Moral Courage' and my son's lack of it. He conveniently forgot that the entire ship also exhibited this same lack of 'Moral Courage'.

Day 3 - Tape 4 – 01:04:25

> Our Barrister
>> *"Up to this point nobody seems to have thought that the policy indicated they should wear a harness. The photographers show that, don't they? Up they go, they lean over and they've taken the photographs we can see. No-one stopped them. No-one's pointed it out to them. They hadn't thought about it, and we can see what they did."*
>
> Lt Cdr Brewer
>> *"Yes"*
>
> Our Barrister
>> ***"It wasn't working, was it?*** *The policy. Whatever was happening, it may have been written down.* ***It wasn't working, and it wasn't being enforced.*** *Was it?"*
>
> Lt Cdr Brewer
>> *"It was being enforced by those who wished to enforce it. Because I would not that any...I mean... I myself would walk round the ship and if I saw something*

*wrong, I'd tell them. It comes about people having the **moral courage** to stop someone doing work. And that might upset many it may take more time.. but it's all about **moral courage** and being in command. Having leadership. Being the, whatever rank you were, you are responsible for someone. And in that instance **Lt Woodhouse, being a Lieutenant with commission, he was responsible for himself and also for Petty Officer Fulton going up there in my eyes.** And therefore **he** as an engineer trained in safety and we've heard today about all the courses he's done in safety should have known the risk and what he should have been doing to go up there. As a commissioned officer having done a normal board with myself"*

    Our Barrister

*"We'll come back to that again in a moment."*

We knew where Lt Cdr Brewer was heading, and all we had to do was wait a very little while. And so we waited as the barrage of words continued attacking our ears.

We only had to wait three minutes to hear how he possessed this admirable 'Moral Courage' that he had described to us. He, Lt Cdr Brewer, had the 'Moral Courage' to enforce Health and Safety on HMS Ocean: the 'Moral Courage' which he informed us that my son did not possess.

Day 3 - Tape 4 – 01:07:14

Talking about the monthly Safety Rounds

    Lt Cdr Brewer

*"When they do the rounds they probably discuss things, but it was, like I said… The rounds themselves were detailed more to ensure the place was there….. So if you see someone work, I am sure, I'd like to think, I know when I do my rounds and I used to walk the ship, I used to walk the ship every day. I mean that is part of my job. I chat to people, and if I saw anything I question it. And if they weren't doing it correctly **I make them** go and get the PPT etc. So I'd like to think others have **that courage as well** to do the same."*

Hang on a moment. If we have such a fine Health and Safety Officer on board

HMS Ocean, then why was HMS Ocean such a tardy Health and Safety ship? Surely when you had such a fine leader as this, with so much self-professed Health and Safety Moral Courage, you would have thought some of it would have rubbed off on the crew of HMS Ocean?

It appears that it did not.

## Lt Cdr Brewer – Men Painting

Lt Cdr Brewer did let slip some of the facts that HMS Ocean and the MOD tried to keep from us.

According to US Navy Witness 2, Charleston, at the time of my son's fall there were men painting on the side of HMS Ocean, in the same Bay area where my son was.

We were first alerted to this new bit of information when the second set of US Navy Witness Statements arrived, ten days before the Inquest commenced.

In Lt Cdr Brewer's constant, defensive, non-stop verbal fire, he mentioned that there were men doing painting and maintenance work on the LCVP Bay of HMS Ocean.

He then looked nervous at this slip and, realising his mistake in alerting us to this fact, he quickly countered, "on the opposite side".

Day 3 - Tape 4 – 01:16:43

> Lt Cdr Brewer
> *"Because at this point there was maintenance going on, on there, painting the ship's side, and the ship's bits and pieces."*

> Our Barrister
> *"That's working on the ship's side, painting, but not likely to be on the Davits working on the Landing Craft"*

> Lt Cdr Brewer
> *"Um...I mean...I'm...not sure...they've definitely drawn them there, so they could have been on the Landing Craft or it could have been painting. There was work going on in the LCVP Bays up on the **opposite side** at the time of the incident took place."*

Witness 2, Charleston, tells us he saw men working on a moveable platform by the same Bay where my son was standing.

Witness 1, Philippines, told us he saw feet, and the position he drew the feet fitted in with the statement by Witness 2, Charleston. The moveable platform was in the very LCVP Bay where my son was just before he fell.

By that defensive statement I instantly knew that not only Lt Cdr Brewer, but also Captain Blount, Lt Cdr Pickles, Lt Cdr Lucocq, and WO Clapham also knew that there were men working on the side of HMS Ocean at the time of my son's fall, but were content not to mention it in the Ship's Investigations.

How many other things did they know and not mention?

## Lt Cdr Brewer – The Real Motives Behind the Health and Safety Charade

In the opinion of Lt Cdr Brewer, the Health and Safety Officer of HMS Ocean, the ship was run perfectly with regard to its Health and Safety. That is, except for those renegade people who did not have the 'Moral Courage' to obey the excellent Health and Safety rules on HMS Ocean.

But Lt Cdr Brewer's fiasco and self-deception with Health and Safety bores me.

Health and Safety is not the issue here. A suspicious death is the issue here.

Lt Cdr Brewer, and the Royal Navy officials were using Health and Safety to do two things –

Hide the fact that my son died in suspicious circumstances.
Divert attention from the suspicious death, and turn it into an Health and Safety issue.

- In order to turn my son's death into an unfortunate Health and Safety accident, they wanted and needed to prove –
- Firstly, that HMS Ocean had a perfect Health and Safety culture.
- Secondly, that my son was a renegade officer who broke all the rules, which consequently resulted in his fall. It was his fault, that 'unfortunate individual'.

On both counts they failed.

We will see from the remaining proceedings of the Inquest why they failed.

We were given a most skilful barrister, backed by an equally skilful, and hidden, legal team. And they did work together as a team. I noticed that none took any of the glory, though each could have done, but genuinely attributed it to the entire legal team.

It was a pleasure to watch our Barrister, as the public figure, at work. It was like watching a master swordsman effortlessly disarming his opponents, even though he was blindfolded and had his right hand tied behind his back.

How is it possible not to fall asleep, when the majority of the rest of my son's Inquest is bludgeoned to death by the most boring Health and Safety?

This great feat was accomplished effortlessly, and with the greatest grace, by the barrister who volunteered to defend our son against these most powerful and formidable foes, the Coroner, the MOD, and the Royal Navy.

The whole courtroom waited when our barrister rose to speak.

The MOD failed in their attempts to blacken my son's name.

The MOD failed to prove that they had a perfect Health and Safety culture on HMS Ocean, and in the Royal Navy. At the end of the Inquest the Royal Navy had a Rule 43 slapped on them.

"…..the race is not to the swift, nor the battle to the strong….."

Ecclesiastes 9:11

# Military Justice

And so we came to the end of the first three days of the Inquest proceedings.

Monday had passed when PO Fulton, SIB Wilson and the pathologist were on the witness stand.

Tuesday had passed when PO Fulton, the three Lieutenants, and PO Dot Cottam were on the stand. This is the day that the US Navy Witness statements had been read out. How was it possible for the Jury to make head or tail of these statements presented in such an obscure manner?

Wednesday was a half-day, when only Health and Safety people were on the stand.

And that was the end of that. The majority of the rest of the Inquest was dedicated to Health and Safety.

That Wednesday afternoon I was walking round an English village thinking of these things. It was a hard day for us. It was hard not to feel totally downcast.

This was the value that the MOD placed on a suspicious military death. Two days.

We were allocated this two day window, in which to question the people directly involved with my son's last movements. And this questioning was so limited, and so narrow; this Inquest does not deserve to be called a free, an honest, or a legitimate Inquest. This Inquest did not 'discover the facts', as the Coroner had made very sure of.

This is the Military Justice meted out to my son Joshua.

Thank you for serving your country.

# Health and Safety is our Friend

As we now commenced the fourth day of my son's Inquest it was hard not to think that the Coroner, the SIB, the Royal Navy, and the MOD, had won. This is what they do. This was not a novel experience for them.

And yet, in all of this, Health and Safety was our friend, probably far more than I could have possibly realised.

If it had not been for the Health and Safety aspect of my son's death, there would not have been a Jury.

Without a Jury, the Coroner, the SIB, and the MOD would have done what they do best, what they are accustomed to doing. To rubber stamp a suspicious death. This was just an unfortunate accident where the unfortunate individual was to blame.

We are most grateful my son's Inquest had a Jury.

If it had not been for the Health and Safety aspect of my son's death, then our legal team would have basically nothing to ask the witnesses, especially as they were forbidden from encroaching on the forbidden ground of foul play.

Our legal team were not gagged with regard to Health and Safety, yet they still had to tread most carefully, so as not to anger or alert the opposition.

## Captain Forsey – Chief Staff Officer (Engineering) Surface Ships – RN HQ

There was no Inquest hearing on Thursday, 8th November, 2012. Friday, 9th November, 2012, was Day Four of my son's Inquest, and involved questioning the civilian Health and Safety staff of the Royal Navy. A whole day was spent on this.

It was now Monday, 12th November, 2012, and day Five of the Inquest. Captain Forsey, RN HQ, now came into the witness stand.

For the Coroner, the MOD and the Royal Navy, they could now relax. My son's Inquest had moved on from the uncomfortable area of listening to the testimony of PO Fulton, and then the three Lieutenants, and finally the US Navy Witness statements, to the very comfortable area of discussing Health and Safety, and how it was all my son's fault.

Captain Forsey was a man who had an air that made you feel relaxed and at ease. You could almost picture him sitting in his armchair with a smoking jacket, a glass of port and a cigar, having a very good, very interesting discussion with you. All very comfortable, civilised, and gentlemanly.

Captain Forsey is the man that requested a further Ship's Investigation, for which we shall always be grateful. Captain Forsey could not understand why my son, the Ship's Services Engineering Officer (the one who dealt with the running of all the machines on the ship like refrigeration and hot water systems) was dealing with equipment that belonged to the Warfare Engineering category. The Initial Ship's Investigation was desperately inadequate on numerous fronts, and other people also found it sadly inadequate, even if only on a few fronts.

This second Supplementary Ship's Investigation answered Captain Forsey's questions, and I did wonder whether Captain Forsey ever noticed how it also heightened the suspicious circumstances surrounding my son's death.

# Captain Forsey – Drink-Driving Attack

Let us discuss Captain Forsey. Here was a man who had it all worked out. It was all my son's fault, and he was going to easily show us why. The Coroner began with the questioning.

Captain Forsey sat very comfortably, and reasonably explained to us that military men and women are of a different calibre from the normal man in the street. These are the people with the 'Can-do', 'Up and At Them', 'Fight and Win' attitude, which is vital for their job.

However, Captain Forsey explained, sighing in a most reasonable way, the down side is that this 'Can-do', 'Up and At Them', 'Fight and Win' attitude is not conducive to obeying Health and Safety Regulations in peace time. He now spoke with resignation; this was a big problem. But he made it quite clear it was only the ones and the twos who disobey the Health and Safety rules. The ones and the twos, like my son, who were exactly like the law breaking drink-drivers, the *'hardened number'*. You could tell them all you liked about the dangers of drink-driving, but they would just go ahead and drink-drive. Yes, a real problem. Another sigh of resignation.

This was a very clever tactic, comparing my son to one of those drink-drivers who just never obeyed the laws of the land. I quote from the Inquest transcript below -

Day 5 - Monday 12<sup>th</sup> November, 2012 - Tape 7 – 00:13:13

Captain Forsey
*"I recognise the issue. I think it is something that we have a particular issue with in the Services. On the one hand we are preparing, our primary role, for people to be* **'Can-do', 'Up and At Them'** *,* **'Fight and Win',** *is one element. So we want to train them that way for operations and if we have to go to war."*

*"There's also an element, a lot of our people are young. There is an element of invincibility that sits around people of that age. And I think the third thing is we want them to switch. When we are not on operations, when we are not at war, what we want are people to follow the peace-time rules, which is we want to keep our people super safe. And we want them to follow our safe system of work in this scenario."*

*"And I think it's like many other things that happen in the world today. You have instructions, I mean it could be like Drink-Driving. You know, there are very clear instructions on Drink-Driving. Most people will follow them. There is a proportion that don't, Police will enforce the regulation, that gets an even higher proportion to follow them."*

*"Despite all that, despite, you know, all the stuff that you see on telly etc, the seasonal approach to Drink-Driving at the end of each year, there are still a hardened number who will still do that."*

*"And it's a similar culture to that. We've laid out a very clear safe system of work which most people will follow all the time. But I think, I have in my mind, that there are one or two people who are still in that youth invincibility sort of area, who because it will take time and maybe it's only a short two minute job, they may see it as something that they can just get on and do."*

After the Coroner finished his questioning, it was the turn of our barrister to question Captain Forsey.

To those with untrained legal minds, like the majority of the participants at the Inquest, this drink-driving line of attack seemed perfectly logical and feasible. How would our Barrister attack this? Our Barrister arose, and, with great dignity and composure, quietly stood and paused before commencing his questioning.

We all waited in anticipation.

Captain Forsey was relaxed as our Barrister approached him. I quote from the Inquest transcript

Day 5  - Monday 12th November, 2012  - Tape 7 – 00:59:57

Our Barrister
*"Now in answer to questions from the Coroner, you had identified the example of 'Drink-Drive' as being an example perhaps familiar to all of us of something which is laid down as being something one shouldn't do. It's*

*clear that people sometimes don't follow it. Is that your aim in identifying that?"*

Captain Forsey

*"My aim in identifying that was to show that ........................ most people will follow the instructions they are given. Some people need some encouragement, and then there are those who despite encouragement, and then there are those who despite encouragement, training etc etc etc for whatever reason"*

Our Barrister

*"So people sometimes won't follow orders. That's the point?"*

Captain Forsey – voice lowered – not so confident now

*"I won't go quite that far. But they don't do as directed"*

Our Barrister

*"It's a pretty clear order isn't it, when there is a **criminal offence** of Driving under the influence of Alcohol?"*

Captain Forsey

*"Yes, absolutely"*

Our Barrister

*"**A criminal offence, carrying a prison sentence.** That's a pretty clear order given by the state"*

Captain Forsey – starts coughing – not so comfortable

*"It is"*

Our Barrister

*"And there are **clear lines set for the level of alcohol,** which one cannot exceed, blood test, urine test, breath test. If you past that, Tough. Offence committed. Yes?"*

Captain Forsey

*"Yes."*

Our Barrister

*"**Very clear lines?"***

Captain Forsey

*"Yes"*

Our Barrister

*"**And do you think it is a little different** if things **aren't spelled out quite as clearly,** in for example, a Risk Assessment passed on to crew to help them with a specific task?"*

Captain Forsey

*"Yes sir"*

Our Barrister

*"On a huge ship like this? **Bit different?"***

Captain Forsey

*"Yes, it is different."*
Our Barrister
*"Alright."*

And so our Barrister effortlessly squashed this most reasonable and cunning point made by Captain Forsey, RN HQ. The comfortable look on Captain Forsey's face disappeared. He knew his sophistry had been exposed.

What had he done, this Captain from Royal Navy Headquarters? Why, by discussing the great problem of drink-drivers, he was calling my son a criminal, and therefore worthy of going to prison.

But hang on a moment; I thought my son was the victim.

This is the Military Justice that was meted out to my son. My son was the one branded the criminal by all these respectable people with their gold braid, and very important public titles and positions.

Who are the real criminals in my son's Inquest? Who are the ones that deserve to be put in prison for their part in my son's Inquest?

# Captain Forsey – The Ones and the Twos Disobeying

Captain Forsey told us another bit of information that could not be substantiated. He told us that this group of people who did not obey the Royal Navy Health and Safety were only one or two in every ship.

That is a very small number of people he is telling us about. Let me quote a few of his statements –

Day 5 - Monday 12th November, 2012 - Tape 7 – 00:13:13

*"Despite all that, despite, you know, all the stuff that you see on telly etc, the seasonal approach to Drink-Driving at the end of each year, there are still a hardened number who will still do that."*

*"And it's a similar culture to that. We've laid out a very clear safe system of work which most people will follow all the time. But I think, I have in my mind, that there are **one or two people** who are still in that youth invincibility sort of area, who because it will take time and maybe it's only a short two minute job,*

*they may see it as something that they can just get on and do."*
And

Day 5 - Monday 12ᵗʰ November, 2012 - Tape 7 – 02:05:00

*"That is the supposition but this is based at the nth degree of the **few percent** who are still not following the detail of what we want to happen. So, widespread yes, because it is probably **one or two people in each ship** who would fall into that. 'I'm young and invicible and will just go and do that' rather than go through this procedure. But, you know, in terms of overall numbers who would do the right thing, most people will do the right thing. But most people is not good enough to me."*

This was just like his previous ploy of the drink-driving attack.

The Inquest showed a different reality to the one the Royal Navy and the MOD painted. The Inquest showed that hardly anyone wore a harness when boarding the LCVP, let alone when climbing onto the roof of the LCVP wheelhouse. Despite what Captain Forsey sat and comfortably told us, it was not the ones and the twos who did not wear a harness. This problem permeated throughout the entire Royal Navy.

## Captain Forsey RN HQ – Heavily [*sic*] Legal Advice

Captain Forsey had the gift of talking and making you feel relaxed and at home in his company.

His conversation was beneficial to us. Captain Forsey started discussing a Service Enquiry and mentioned that the reason they did not conduct a Service Enquiry into my son's death was because they (the Royal Navy) had received 'Heavily [*sic*] Legal Advice' not to do so, let me quote –

Day 5 - Monday 12ᵗʰ November, 2012 - Tape 7 – 02:18:48

Captain Forsey
*"We've also set up a Service Inquiry Panel. You'd be aware that a Service Inquiry was not **conducted** .. um.. on on .. Jo.. Joshua's death and... the reason for that was because it was very **heavily [sic] legal advice** that said, you know, this, it seems to be quite straight forward what's happened."*

Aahh. The curtain is being drawn slightly and we have a peek at some of the events occurring behind the scenes in Royal Navy HQ.

The Royal Navy received Heavy Legal Advice not to conduct a Service Enquiry into my son's death. What other Heavy Legal Advice did they receive regarding my son's death?

Immediately that Captain Forsey spoke of 'Heavily [sic] Legal Advice', the MOD barrister was up and protesting.

Collins interrupts - Tape 7 – 02:18:48
> *"I don't …I don't want to interrupt but obviously, as soon as legal advice is mentioned that sets alarm bells ringing as to whether those are matters which ought to be referred to in court. Um, certainly not a matter that I've discussed with the witness in advance …. "*

What was interesting was that later in the Inquest, during the times of 'private courtroom discussion', when the Jury were not present, the MOD barrister petitioned the Coroner to have the Jury briefed about this statement 'Heavily [sic] Legal Advice', and somehow to eradicate it from their minds. I cannot remember his exact wording, but MOD Collins was so disturbed by this admission of Captain Forsey that he wanted to have it countered.

But we all heard, and no amount of MOD Collins' protestations could wipe that statement from our minds.

Captain Forsey gave us a peep into the discussions in high places concerning my son's death, discussions in Royal Navy HQ. They received Heavy Legal Advice not to have a Service Inquiry, and he started stammering when speaking of it and my son's death.

From this statement we can only conclude that the top people in the Royal Navy knew that my son's death was suspicious.

## Lt Cdr Pickles – ISI - First Attempt Fails

Lt Cdr Pickles, Lt Cdr Lucocq, and WO Clapham were tasked with investigating my son's death. This is a solemn responsibility.

They interviewed PO Fulton and PO Dot Cottam. We have no idea how long they spent interviewing PO Fulton. All we know is that this vital investigation was completed and signed by the 9th August, 2010, three days after my son's fall.

In their first investigation, the ISI, Lt Cdr Pickles, Lt Cdr Lucocq, and WO Clapham very squarely put the blame solely on my son for his own death. I quote below from Item 26 of their report.

*There is insufficient evidence to establish the exact reason that caused Lt Woodhouse to fall from N4 LCVP on 6 Aug 10, but based on the evidence provided, it appears to have been a tragic accident **due to him losing his balance**, after having jumped or fallen onto the deck from the wheelhouse roof.*

***The primary factor was a lack of judgement*** *which led Lt Woodhouse and PO Fulton to proceed aloft without wearing the correct safely equipment, as detailed in SGOs.*

So important was this conclusion of the Initial Ship's Investigation, that Captain Forsey RN HQ states the following in his letter of the 2nd September, 2010.

Item 1

*HMS OCEAN's ISI into the circumstances leading to a fatal incident onboard on 6 Aug and the Commanding Officer's covering letter has been received by NCHQ.*

***The report clearly identifies*** *that the **unfortunate individual was ultimately at fault** for failing to ensure his own safety whilst working at height which consequently lead to the fatal accident.*

And yet something was wrong, for Captain Forsey found the ISI so lacking, so unsatisfactory, so inferior, that he asked for a second investigation. The result was the Supplementary Ship's Investigation, (SSI), completed just over a month later on the 12th September, 2010. Unfortunately, we were not allowed to see this second investigation till one and a half years later, when the Coroner, with great magnanimity, released more information to us. Up to that time all we had was the ISI, and my son's Post Mortem.

In this second Ship's Investigation, Lt Cdr Pickles and Lt Cdr Lucocq had the opportunity to undo the great wrongs they had committed in their first Investigation. They interviewed PO Fulton again; we hope in more depth this second time around.

The results of this second investigation were even more damning for PO Fulton than the first investigation.

## Lt Cdr Pickles – 'The Report is Wrong'

We were full of interest. Who was this person? What was he like? How would he answer our Barrister's questions?

Our Barrister questioned Lt Cdr Pickles regarding his statement blaming my son for emailing Billy Connolly. I quote from part of the Inquest Transcript below –

Day 5  - Monday 12th November, 2012  -  Tape 7 – 03:44:43

> Our Barrister
> *"Summarising. PO Fulton has told us that Lt Woodhouse had been enquiring of him on a monthly basis. So, if that's right, okay, the Jury have heard this evidence, your report that reads, it's paragraph 12"*
>
> > *"For reasons we shall never understand, Lt Woodhouse did not consult with PO Fulton or PO Dot Cottam prior to emailing WO1 Connelly."*
>
> *"If in fact PO Fulton said that Lt Woodhouse was emailing him and asking him, then that part of the report is wrong, isn't it?"*

Our Barrister points out that my son had been industrious and meticulous in his attempts to come to the bottom of the mystery of the missing davit hoses. Yet in this statement, Lt Cdr Pickles castigates my son for emailing Billy Connelly, saying that my son did not take the trouble to first find out whether the hoses had been changed from either PO Dot Cottam or PO Fulton.

Our Barrister informs Lt Cdr Pickles that evidence from PO Fulton contradicts this statement; therefore that part of Lt Cdr Pickles' Investigation is wrong.

Will Lt Cdr Pickles admit he is wrong ?

Lt Cdr Pickles
> "Yuh. It's only the investigation from what I've written here would indicate that at the time I **was informed** that they hadn't been chased up at all."

Lt Cdr Pickles puts the blame on the information that he received. (see full transcript on website)

## Lt Cdr Pickles Receives Faulty Information

Our Barrister asks Lt Cdr Pickles to confirm the origin of this faulty information that led him to make his wrong statement.

Day 5 - Monday 12th November, 2012 - Tape 7 – 03:45:49

Our Barrister
> "That information would have come from **in particular,** Petty Officer PO Fulton?"

Lt Cdr Pickles
> "Um, **both** PO Fulton and PO Dot Cottam were interviewed as part of this investigation so it would have come from **both** of them."

Our Barrister
> "Yes, thank you."

Lt Cdr Pickles, sitting in the witness stand, is trying desperately to disguise the enormous failings of his investigation by linking both men together. PO Fulton's suspicious account with that of PO Cottam's credible account.

## Lt Cdr Pickles Knows PO Fulton is Hiding Something

We must remember that our Barrister had to be very careful in his questioning, as he was prohibited from asking any questions regarding Foul Play. Our Barrister could not risk the wrath of either the Coroner or the MOD which would scupper the entire Inquest.

Our Barrister very carefully questions Lt Cdr Pickles regarding another of the suspicious statements that PO Fulton made.

PO Fulton had explained that he had not informed my son the hoses had been changed, even when my son was enquiring, as PO Fulton personally wanted to check the work for himself. This is very strange behaviour, but we shall continue.

For three whole months PO Fulton did not check the hoses. In this time my son had started enquiring about the hoses again, and PO Fulton still would not check them, nor would he inform my son that he knew they had been changed. More strange behaviour.

Our Barrister questions Lt Cdr Pickles on this. I quote from the Inquest transcript below

Day 5  - Monday 12th November, 2012  -  Tape 7 – 03:38:05

> Our Barrister
> *"And equally, PO Fulton, when you were enquiring, had not explained why he hadn't checked the work from May right up till August?"*
> Lt Cdr Pickles
> *"That is correct.* **We did pursue that avenue of questioning,** *and he wasn't able to give an answer."*
> Our Barrister
> ***"What did you make of that?"***
> Lt Cdr Pickles
> *"…….Um……… it clearly ……um …made it difficult to be able to make a* **full judgement on what had actually happened.** *Um, whether he was unable to provide an explanation due to the fact he literally didn't know whether ….. um….. there were other reasons….we were not able to establish and as a Ship's Investigation…. um…..we* **have limited powers** *of being able to pursue a line of questioning if someone is unable to provide an answer."*
> Our Barrister
> *"If they're not going to tell you, you can't ram their arm behind their back and force them. Alright."*

Limited Powers. With this one statement, Lt Cdr Pickles is telling us all, and he is telling the whole world, that he knows PO Fulton is hiding something.

# Limited Powers – Really?

Lt Cdr Pickles has told us that he has *"limited powers"*, hence he was unable to unravel the suspicious aspects of PO Fulton's account.

What attempts did he make to get more information that would shed light on the suspicious circumstances of PO Fulton's account? What attempts did Lt Cdr Pickles make to get more information from other sources?

Did Lt Cdr Pickles investigate the Disciplinary Records of HMS Ocean? We were denied these time and time again by the Coroner. Lt Cdr Pickles was tasked with the investigation of my son's death; surely he could have studied the Disciplinary Records of HMS Ocean that were refused us?

Did Lt Cdr Pickles or Lt Cdr Lucocq know why PO Fulton was demoted? Did this have any bearing on the Ship's Investigation?

Why did Lt Cdr Pickles and Lt Cdr Lucocq have to be asked by RN HQ to conduct a further Investigation, if the first one was adequate?

We know that the bridge of USS Mitscher contacted the bridge of HMS Ocean immediately they saw my son falling. Witness 2, Charleston, was on the bridge of USS Mitscher; he saw my son falling and contacted the bridge of HMS Ocean immediately.

Did Lt Cdr Pickles or Lt Cdr Lucocq ask to interview the US Navy Witnesses in order to do their job properly, the investigating of my son's suspicious death?

It is not the *"limited powers"* that are responsible for the flawed investigation that Lt Cdr Pickles and Lt Cdr Lucocq held. It is the fault of Lt Cdr Pickles and Lt Cdr Lucocq.

# The Hewitt Review - All is Well with the World

It is still Monday, 12th November, 2010, the fifth day of my son's Inquest. It had been a full day. Captain Forsey and Lt Cdr Pickles had been on the witness stand.

There was a third witness that was due to go on the witness stand today. His name was Lt Cdr Hewitt. He wrote the Hewitt Review stating that all the recommendations following my son's death had been put in place.

But this was only in writing. During the visit to HMS Ocean by the Coroner, the MOD legal team, and our legal team, a crew member on board HMS

Ocean had jumped up onto the roof of the LCVP, saying that this is the way they would do it, without a safety harness.

> "We made a careful note of the statements that were made during the tour. One of the marines giving the tour was asked by our Counsel, in the presence of yourself and the Ministry of Defence legal team, **how he would now gain access to the LCVP when it was 'in bed'.** He said that he would climb up the ladder/s (squeezing through the metal hoops on one of the ladders) and, when asked about the use of a harness, he said **he would do it without a harness** because a harness was 'more a hindrance than a help'."

Our legal team were very concerned with this behaviour. I quote from their letter of the 27th June, 2012 to the Coroner –

> "This seems to us to contradict some of the evidence that has been supplied to you. This evidence is to the effect that, **since the accident**, steps have been taken to ensure that procedures are now in place to seek to **prevent a similar accident in the future.** The evidence currently before you records that a harness and a hard hat should have been worn (Lt Cdr Brewer Aug 2010). The report of the ISI (Sept 2010: para(1)) recorded that recommendations have been implemented to avoid a repetition of the accident. You may also want to consider **the Lt Cdr Hewitt review** (dated 15 January 2012: paras 6, 12, 16, 17-20) which suggests that the necessary safety measures **have now been implemented.**"

(the full letter can be viewed on the web site)

It was very important to question Lt Cdr Hewitt, and to endeavour to find out how he could possibly say that he is "satisfied that **all recommendations** from HMS Ocean's ISI have been implemented."

> *Item 12*
>
> From my efforts to establish follow up actions, **I am satisfied that all recommendations from HMS OCEAN's ISI have been implemented,** in addition to COMDEVFLOT conducting an assurance visit 16 Sep 10, and a full Safety, Health and Environment Audit conducted on the 19 Jan 11. Both were able to provide assurance that a safe PTW system in HMS OCEAN is in place, of note the tragic accident was said to have had a seismic affect on HMS OCEAN's safety culture and has resulted in an emphatic Command Focus on tightening up PTW and

*other safety routines.*

And let us quote the recommendations from the Immediate Ship's Investigations that have been implemented, according to Lt Cdr Hewitt

29. A whole ship brief should be conducted to re-educate personnel on the risks associated with working aloft and the regulations regarding the **wearing of safety equipment.**

30. The **requirement to wear a safety harness when working on housed LCVPs** should be referred to as a specific example in SGOs.

31. A warning sign should be placed at the bottom of all ladders that provide access to workspaces greater than 2m above the deck, or lower if a risk of significant injury exists, to remind personnel of the requirement to wear safety harnesses when working aloft.

# MOD Collins to the Rescue

Lt Cdr Hewitt had been sitting all day at the Inquest, waiting to take his turn on the witness stand.

He had watched as Captain Forsey had his clever but false reasoning regarding drink-driving skilfully squashed, and that publically, by our Barrister.

He had watched as our Barrister had questioned Lt Cdr Pickles.

Lt Cdr Hewitt had made sweeping statements in his report, and he knew that he would have to explain them.

The time was 3:30pm when the questioning of Lt Cdr Pickles came to an end, and the Coroner thought it best to postpone Lt Cdr Hewitt's questioning till the next day, as he suspected that our Barrister's questioning of Lt Cdr Hewitt would not be a quick, short affair.

Day 5 - Monday 12th November, 2012 - Tape 7 – 04:02:22

Coroner
*"It's now half past three, the next witness is Lt Cdr Hewitt. I'm mindful of the fact we've been hearing evidence for getting on for an hour and a half. I'm just wondering how long we're going to be with this*

witness. Whether we in fact proceed this afternoon or whether we stop until tomorrow. Because I don't want to leave a witness in the situation where overnight he can't speak to anyone. It's different for coffee break, or lunchtime, but .. Mr. X, how long do you anticipate being this witness?"

Our Barrister

*"I do have some questions for this witness who has written a fairly comprehensive Review of the case, so for that reason **I am not going to be very short.** I doubt I could complete in an hour."*

Coroner

***"I didn't think you would. I didn't think you would be.*** *Collins, I mean obviously, a lot of what you are going to ask will be based on the answers that he gives to questions from myself, the Jury, and Mr. X."*

MOD Collins did not want this witness questioned thoroughly, and the only way to accomplish this was to ask to have him questioned today, and quickly. Job done, all finished, we can breathe easily now, next witness please.

Strangely the Coroner did not grant MOD Collins his request on this occasion. Instead we were all subjected to melodrama and comings and goings when Hewitt did finally take the stand on the Wednesday. I quote below -

Day 5 - Monday 12th November, 2012 - Tape 7 – 04:02:22

Collins

*"Yes, indeed. Two things to say, firstly the evidence is a review of other documents. It may indeed be that it doesn't take quite as long as Mr. X suspects, but of course I am in his hands to ask the questions that are appropriate. Having said that, um..I wouldn't have difficulty with um..the witness being unable to speak about the case overnight. I'm sure he has other things that he would be able to speak about in the course of an evening, if you are content for him to be further from this afternoon until tomorrow, not an unfamiliar situation."*

Coroner

*"The thing is we have been sitting for about an hour and a half now and if I were to break to give the Jury a chance to refresh themselves. There's not going to*

be an awful lot of time for my questions and Mr. X. I
don't want us to get into it and have to break it off at
an early stage. Because obviously the Jury are going to
need to understand what the witness says, and as much
as anything else, I want them to approach it fresh."

Collins

"Indeed, Sir, I don't know what time you are thinking of
sitting until this afternoon."

Coroner

"Well, I don't think, if I take a break, by the time we
get back in, I'm not going to have much more than an
hour maximum. I think... Lt Cdr Hewitt, can you come
tomorrow?"

Lt Cdr Hewitt

"Yes sir, I'm free."

Coroner

"There's no problem at all? Well I think that's the
answer isn't it? And then you may be able to help me
on that other question that I set the Ministry of Defence
the end of last week, whether anyone can help us on
these anchorage points for harnesses"

Collins

"Sir we will certainly..."

Coroner

"There's been no progress on that so far, I take it."

Collins

"There hadn't at lunchtime, I can't say.."

Coroner

"I think I will, I don't want, I don't want anyone to have
to stop in the flow. Lt Cdr Hewitt, me, the Jury or Mr. X,
and indeed yourself. I think"

Collins – talking at same time as Coroner

Coroner

"I think we will adjourn at this point. If we adjourn at
this point it may give us more time as well to sort out
what is going to happen about somebody helping us on
the question of secure mounting points for harnesses.
Are you happy to adjourn now Mr. X?"

Our Barrister

"Certainly, I would just like to know the answer to that
question before I embark..."

Collins

"Sir, can I suggest this Sir. Shall we let the Jury rise at this point? It sounds likely that you are going to adjourn. But there are some other, there have been some developments this afternoon. **It may be we can conveniently discuss them while the Jury have a cup of tea and if it emerges that we are not going to be able to carry on this** afternoon, we can then send them away."

Coroner

**"It's just wasting more time, even less of a window to proceed in this afternoon."**

Collins

"Well if, .. the reason why I ....."

Coroner

"I would rather let the Jury go and if you update me afterwards and then we'll all stop."

Collins

"Well, simply this Sir, if there is going to be another witness, which may follow from the enquiries that you've asked us to make ...um....and it may be that they are available tomorrow morning **and if we lose time further from tomorrow morning because we rise early this afternoon** that will make logistical difficulties, that's all. Sir, it may be that we encourage you in light of that to see if we can make some more progress this afternoon. But if you are set on adjourning now ........ straightforward.... send the Jury away."

Coroner

"I think I will, because we are not up against a deadline on hearing evidence. The only problem is that we can't use this room tomorrow afternoon because there is going to be a Portsmouth City Council meeting in here. Nothing prevents us then using it again for the rest of the week."

Collins

"Indeed. Very well sir"

Coroner

"So, I think I will. I don't want,....I....I...I...I... I don't want to put any unfair target times on either the witness or the questions or the Jury. So, I think I have the Jury taken out. Members of the Jury we are finishing early but we have been hearing evidence all day today so......"

And so the Inquest was adjourned till the next day, Tuesday, 13th November, 2012. The following day, an additional witness, Mr Sanders, was brought to the Inquest to answer questions on anchor points for safety harnesses on the LCVP.

Tuesday, 13th November, was a half day, as the rooms were to be used by Portsmouth City Council.

Lt Cdr Hewitt was not to take the witness stand till Wednesday, 14th November, 2012, the 7th Day of the Inquest.

## The Evidence is......

It is now Tuesday, 13th November, 2012, Day Six of the Inquest.

Before the Jury were brought in, MOD Collins informed the Coroner, that, as per his request, an expert had been found who could testify concerning anchor points for the safety harnesses on the LCVP.

Our Barrister noted that the Coroner was only concerned about anchor points whilst climbing on and off the wheelhouse roof. Our Barrister pointed out that he would like the questioning of this witness to be broadened to include anchor points also for the deck area of the LCVP.

During this discussion, the Coroner had the audacity to say that the *'evidence is'* that my son fell whilst climbing down from the wheelhouse roof. I quote below –

Day 6 - Tuesday 13th November, 2012 - Tape 8 – 05:21:05

> Coroner
> *"But of course poor **Joshua didn't fall, didn't fall from the deck**, he.. **the evidence is** that he fell climbing down from the wheelhouse. And so it's the location of,... would a safety harness located somewhere up, somewhere there, have prevented his fall."*

We knew the entire Inquest was rigged, but here was the Coroner giving us 'evidence' only from the chief suspect. Two men went to do a job, and only one came back, and his account is shot through with holes.

The Coroner tells us that 'of course' the *'evidence is'* that my 'poor' son fell down from the wheelhouse roof.

Our Barrister instantly countered this statement. I quote below

Day 6 - Tuesday 13<sup>th</sup> November, 2012 - Tape 8 – 05:21:05 (see website)

> Our Barrister
>> *"Sir, with respect, the Los Angeles witness does not describe that. The Los Angeles witness has Lt Woodhouse at the back of the wheelhouse, and coming around the side. And one needs to embrace that, we submit, within the scope of this Inquest."*
>>
>> *"He describes himself as having the best view from the USS Mitscher of all of those witnesses. And he has Lt Woodhouse…"*
>
> Coroner interrupts
>> *"Well, it will be down to the Jury at the end of the day which version they accept* … and I will be advising them on that when, directing them on that when, at the appropriate time."
>
> Our Barrister
>> *"Of course."*
>
> Coroner – **sighs heavily**

We are left speechless.

# Lt Cdr Hewitt

It is Wednesday, 14<sup>th</sup> November, 2012, day seven of the Inquest. Lt Cdr Hewitt had been nervously waiting to come to the witness stand since Monday, 12<sup>th</sup> November. It was now his turn to be questioned.

Lt Cdr Hewitt was to continue in the ducking culture that was prevalent in this Inquest, and as MOD Collins always jumped up to protect him, he had nothing at all to be concerned about.

What was the main thrust in his review? Everything was now perfect. But there was more. Lt Cdr Hewitt continued with Captain Forsey's falsehood that it was only the very small percentage that never obeyed the rules.

I quote from the Inquest transcript below –

Day 7 - Wednesday 14<sup>th</sup> November, 2012 - Tape 9 – 01:15:51

Lt Cdr Hewitt

*"**The steps have always been in place** on HMS Ocean, as your Investigation found out, there is, there is, as Captain Forsey alluded to, there is always that percentile that won't follow the proper course of action, but the safety chain was there."*

Why was it very important to question this witness and expose his false statements?

There were two sets of false statements propagated here. One, that the Health and Safety culture on HMS Ocean at the time of my son's fall was perfect, except for the ones and the twos, very pointedly placing my son in that number. Therefore, the Royal Navy wanted to blame my son for his death, and not expose their faulty Health and Safety culture. This statement was discredited when we heard from PO Dot Cottam and PO Fulton that it was customary not to wear a safety harness for any job on the LCVP that was just a few minutes in duration.

The second set of false statements put forward by Lt Cdr Hewitt in his Review was that all recommendations from HMS Ocean's ISI had been implemented, and that there has been a seismic effect on the safety culture of HMS Ocean following my son's death. See Item 12 of his review -

*Item 12*

*From my efforts to establish follow up actions, **I am satisfied that all recommendations from HMS OCEAN's ISI have been implemented**, in addition to COMDEVFLOT conducting an assurance visit 16 Sep 10, and a full Safety, Health and Environment Audit conducted on the 19 Jan 11.*

*Both were able to provide assurance that a safe PTW (Permit to Work) system in HMS OCEAN is in place, of note the tragic accident was said to have had a **seismic affect** on HMS OCEAN's safety culture and has resulted in an emphatic Command Focus on tightening up PTW and other safety routines.*

What were the recommendations of the ISI that Lt Cdr Hewitt tells us have been implemented? I list them below.

**Recommendations**

29. A whole ship brief should be conducted to re-educate personnel on the risks associated with working aloft and the **regulations regarding the wearing of safety equipment.**

30. The **requirement to wear a safety harness when working on housed LCVPs** should be referred to as a specific example in SGOs.

31. A warning sign should be placed at the bottom of all ladders that provide access to workspaces greater than 2m above the deck, or lower if a risk of significant injury exists, to remind personnel of the requirement to wear safety harnesses when working aloft.

Our Barrister endeavoured to show the falseness of both these premises. And in the process we had MOD Collins constantly jumping up like a rabbit out of a magician's hat, and we had the Coroner not able to maintain the mask of his kind, fatherly exterior, and giving our Barrister a sound telling off and also sending the Jury out of the court room on two occasions.

# The Jury Sent Out – Our Barrister Fights on

The Jury had been sent out; the Coroner was agitated and self-righteous. Our Barrister had fought for his right to be allowed to question Lt Cdr Hewitt fully, and expose the false statements and hypocrisy of the Hewitt Review.

I quote some of our Barrister's brave attempts to fight on against all odds –

Day 7 - Wednesday 14th November, 2012 - Tape 9 – 01:22:27

> Our Barrister
> *"With respect Sir, it does go wider than that because in so far as a Culture is still prevalent in June 2012 we submit that what we saw on board indicates that, it's relevant to the strength..."*
> Coroner
> *"I may or may not share that view, but I heard it as well."*
> Our Barrister
> *"Well Sir, that's of course right. But **we are entitled in my submission** when we are exploring a Culture of*

non-compliance to explore the extent to which it still continues notwithstanding the many corrective steps this witness has spoken about."

"And that is directly indicative, we submit, of the **strength of such a Culture**, particularly when that Culture appears to persist when it is demonstrated in front of HM Coroner, the MOD legal team and the family's lawyers."

"And that in my respectful submission is a compelling point as to the strength of that Culture, and the failure of training. And that's a continuing process, it's not as if failures happened immediately after Joshua fell and subsequently died. It's on going shortcomings"

Coroner

"I think the evidence has established that that Culture existed at the time of Joshua died. That's the point for the Jury. Whether it still exists now is something for me as Coroner. "

Our Barrister

"The strength of it, we submit, is a highly relevant point, because the stronger the Culture the more likely it is to **have driven decisions on the day.** And a strongly held and widespread Culture is one which we submit will be resistant to all the steps this witness has spoken about, and so strong, that when a Coroner comes on board and the question is asked, 'How would you do it?' that Culture still persists."

"And we submit that it is highly germane to the very issues this Jury is having to consider."

"Was there such a Culture? Was it recognised? Was it identified? And were adequate steps taken to overcome it so that incidents such as this did not happen?"

"We've identified that Culture with a number of witnesses and **I'm entitled** in my submission to explore its strength, depth, and prevalence, and that's what I propose to do."

And continuing a few minutes later

Day 7 - Wednesday 14th November, 2012 - Tape 9 – 01:32:22

Our Barrister

*"Sir, I'm grateful for that indication. Certainly as and when we reach that point I'd certainly like to take you up on that."*

*"However, we submit that there remains a **very real difficulty here**. Because you said rightly that you would not want the Jury to be coloured by events subsequent to the fall."*

*"But this witness has been permitted to give by virtue of his report, evidence entirely positive to the Navy, and helpful to the Navy, in terms of the Culture, the ease with which it could be overcome, and the steps that have been taken, and that we submit is **a fundamentally misleading** position in which to lead this Jury."*

*"Because that Culture, and all those steps, are not sufficient, when they **clashed** when we were aboard HMS Ocean in June, to prevent a witness tasked with demonstrating in front of HM Coroner, MOD and family's lawyers how he'd go about it to do it in the way that our letter reveals."*

*"And we submit that to **leave the Jury blind** to that when all this positive evidence is placed before them **is to mislead them** and it goes directly to the strength and prevalence of the Culture."*

*"And that is the point which is **central to this Inquiry**. The picture we are left with is, the steps that have been taken, were easily able to sort it out. This witness said in terms, in answer to questions to you, Sir, at the very outset before I was even on my feet, that he was selected because he had recent sea experience. He says, Health and Safety was prevalent on board, it was adhered to, meetings took place regularly, they cascaded down, it only takes a few minutes to get the correct Personal Protective Equipment."*

*"This is evidence which is **positive** and **supportive** and yet what we find almost two years after Joshua's death, is what we saw when we went aboard. **And that picture should not be left uncorrected.**"*

Coroner

*"That point's not lost in my mind, as I said to you a moment ago."*

Our Barrister

*"**The Jury's mind,** we submit, we should be considering now, we're in the Jury..."*

Coroner

*"But that can't colour their decision on what happened in 2010."*

Our Barrister

*"It will, we submit, if they are left with the impression that the Culture wasn't so prevalent that it couldn't be overcome with these corrective measures. It was **so pervasive, so strong,** we submit, that what happened when we went on board happened. **And that is relevant.**"*

# This was Flagged Immediately after Ship's Visit

Our Barrister went on to remind the Coroner that our legal team were so concerned with the bold statements in the Hewitt Review, following the ship's visit of June, 2012, that they immediately wrote to the Coroner, asking for evidence to verify Lt Cdr Hewitt's statements that all was well with the Health and Safety on HMS Ocean and the Royal Navy –

27/6/2012 – Our legal team's Letter to Coroner (the entire letter can be viewed on the website)

### Use of Safety Equipment –

*"We made a careful note of the statements that were made during the tour. One of the marines giving the tour was asked by our Counsel, in the presence of yourself and the Ministry of Defence legal team, how he would now gain access to the LCVP when it was 'in bed'. He said that he would climb up the ladder/s (squeezing through the metal hoops on one of the ladders) and, when asked about the use of a harness, he said he would do it without a harness because a harness was 'more a hindrance than a help'."*

*"This seems to us to contradict some of the evidence that has been supplied to you. This evidence is to the effect that, **since the accident**, steps have been taken to ensure that procedures are now in place to seek to **prevent a similar accident in the future**. The evidence currently before you records that a harness and a hard hat should have been worn (Lt Cdr Brewer Aug 2010). The report of the ISI (Sept 2010: para(1)) recorded that recommendations have been implemented to avoid a repetition of the accident. You may also want to consider the **Lt Cdr Hewitt review** (dated 15 January 2012: paras 6, 12, 16, 17-20) which suggests that the necessary safety measures **have now been implemented.**"*

The Coroner replied to this letter, saying that he would allow our Barrister to question the witnesses on this.

It is the Hewitt Review that our legal team were concerned with, and the Coroner assured them that they could question this witness, and in respect to this particular episode. I quote from the Coroner's reply.

### Use of Safety Equipment –
*"Whilst I note what you say on this issue, I consider it is a matter **which can be explored with the existing witnesses** rather than further evidence."*

see the Coroner's full letter dated 4th July, 2012, on the website.

But despite this letter and the reply from the Coroner, our Barrister is stopped from questioning Lt Cdr Hewitt, and the Jury has been sent out so that this can be discussed in private.

What is there to discuss? Our legal team had pointed out their grave concerns about the whitewash statements of the Hewitt Review, and they were told that they could question the witnesses at the Inquest, but now it appears our Barrister had to remind the Coroner of his promise.

I quote from the Inquest transcript below -

Day 7 - Wednesday 14th November, 2012 - Tape 9 – 01:40:40

Our Barrister – quoting the Coroner's Letter of the 4th July, 2012
*"Indeed, yes Sir. Of course I'll give you a moment to read it fully so I identify the right paragraph. The heading is 'Use of Safety Equipment' about half way down the first*

*page and that corresponds therefore with the heading 'Use of Safety Equipment' in our letter in which you say"*

—

Use of Safety Equipment
*"Whilst I note what you say on this issue, I consider it is a matter which can be **explored with the existing witnesses** rather than further evidence."*

*"And we had no submissions from any quarter to the contrary, and you'll see Sir, that our letter specifically ties the relevance of this to the Hewitt review. We **identify the concerns** about the Hewitt Review and what it says, **which is why we flagged up very much from the outset** that that's where we propose to go with this."*

Coroner
*"Well, I'm sorry, but I think, …..with the greatest of respect to you, that isn't what I intended in my letter, to open up to the Jury to consider post death events when reaching their verdict on how and in what circumstances Joshua has died, and **I'm not going to let you do that."***

# Coroner Threatens and Mocks Us

After forbidding our Barrister from questioning Lt Cdr Hewitt regarding the events on the visit to HMS Ocean in June, 2012, the Coroner then threatens our Barrister, telling him that he would be quite happy to adjourn the entire Inquest proceedings here and now.

Day 7 - Wednesday 14th November, 2012 - Tape 9 – 01:41:35

Coroner
*"If you're not happy with it, **if you want to adjourn these proceedings now** and take it further elsewhere, I'm quite happy to do so."*

The Coroner knows that to adjourn the Inquest proceedings would only delay this phoney Inquest for a further one to two years. He has already delayed it two years and three months.

And so he can laugh at our Barrister as he forbids him from questioning Lt Cdr

Hewitt, and then smilingly threatens him with the mocking statement that we can have a Judicial Review on him.

As if it was possible, without a lot of money and a lot of influence, to ever have a Judicial Review on any Coroner.

Day 7 - Wednesday 14ᵗʰ November, 2012 - Tape 9 – 01:42:15

> Our Barrister
> *"Sir, I'll take that as the ruling on that subject."*
> Coroner
> *"Yes. That is the ruling. And as I said, **if you are not happy with that ruling, please say so now, and I'll adjourn the proceedings so you can go away and .....  and...and..........Judicially Review me on it."***

In all probability there will never be a Judicial Review of the Coroner's behaviour on this earth, but there will certainly be one in the future, and it will be by a Righteous Judge. .....

> *But the LORD shall endure for ever:*
> *He hath prepared his throne for judgment.*
> *And he shall judge the world in righteousness*

Psalm 9 : 7,8

# Jury Brought Back In

The Jury were brought back after over one hour of debating and twenty five minutes of private consultation. Our Barrister was forbidden from questioning Lt Cdr Hewitt regarding the visit to HMS Ocean in June, 2012. This visit contradicted Lt Cdr Hewitt's statements that all recommendations in the ISI following my son's death had been implemented -

> *"I am satisfied that **all recommendations** from HMS OCEAN's ISI have been implemented"* Item 12, and

> *"and **I am satisfied** that their recommendations and observations have been taken accordingly."* of Item 17, and then again

> *"**I am satisfied that this report has reviewed all***

*recommendations for follow up action, and that those of greatest immediate importance have been implemented."*
of Item 20

And it was in this time that our Barrister was threatened with a complete stop to the Inquest proceedings if he persisted in seeking to question Lt Cdr Hewitt on these fundamental points and the June visit, as promised to us by the Coroner in his letter of the 4th July, 2012.

The Jury remembers that they were ordered out of the courtroom when our Barrister brought to Lt Cdr Hewitt's attention the visit to HMS Ocean of June, 2012. What could possibly have happened at this visit to HMS Ocean?

Now that the Jury had been brought back in, our Barrister was invited to continue his questioning of Lt Cdr Hewitt.

Day 7 - Wednesday 14th November, 2012 - Tape 9 – 02:27:44

> Coroner
> > *"Mr R you were asking questions of Lt Cdr Hewitt, do you want to proceed with that?"*
> Our Barrister
> > **"I have no further questions."**
> Coroner
> > *"You have no further questions. Thank you very much"*

Our Barrister sat in his place and with a gentle flurry of his hand crossed out all the questions he hoped to ask Lt Cdr Hewitt. Had the Jury noticed?

Had the Jury noticed the double standards of this mock Inquest into my son's death? Were the Jury aware that the entire Inquest consisted of hiding, manipulating, and creating information?

# The Two Pillars – 'All'

As I thought about this last witness, Lt Cdr Hewitt, my mind then went back to the very first witness, Lt Cdr Wilson, SIB, Royal Navy Police.

It was very telling that both the last witness and the first witness, like two great pillars, symbolised the entire Inquest for me.

As I think of Lt Cdr Hewitt's Review, I see the use of the word 'all'. I quote from his Review -

> "From my efforts to establish follow up actions, I am satisfied that **all** recommendations from HMS OCEAN's ISI **have been implemented**, "

> "the tragic accident was said to have had a **seismic** affect on HMS OCEAN's safety culture and has resulted in an emphatic Command Focus on tightening up PTW and other safety routines."

> Item 20
> "I am satisfied that this report has reviewed **all** recommendations for follow up action, and that those of greatest immediate importance have been implemented."

And I am reminded of the use of the same word by SIB Wilson, who told us in equally bold statements that

> In Item 22 of his report
> The aim of the investigation was to examine **all** circumstances that led up to the incident and **all** circumstances surrounding it. The investigation was to be conducted with an 'open mind' taking into account **all** possible explanations motives and lines of inquiry.

> Item 34 states -
> "OIC SIB was satisfied that the SIB team had pursued **all** reasonable lines of enquiry to establish the facts and had concluded that 'foul play' and suicide had not been contributory factors to Lt Woodhouse falling.

> Item 36 states –
> "From the outset, **all** available lines of inquiry were followed, including the obtaining of **all** information relating to the LCVP deck."

> Item 38 states –
> "The receipt of the US statements meant that OIC SIB was able to conclude with the **honestly held belief**, that having established the facts and gathered **all** available evidence, Lt Woodhouse had not been the victim of an intentional act or suicide. The investigation then concentrated on all other matters relating to the incident which are contained within RNP SIB report 100025/10.

Item 39 RN SIB Investigation Process states

> *"RNP SIB is satisfied that it has followed **all** reasonable lines of enquiry and there is nothing further of evidential substance to be investigated, regarding the immediate circumstances of death.*

And so I thought on the similarity between these two witnesses and their two important reports, on which the whole Inquest was founded. These reports were like two great pillars on which the Coroner had built the entire edifice of my son's Inquest.

The first great pillar, the SIB Criminal Investigation Summary into my son's suspicious death, stood as a towering and powerful plaster cast of untruths and hypocrisy.

The second great pillar, the Hewitt Review, stood as another towering plaster cast of equal untruths and hypocrisy.

What held up these two great pillars of falsehood? All the power of the Ministry of Defence, and all the power of the Royal Navy, headed artfully and willingly by none other than HM Coroner David Horsley.

This is my experience of the Military Justice given to my son by the United Kingdom.

# What Verdict are the Jury to be Allowed?

The last witness had finished, the Jury had been sent out, and now commenced the submissions to the Coroner from each Barrister on the verdict that the Coroner would allow the Jury.

I am not a legal person, and all this legal speak is new to me. It appeared that the Coroner was to decide what verdicts the Jury would be allowed to give. I list below the possible verdicts permissible in an Inquest, obtained from the url - http://www.inquest.org.uk/help/handbook/section-4-3-verdicts

> *"There are a number of verdicts that can be given including:*

> - *natural causes;*
> - *industrial disease;*

- *dependence on drugs/non-dependent abuse of drugs;*
- *want of attention at birth;*
- *suicide/killed him or herself whilst the balance of his or her mind was disturbed;*
- *accident or misadventure (which means almost the same thing);*
- *disaster which is the subject of a public inquiry;*
- *attempted or self-induced abortion;*
- *lawful killing;*
- *unlawful killing;*
- *open verdict – this means that the cause of death cannot be established **and doubt remains** as to how the deceased came to their death;*
- *stillbirth;*
- *narrative verdict - A form of verdict letting a Jury give a longer explanation of what they think are the main or important issues."*

The Coroner had intimated that he wanted to go the route of a Narrative Verdict, and both Barristers were agreed with this course of action.

Both Barristers therefore worked together to come up with a set of prospective questions for the Coroner, from which he would compose his own questions for the Jury. The Jury's answers to these questions would form the resulting Narrative Verdict.

Our Barrister was a gentleman to the end, and despite the totally misused power wielded by the Coroner and the MOD Barrister, in this phoney Inquest, he worked with them, and never reciprocated any ill will or rancour, despite, at times, open mockery and humiliation.

Our Barrister and the entire legal team fought hard and fought long, and fought to the very end with all of their might.

We shall never forget.

They had one end in mind. They wanted the best verdict for my son under impossible circumstances, and thus endeavoured to open the way for us to obtain some sort of justice after the Inquest, if that was at all possible.

## MOD Collins Makes his Submission

And so MOD Collins commenced with his submission, full of absurdities and false statements to the very end. Someone has to defend the indefensible.

I am reminded of the purpose of an Inquest, to discover the facts, see Ministry of Justice – Guide to Coroner Services

> https://www.gov.uk/government/uploads/system/uploads/attachment_data/file/363879/guide-to-coroner-service.pdf
>
> *An inquest is different from other types of court hearing because there is no prosecution or defence.*
>
> *The purpose of the inquest is to **discover the facts** of the death. This means that the coroner (or Jury) cannot find a person or organisation criminally responsible for the death.*
>
> *However if evidence is found that suggests someone may be to blame for the death the coroner can pass all the evidence gathered to the police or Crown Prosecution Service.*

We heard MOD Collins come out with the same old statements from the very first pre-Inquest. Such absolutes were used as -

> *"there is **no evidence whatsoever of Foul Play** in this case"*

and we go on with more absolutes,

Day 7 - Wednesday 14ᵗʰ November, 2012 - Tape 9 – 02:56:20

> *"Sir, you were clear at that stage, that **there was before you no such evidence.** You invited any such evidence to be produced if there was any. **None has been**, and none has emerged in the court of this Inquest."*

How can MOD Collins say this?

Nevertheless, MOD Collins gets even more absurd when he goes on to make the following statement –

*"What is particularly clear is **that no questions have been put to witnesses,** and no evidence has been given by witnesses which would lend themselves to the possibility of such a verdict."*

Perhaps MOD Collins has forgotten that our legal team were prohibited from putting any questions to any witnesses that at all encroached on Foul Play? Could this be the reason that there were no questions put to the witnesses concerning Foul Play?

I have added this portion of MOD Collin's submission in the web site.

## Our Barrister Makes his Submission

Our Barrister reminds the Coroner of the discrepancies in the account by PO Fulton, and refers to them as 'oddities'.

Why did he so gently call them 'oddities'? For no other reason than that the entire Inquest was one big, engineered episode, and he could not afford to anger the one who held centre stage and all the power.   He could not afford to anger the Coroner, who would this very night go and put together the list of questions for the Jury.

Our Barrister in his submission to the Coroner points out that

Day 7 - Wednesday 14th November, 2012 - Tape 9 – 03:30:13

> *"we have not been in a position to put **a positive case that there was a push,** for example."*

and a few minutes later he says

> *"**Those issues are there.** We could not put **a positive case of a push,** all we could do was explore the evidence, and we have done so."*

(the limited evidence that was allowed, with the limited exploration that was allowed)

Why was it that our Barrister could not put a positive case that there was a push?

Because the Coroner had forbidden any questions on Foul Play; so here was our Barrister making his point that all we could do was explore the evidence, and only the evidence which we were allowed to explore.

Our Barrister's submission can be viewed on the website.

# To the End

Time forbids me mentioning the other characters in my son's Inquest, or even giving the present characters the due time they deserve.

Time forbids me from speaking in depth of Mr Andrew Wheeler, the civilian Health and Safety officer of the Royal Navy. In this man I saw remorse, great remorse. In him I saw sadness at the death of my son, and so to you I say thank you for this show of compassion. It was no small comfort to us in this comedy-tragedy that was my son's Inquest.

Time also forbids me telling of the mammoth work and skill that our entire legal team did in bringing the hypocrisy of the Royal Navy Health and Safety to the light of day. Our Barrister explained to all at my son's Inquest the Health and Safety rating system on board HMS Ocean, the Risk Assessments, and how they worked. He meticulously showed us that if my son were to look up the particular Risk Assessment for the LCVP wheelhouse roof, he would find that the danger was rated as low, and the need for a harness was marked as zero.

Our Barrister showed that my son was indeed obeying the Health and Safety Risk Assessment for the wheelhouse roof and was abiding by the Health and Safety culture prevalent on HMS Ocean. My son did nothing that he should not have done, and neither did he omit to do anything that he should have done – these are the words of Captain Blount to our party.

This great feat of uncovering the hypocrisy of the Royal Navy was accomplished by the entire legal team working as one, with our Barrister as the talented front player in the theatre of this Inquest setting. This account of mine which details just some of the events concerning my son's Inquest does not give the legal team the full credit they deserve, but it is a small way for me to be able to say thank you.

And now we waited for the Coroner to take the submissions from the two Barristers and prepare a question sheet for the Jury.

It was another hard time as I became aware again of the impossibility of expecting anything approaching a fair verdict from the Jury, under these engineered circumstances of my son's Inquest.

# Before the Jury is brought in

It was Thursday, 15th November, 2012, day eight of my son's Inquest. The previous day the Coroner had been given submissions, and suggested Jury questions, by the two barristers; from these he would prepare his own list of Jury questions.

There was much continued prayer for these questions.

Before the Jury was brought in, the Coroner read out his list of Jury Questions and asked for the Barristers' comments.

There was one question that was so important to us; it was Question 3.

> Are you able from the evidence, to say what caused him to fall?

In answering this question, we would know whether the Jury had believed the false account of the SIB Royal Navy Police, the MOD, the Royal Navy, PO Fulton, and the Coroner.

And we would totally understand if the Jury had believed the united false statements of the establishment. How was it possible to see past those two great mammoth pillars on which the Coroner had based his Inquest, the SIB criminal investigation and the Hewitt Review?

Did the Jury notice the discrepancies between PO Fulton's account and that of US Witness 3, Los Angeles?

Did the Jury notice the endless weavings and implausible statements of PO Fulton, the man with my son when my son suspiciously fell to his death?

We would not have to wait very long to hear the Jury's verdict.

# Members of the Jury, Good Morning

Once the discussions regarding the Jury questions were finished, the Jury were brought in.

The Coroner very solemnly addressed the Jury, informing them of the weighty responsibility before them. He gave them a summary of the evidence, and kept stressing that the summary of evidence was only his opinion, and that they were free to make up their own minds. I quote below –

Day 8 - Thursday 15th November, 2012 - Tape 10 – 00:27:57

*"Members of the Jury, Good Morning. We've now reached the stage in the Inquest, where we've heard all the evidence relating to the death of Joshua and **it's now my duty to sum it up for you…."***

*"Now my summing up won't be a repeat, word for word, of everything that's been said in evidence over the last few days. Rather, it's me drawing your attention, to the salient points of evidence **as I see them to be**….*

*"At the end of the day, **it is you,** who are the judges of fact in this Inquest, not me. It is you, who very shortly will decide which of the evidence is relevant, and from that you will decide the facts of the case."*

Day 8 - Thursday 15th November, 2012 - Tape 10 – 00:29:12

*"It is entirely **open to you to disagree with my opinions** about the evidence and what represents the truth, **because you are the judges of that."***

*"However, I must point out that you have to reach your verdict, **only on evidence you heard in court** and not upon facts or opinions that have come to you from elsewhere."*

This was all very well and good, telling the Jury that they were allowed to have a different opinion to that of the Coroner.

Despite his fine words, it would be almost impossible for the Jury to have a different opinion to that of the Coroner, when it was the Coroner who had elevated the prime suspect to the position of prime witness.

## It is your Duty

Time forbids me from remarking on all of the Coroner's address to the Jury, but it was summed up in the following grave and weighty admonition he gave them. He stresses the importance of their role by telling them three times what their duty is.

Day 8 - Thursday 15th November, 2012 - Tape 10 – 00:46:03

> *"**Your duty** is to find the facts and reach a conclusion from the evidence, and this **duty** must transcend your feelings of sympathy for anyone."*

> *"You must perform **your duty,** even if your conclusions seem unkind or critical to some person or persons, indeed even Joshua himself."*

This statement made me think of that great man, Admiral Horatio Nelson, who famously gave the following signal in his last battle –

> *"England expects that every man will do his duty."*

From Lord Nelson we are all happy to receive such a call. Lord Nelson served and died for his country; he gave the ultimate sacrifice in doing his duty for his country.

But here we have HM Coroner reminding the Members of the Jury of their great duty in this most solemn and grave position that they were holding.

And we have to turn our gaze onto HM Coroner David Horsley. To this man who tells the Members of the Jury to do their duty, whilst he refuses to carry out his own duty.

## The Jury's Verdict

After the Coroner completed his address to the Jury, it was now time for the Jury to leave the Inquest setting and decide on their verdict.

The Jury was given two days to come to their decision, but it was reached within a few hours.

This was telling.

Their answer to question Three *"Are you able from the evidence, to say what caused him to fall?"* summed up their verdict

> *"From the evidence, we are unable to say what caused Lt Woodhouse to fall."*

To them it was obvious that the Coroner, SIB Military Police, the MOD, the Royal Navy, and PO Fulton, were covering my son's suspicious death.

The Jury rejected their accounts.

## To the Jury

As a family we are grateful to the Jury. We do not know you, but we thank you. During the Inquest we were informed that one of the Jurors was in deep pain due to back problems, but rather than being excused, she wanted to stay. They wanted to give us an honest verdict.

Within a few days of the start of the Inquest another member of the Jury lost her nephew in a traffic accident. She did not want to be excused, despite her great personal grief; instead she stayed and gave us a rightful verdict.

We are very grateful for the verdict that you had the courage to give.

We are very grateful that you had the wisdom to see through the false statements of the Establishment, as they stood united in their efforts to deprive my son of an honest criminal investigation and an honest Inquest into his violent and suspicious death. Thank you.

## If it were not for

If it were not for the Royal British Legion, who commenced an Inquest Advice Service one month before my son's death, we would not have received the verdict we did.

If it were not for the full legal team that the Royal British Legion contacted, and who volunteered to represent us Pro Bono (totally free of charge), and selflessly, we would not have received the verdict we did.

If it were not for the good hand of our God, the Lord Jesus Christ, who brought these people, all with one heart, to help us defend our son's name, to help us endeavour to break the MOD fortress of fables and deceit, we would continue to be that unheeded, unwanted, bothersome family who hoarsely cried for 'justice'.

But the great Jericho fortress of MOD fables and deceit still proudly stands, defying any to take her.

The first step has been accomplished. The walls of Jericho are down. Despite their great power, and against all odds, the MOD did not get the verdict they wanted of accidental death.

The Jury did not believe the great fortress of falsehoods that was built over my son's innocent blood, which still cries from HMS Ocean.

## More Checks and Balances – Chief Coroner Peter Thornton

After my son's Inquest, when the Jury rejected the account fed to them by the Military, the legal team chose to go further. They did not have to. They had given totally of themselves. It had cost them dear; a two week Inquest not just an Inquest of a few days, and the huge amount of work to reach that stage.

The legal team wrote to the newly appointed Chief Coroner, and also included a document that I had written, outlining just some of the actions the Coroner constructed to cover the facts surrounding my son's suspicious and violent death. See the web site for some of these documents.

With these documents in front of him, we waited to see what the newly appointed Chief Coroner would do. Was this the man that would finally right the wrongs of the Coronial System?

In keeping with the previous checks and balances, Chief Coroner Peter Thornton did nothing. Chief Coroner Peter Thornton joined the ranks of the Coroner, SIB Wilson, the Royal Navy, the MOD, and PO Fulton. And in joining with them, he contracted their guilt.

The 6th check has failed.

This is the Military Justice given to my son.

# More Checks and Balances – Hampshire Constabulary

After my son's Inquest, the legal team went to great lengths through letters and meetings to explain to the Hampshire Constabulary why it was their duty to investigate my son's suspicious death.

It is that word duty again. We cannot but remember those immortal words of Horatio Nelson

*"England expects that every man will do his duty."*

What has happened in the once great United Kingdom, that truth and right have fallen in the streets, and that duty is likewise tossed to the wind?

In keeping with the previous checks and balances, the Hampshire Constabulary refused to do their duty.

What has happened to the United Kingdom, that we have to beg Hampshire Constabulary to do their job?

After one and a half years of letters and meetings with Hampshire Constabulary, they refused to investigate my son's suspicious death. They refused to pick up the pieces of my son's broken life, when their job demanded it of them.

So now Hampshire Constabulary joined with the Coroner, SIB Wilson, the Royal Navy, Captain Blount, Captain Forsey, Lt Cdr Pickles, Lt Cdr Lucocq, WO Clapham, MOD Collins, the MOD, PO Fulton, and Chief Coroner Peter Thornton, and together with them hold the guilt of my son's blood on their united heads.

The 7th check has failed.

# On and on and on and on ......

What could we do now? We could write to our MP and then wait. Wait for the same highly inventive reasons that all previous seven checks have given to date.

And so we would go on, and on, and on, and on. I could write to the Queen.

What would the outcome in all probability be?

A long passage of time is what the outcome would be. We would be given so many reasonably sounding arguments why the person we had just contacted could not do anything. Look at the results from Hampshire Constabulary and Chief Coroner Peter Thornton.

If the person I contacted was sympathetic, he might possibly recommend another person that we could write to, and so the years would roll on. Look at the Deepcut military families.

Lt Cdr Pickles, Lt Cdr Lucocq, WO Clapham, Captain Blount, Lt Cdr Brewer, SIB Wilson, Captain Forsey, the Coroner, the MOD, Hampshire Constabulary, and Chief Coroner Peter Thornton have all failed in their duty to bring my son's suspicious death to the true light of day.

I have the option to spend my last years begging government officials to do what the country has paid them to do.

And then I have the option to write this book, and leave not only the writing of it, but the outcome, to my God, the Lord Jesus Christ, and this is the choice I have made.

# Can I Dream?

Am I allowed to dream? If so, what would I want?

I would want the existing coronial system completely overhauled, and the rules of disclosure changed, so that never again would a Coroner be able to withhold evidence. I would want Coroners stripped of their immense power, and all Inquest proceedings to be in the open, and founded on truth and justice.

I would like my son given an honest investigation into his death. Is there anyone fit to give my son an honest investigation into his death? Can such a thing occur in the real world? Can such a thing occur in the United Kingdom, or is it only in dream land?

I would like the people who covered my son's suspicious death in a concerted and united effort to be held accountable for their actions. Can this possibly occur, or will you join me in dream land?

I would like no other family to receive what we received at the hands of the

Military Justice of the United Kingdom of Great Britain.

This is my dream. This is my cry.

# How Many other Military Deaths?

I do not believe that the intentional and concerted coverup of my son's death is an isolated incident, nor an unusual occurrence in the Military of the United Kingdom.

One of the legal team informed us that he was dealing with a case similar to ours. My heart went out to the family. A case similar to ours. How tragic.

How many other families have been told that the death of their beloved son, husband, daughter, wife, was an unfortunate accident or a suicide? And to make matters worse, always blaming the victim. It was their fault. The dead cannot speak. The dead cannot defend themselves.

The MOD has robbed this family of a dear member, and they have also robbed the victim of his human right to an honest investigation. And if that was not enough, the MOD have destroyed the good name of the victim, and smothered it with shame. It was all the fault of the victim.

This is what the MOD hand over to the family; a corpse, a fine funeral, and a name of shame. This is how the United Kingdom rewards its Military. Don't forget to put the flag at half-mast.

How many other families have been fed MOD fables, rubber stamped in a phoney Inquest?

How many other families are powerless like us? How many other families are sitting in darkness, because the MOD, working with Coroners, has ensured that they remain ignorant, and are only fed MOD fables?

Why did the Royal British Legion set up the Independent Inquest Advice Service if there was not a terrible abuse and outcry in the Military?

This great army of our fallen Military men and women, who now lie silent in cold graves, cannot speak. They cannot tell us how or why they died. But they are a great army, and as a great army they shall rise and stand once more on that Great Judgment Day when the books are opened, and then they shall speak.

# The Stifling Blanket of Time

For every year that passes another stifling blanket of time drops heavily over my son's suspicious death.

At this present time, August, 2016, six years of time have covered my son's death.

This blanket of time has fallen over the accounts of the three independent US Navy witnesses. Are they even alive? Can they even be traced?

This blanket of time has somehow separated the actions recounted in this book from the people who have committed them and left them guiltless.

This blanket of time threatens to turn this book into an interesting historic read that we are not responsible for, and that we, living in the present, do not have to give account for.

This stifling blanket of time surely has blunted the first sharp emotions of indignation at what has been done to my son.

Each blanket of time threatens to extinguish that tiny flame of hope that is ours and is still struggling to shine forth. This book is an attempt to throw off the stupefying thick layers of this blanket and to reveal to the world the Military Justice that the United Kingdom of Great Britain gave to my son.

And in so doing to leave it to those who read this book and who live in the present to rectify this terrible wrong and ensure that this Military Justice never occurs again.

# Is this the End?

The Jury did not believe the account given by Coroner David Horsley. The Jury did not believe the account given to them by the Royal Navy, by the SIB Royal Navy Military Police, and by the MOD, neither the account given by PO Fulton.

What did the authorities do with the Jury's verdict?

Nothing.

Throughout the Inquest we were aware that the comedy-tragedy, that they called an Inquest, was merely a highly polished professional rubber stamping exercise.

The Coroner had blocked the evidence, had forbidden any questions on foul play, had refused to hand over the case to the police, and had thus impeded justice.

Yet, despite these great obstacles, and with the help of our legal team, the Jury were enabled to see that there was another side to the story. There was a side that the MOD did not want them to see. The result was that despite the stranglehold of control exercised upon the Inquest, the Jury did not buy the fables presented to them.

Wonderful as the verdict was, that is the sum total of all that my son received at the hands of the United Kingdom.

We still do not know how my son came to die.

My son's death still remains a suspicious death that has not been allowed an honest investigation, nor an honest Inquest.

This is my experience of the Military Justice given to my son, Lt Joshua Woodhouse RN, by the United Kingdom of Great Britain.

**O our God, wilt thou not judge them?**
**for we have no might against this great company that cometh against us;**
**neither know we what to do:**
**but our eyes are upon Thee**

2 Chronicles 20:12